# SCRIPTURE IN
# THE TRADITION

# SCRIPTURE IN THE TRADITION

## HENRI DE LUBAC, S.J.

*Translated by* Luke O'Neill

*Introduction by* Peter Casarella

*A Herder & Herder Book*
The Crossroad Publishing Company
New York

The Crossroad Publishing Company
481 Eighth Avenue, New York, NY 10001

Originally published under the title *L'ecriture dans la tradition*
© 1967 F. Aubier, Editions Montaigne, Paris
English translation copyright © 1968  by Herder & Herder
Introduction to the 2000 Edition copyright © 2000 by
The Crossroad Publishing Company

*Nihil obstat:* Leo J. Steady, Censor Librorum

*Imprimatur:* Robert F. Joyce, Bishop of Burlington

August 20, 1968

Printed in the United States of America

Library of Congress Card Number: 00-110770

ISBN: 0-8245-1871-3

1  2  3  4  5  6  7  8  9  10  04  03  02  01

# CONTENTS

# FOREWORD

This book is not the place to look for a complete history of biblical exegesis in the Church, or for a doctrinal explanation of the connection between Holy Scripture and Christian Tradition. They are subjects too vast and too intricate to be readily compressed. In any event, they are not the subjects which we undertook to treat. Starting from somewhat different perspectives, we propose to the reader a series of approaches which share a single focus: the spiritual understanding of the Scriptures, as it existed during the Christian centuries. The first chapter, a simple historical sketch, originally appeared as the conclusion of *Histoire et Esprit* (1950). The second chapter was taken from the first volume of *Exégèse Médiévale* (1959), where it appeared as the fifth chapter. The five sections which constitute the third and last chapter of this book were taken from the second, third, and fourth volumes of that work (1959–1964).

We have often had occasion to note that five large volumes are within the reach of only a small number of readers, whereas their principal themes might well be of interest to many more. We have also been told that study of these themes would be useful to many and would lead to a better assimilation of the teaching contained in the recent constitution, *Dei Verbum*. We are, of course, aware that a collection of this kind, even though homogeneous, cannot fully sustain itself. We have had to exclude a number of longer discussions which, in some instances anyway, would have shed light on the great variety which is to be found within centuries, individuals, and schools; the need to make a choice required the sacrifice of many explanations which would have supplemented and added nuances to the passages we have retained. The footnotes, too, have been significantly abridged. It was not, in fact, without some hesitation that we consented to the publication of this book, and we would ask all those who would not be wearied by the effort to refer back to the original volumes.

The methods of exegesis have, of course, varied greatly through the centuries. The interest aroused by the history of spiritual interpretation and its modes of expression has made us aware of the need to employ the most appropriate methods, the best methods of our time. Even so, we are of the opinion that this history, considered in its doctrinal foundations rather than in its implementation, with its wealth of ancient detail, has an ever-present importance. There *are* constants in Christian exegesis. A man of such learning and faith as Père Lagrange was completely convinced that scientific research and reflective faith —or to use the language of the ancients, history and spirit— were by no means incompatible, and that their union was, in point of fact, indispensable for a thorough study of the word of God. The two letters from his alter ego, Père Hugues Vincent, which are to be found in the appendix, make this abundantly clear, while helping us to see our own objective more precisely. And it is something which the text of *Dei Verbum* frequently brings to mind.

In two consecutive paragraphs devoted to scriptural interpretation, what, really, does the third chapter of *Dei Verbum,* on divine revelation, say if not that we must first, by purely scientific study, determine as best we can the "intention" of each of the human authors, and that only then, in order to better grasp the meaning, should we read it and interpret it as a whole "in the light of the same Spirit who caused it to be written"? When the sixth chapter advises us to "study the Holy Fathers, those of the East as well as those of the West," so as to obtain this increased understanding, does this not indicate that there must still be profit to be derived from a study of the exegetical tradition which stemmed from the Fathers? And when we are told, in the constitution's introduction and frequently throughout the text, that the Word of God contained in Scripture is none other than the Word made flesh, and that "the entire revelation of the most high God is fulfilled" in Jesus Christ, do we not hear the traditional theme of the *Verbum abbreviatum* and many other expressions, to be found in this book, of this basic truth?

When the Council, in its brief but plain way, points out the permanent teachings which the books of the Old Testament, in their literal meaning, contain, it does something else as well. It recalls to our attention another truth which, though never lost from sight, was sometimes obscured in the past by the insistence on showing how outmoded the Old Covenant was. This may have been done to safeguard the Christian conscience, or it may have been a by-product of controversy, or it may simply have been done for the pure joy of contemplating the definitive unity which was achieved in Jesus Christ. The faith which Jesus wants to bring to perfection in us is the faith of Abraham, Moses, and the Prophets. And this may bear repeating here. But the Council, in its chapter on the Old Testament, using an expression whose most famous exponent was St. Augustine, no less forcefully declares the mutual implications of the two Testaments: *Novum in Vetere latet, Vetus in Novo patet.* Thus it canonizes the key idea which, since apostolic times, has dominated the doctrine of spiritual understanding of the Scriptures as elaborated through the ages. The Council thus affirms—or, rather, confirms—the foundation of what was in the beginning and will always remain the Christian newness.

# INTRODUCTION TO THE 2000 EDITION

Looking back over a now-completed century of Christian thought, Cardinal Henri de Lubac, S.J. (1896–1991) emerges as one of its most important voices. No label fits him, and his notoriety arose from an unusual set of circumstances. Eager to collaborate on the influential patristic series *Sources Chrétiennes*, he was nonetheless forced to work in isolation for many years. He did not aim to gratify the more timid ecclesiastical authorities and for ten years had to give up his chair in theology. Likewise, his prodigious output on atheism and the spiritual predicament of the modern age offered no consolation to the Church's cultured despisers.

In spite of these many obstacles, all his efforts yielded lasting results. By mid-century, de Lubac had helped spawn what others called "the new theology," and his tireless advocacy of a return to the sources paved a path that was followed in the development of the theology of the Second Vatican Council.[1] His research into the question of our natural desire to see God according to his essence had a profound effect on the debate about nature and grace.[2] His inquiry into the social aspects of dogma recovered the true meaning of the sacramental body of Christ and charted a course still guiding theologians of the Church.[3] When de Lubac delved into what the Fathers and medieval thinkers found in the Scriptures, these broader developments were also in view. Here as elsewhere,

---

[1] Cf. Joseph Komonchak, "Theology and Culture at Mid-Century: The Example of Henri de Lubac," *Theological Studies* 51 (1990): 579-602.

[2] Cf. David L. Schindler, "Introduction," in Henri de Lubac, *The Mystery of the Supernatural* (New York: Crossroad, 1998), xi-xxxvii.

[3] See, for example, Paul McPartlan, *The Eucharist Makes the Church: Henri de Lubac and John Zizioulas in Dialogue* (T&T Clark: Edinburgh, 1993).

however, Fr. de Lubac's herculean labors continue to attract loyal followers and passionate critics.

## 1. Spiritual Exegesis and Theological Renewal

The ancient practice of spiritual exegesis is once again being applied to the Scriptures.[4] The current renewal represents a late blossoming of the strenuous efforts initiated about fifty years ago not only by de Lubac but also by Jean Daniélou, S.J., Louis Bouyer, and the poet Paul Claudel.[5] The present revival, like the earlier attempt, has met with mixed reactions. Some see de Lubac as the standardbearer for a new synthesis of history and theology. Robert Wilken, for example, argues that de Lubac undertook a study of traditional spiritual exegesis not to supplant historical research but to counter the growing tendency to treat the Christian past as a mere relic.[6] Others express the same sympathy for de Lubac's project but urge caution in straying too far from the current standards of biblical criticism. Susan Wood, for example, considers spiritual exegesis not to be in line with contemporary exegesis. In her view, contemporary theology can nonetheless learn from the liturgical, spiritual, ecclesiological, and eschatological doctrines embodied within its mystagogy.[7] Still others predict that the current revival

---

[4] See, for example, Denis Farkasfalvy, O.Cist., "The case for spiritual exegesis," *Communio: International Catholic Review* 10 (Winter 1983): 332-50; Luke Timothy Johnson, "So What's Catholic about It? The State of Catholic Biblical Scholarship," *Commonweal* (Jan. 16, 1998): 12-16; David S. Yeago, "The New Testament and the Nicene Dogma: A Contribution to the Recovery of Theological Exegesis," *Pro Ecclesia* 3 (Spring 1994): 152-64; and Robert L. Wilken, "*In Dominico Eloquio*: Learning the Lord's Style of Language," *Communio: International Catholic Review* 24 (Winter 1997): 846-66.

[5] Cf. Marcellino D'Ambrosio, "Henri de Lubac and the critique of scientific exegesis," *Communio: International Catholic Review* 19 (Fall 1992): 365-88; John L. McKenzie, "A Chapter in the History of Spiritual Exegesis: De Lubac's *Histoire et Esprit*," *Theological Studies* 12 (1951): 365-81; and Ignace de la Potterie, "The spiritual sense of Scripture," *Communio: International Catholic Review* 23 (Winter 1996): 738-56.

[6] Robert Wilken, "*In Dominico Eloquio*," 849.

[7] Susan Wood, *Spiritual Exegesis and the Church in the Theology of Henri de Lubac* (Grand Rapids, MI: Eerdmans, 1998), 141.

will set us back. Joseph A. Fitzmeyer, for example, admits that the report of the Pontifical Biblical Commission, *The Interpretation of the Bible in the Church*, does not rule out spiritual exegesis.[8] Fitzmeyer would nonetheless prefer that its more ardent proponents revert instead to what the Commission's report terms the "actualised" literal sense as ascertained by the historical-critical method.[9] Unlike Wood, Fitzmeyer shows little enthusiasm for the theological insights of pre-modern approaches. These differences of opinion occasion a need to look closely at what de Lubac and others intended when they re-introduced spiritual exegesis into the theological landscape.

Fitzmeyer's remarks illustrate how de Lubac's recovery of spiritual exegesis could be misunderstood as an attempt to repristinate an earlier approach to reading the Bible. Nothing could be further from the truth, however. Henri de Lubac knew that there are always some who prefer to remove the dust from classical artifacts rather than face the challenge of the future, but he himself did not retreat to the past. By the same token, the axiomatic application of the historical-critical method can provoke a negative reaction. In the face of mere historical positivism, some are understandably drawn to the sweeter air of symbolic, ecclesial interpretation.[10] Yet neither nostalgia nor the search for a more refined hermeneutic approximates the real motivation for de Lubac's project.

The French Jesuit believed that modern exegesis had begun to lose sight of fundamental questions about existence itself. The pursuit of specialized disciplines, while legitimate as one aspect of scriptural interpretation, had come to an inquiry into understanding

---

[8.] Joseph A. Fitzmeyer, S. J., "The Senses of Scripture Today," *Irish Theological Quarterly* 62 (1996-97): 114.

[9.] On *actualisation*, see Joseph A. Fitzmeyer, *The Biblical Commission's Document "The Interpretation of the Bible in the Church". Text and Commentary* (Rome: Editrice Pontificio Istituto Biblico, 1995), 170-6. Fitzmeyer's comment is a reaction to the moderated defense of spiritual exegesis found in Avery Dulles, *The Craft of Theology* (New York: Crossroad, 1992), 85.

[10.] For example, J. Châtillon says of the 12th century mystics: "Scripture is no longer the locus *theologicus* from which the scholar gathers his premises, but is now the *hortus conclusus* where the soul meets the Spouse, listens to his voice and inhales the fragrance of his perfumes." *Revue du moyen âge latin* 4 (1948): 439.

reality as a whole. De Lubac's research into the doctrine of the senses of Scripture, writes Hans Urs von Balthasar, is not simply "a curiosity of the history of theology" but "an instrument permitting the discovery of the profound *interconnections* within the history of salvation."[11] De Lubac was not rejecting the idea of a scientific exegesis but searching for its foundations in Christian wisdom. He felt that the exegesis of the future would certainly have to incorporate *all* that had been discovered by modern archaeology, history, and the literary sciences, but not without attempting to breach the growing gulf between the theoretical axioms of scientific criticism and the practical advice of Christian wisdom.

De Lubac wanted to renew both theology and the Church.[12] He knew that renewal demanded a careful, critical scrutiny of ancient exegetical practices. In his view, the individual methods practiced by the Fathers and the scholastic doctors, particularly when accompanied by an overly systematic form of allegory, were never to be slavishly imitated. De Lubac paid as much attention to the overall effect of their methods as their individual results. He was more interested in showing their abiding truth than in documenting a history of exegetical techniques. In its scope (but not its erudition), de Lubac's account of the medieval period differs from a noteworthy historical study such as that of Beryl Smalley.[13] Above all, de Lubac wanted women and men of the Church today to encounter the very best of their Christian past.

## 2. *Scripture in the Tradition* and *Dei Verbum*

Even though this work has been called "his synthetic book," de Lubac was hesitant to see it published.[14] Since even in its first

[11] Hans Urs von Balthasar, *Le Cardinal de Lubac: l'homme et son oeuvre* (Paris: Lethielleux, 1983), 100, as cited in Susan Wood, *Spiritual Exegesis and the Church*, 26.

[12] Cf. Robert Wilken, "Foreword," Henri de Lubac, *Medieval Exegesis*, I, *The Four Senses of Scripture*, Marc Sebanc, tr. (Grand Rapids, MI: Eerdmans, 1998), x.

[13] Beryl Smalley, *The Study of the Bible in the Middle Ages* (Notre Dame: Univ. of Notre Dame Press, 1964).

[14] Ignace de la Potterie, S.J., "The spiritual sense of Scripture," 745.

appearance it was a reprinting of what had been treated in greater detail elsewhere, de Lubac feared that its publication might prevent his readers from studying the more carefully nuanced presentation in his book on Origen, *L'Histoire et Esprit* (1950), and the four massive volumes of *Exégèse médiévale* (1959-64). These latter books revealed the full grandeur and complexity of the subject matter; the present anthology was meant to whet the reader's appetite. His reluctant acquiescence to the desire of a publisher nonetheless reveals quite a bit about the purpose of spiritual exegesis.

Originally, the preface was the only new material that the author agreed to have published. The publication of the original French in 1966 came on the heels of the promulgation of the Second Vatican Council's Dogmatic Constitution on Divine Revelation, *Dei Verbum*.[15] In fact, de Lubac's own testimony and independent historical research confirm that the author saw the two endeavors as mutually enriching.[16]

The first clue to understanding de Lubac's intention in releasing his research for republication is found in his memoirs. Here he explains the tangled course of events that led to the first publication in English of this volume:

America is also responsible for *L'Écriture dans la tradition* (1966), a book that contains nothing new, being composed solely of texts taken from *Histoire et Esprit* and *Exégèse médiévale*. A woman from New York held the rights to the book. . . . When the project was sent to her, a little late, she no longer wanted it. She thought that the winds had changed and preferred to devote herself to religious syncreticism. Madame Gabail. . .then wanted to publish the volume in French; two letters from Père Vincent, of Jerusalem, were added in an appendix. I don't think that it had much success. However, another American editor made a translation of it. You can't imagine my shock when I read *The Sources of Revelation* (1968) on the cover! And I was the one who had battled against the famous theory of "the two sources"! Was this the gaffe of an unknowing editor? Or perhaps (what I no longer believe) a conscious act of malevolence?[17]

[15.] The document was promulgated on November 18, 1965.
[16.] Ignace de la Potterie, "The spiritual sense of Scripture," 749-51.
[17.] Henri de Lubac, *Mémoire sur l'occasion de mes écrits* (Namur: Culture et Verité, 1989), 123.

Thus, the reprint was originally intended for an American audience. After the first American effort failed, changes were introduced. The French editor added two letters communicating the approbation of de Lubac's research by a well-known pioneer in the historical-critical method, Marie-Joseph Lagrange (1855-1938).[18] This correspondence, also included in the present reprint, shows that from the perspective of the emerging scientific standards de Lubac never sought to abandon historical criticism.

The second change was far less welcome. The subsequent English translation adopted a title that—at least by implication—contradicted the efforts of renewal at the Second Vatican Council. De Lubac had wanted to show that Scripture and Tradition were not in fact two, wholly separate sources of revelation.[19] Not without considerable and protracted debate, a highly significant modification of the so-called "two-source theory" was incorporated into the following conciliar formula:

Sacred Tradition and sacred Scripture, then, are bound closely together, and communicate one with the other. For both of them, flowing out from the same divine well-spring, come together in some fashion to form one thing, and move as towards one goal.[20]

The translator's rendering of *L'Écriture dans la tradition* as *Sources of Revelation* undercut one of the Council's boldest and hard-won results. For de Lubac, there is but one source of revelation, Christ himself, who in turn norms both the written Scriptures and the

[18.] Lagrange was the author of *La méthode historique: La critique biblique et l'Église* (Paris: Cerf, 1966), which at the time was said to represent "the programme of the biblical school of Jerusalem." Ignace de la Potterie, "The spiritual sense of Scripture," 739.

[19.] See Francesco Bertoldi, "Henri de Lubac on Dei Verbum," *Communio: International Catholic Review* 17 (Spring, 1990): 92.

[20.] *Dei verbum* 9, as cited in *Vatican Council II: The Conciliar and Postconciliar Documents*, Austin Flannery, ed., (Northport, N.Y.: Costello, 1987), 755. On the historical development of the conciliar formula, one may consult Riccardo Burigana, *La Bibbia nel Concilio: La redazione della costituzione "Dei verbum" del Vaticano II* (Società Editrice Il Mulino, 1998) and Charles Moeller, "Le texte du chapitre II dans la seconde période du concile," *La révélation divine*, 1, B.-D. Dupuy, ed. (Paris: Cerf, 1968), 305-44.

Church's teaching tradition.[21] Without relinquishing the mandate to read the Bible in the Church, the Council Fathers had maintained that the integral and incarnate Word stands above the witnesses of Scripture and Tradition.[22] This unified and unifying source of truth makes it difficult to conceive of Scripture and Tradition as opposed fractions.[23] The reference to plural "sources" in the earlier American title conjured up for de Lubac an unnecessary fragmenting of the wholeness of the divine person who communicated his very self to us through the words of Scripture.

With the present reprint, we have thus restored a more accurate rendering of de Lubac's own title, yet even this correction could lead to misunderstanding. For example, it would be a grave error to think that the title *Scripture in the Tradition* makes this either a historical study or a neo-Tridentine rebuff to the sixteenth-century cry of *sola scriptura*. In fact, the seemingly innocent prepositional phrase "in the tradition" deserves close inspection. The restored title forces us to ask, "Can 'tradition' be conceived of other than as either mere history or the isolated counterpart to scriptural truth?"

To answer this question, one needs to consider de Lubac's debt to his contemporaries. De Lubac was a vocal supporter of the controversial Catholic philosopher Maurice Blondel and wrote several commentaries on his correspondence.[24] De la Potterie, sees in de Lubac's title a "distant echo" of Blondel's critique of all exegesis that did not account for "the vital role of tradition."[25] This obser-

---

[21.] Henri de Lubac, "Commentaire du préamble et du chapitre I," in *La révélation divine*, 1, 273-9.

[22]*Dei verbum* 9 also states: "The Church does not draw her certainty about all revealed truths from the holy Scriptures alone."

[23.] Cf. E Schlink, "Écriture, tradition et magistère selon la Constitution *Dei Verbum*," in *La révélation divine*, 2, 504; George Lindbeck, *The Future of Roman Catholic Theology. Vatican II—Catalyst for Change* (Philadelphia: Fortress Press, 1970), 108-16.

[24.] *Blondel et Teilhard de Chardin; Correspondance*, with commentary by Henri de Lubac (Paris: Beauchesne, 1965) [ET: *Pierre Teilhard de Chardin, Maurice Blondel: Correspondence* (New York: Herder, 1967)]; *Blondel et A. Valensin: Correspondance,* with commentary by Henri de Lubac (Paris: Beauchesne, 1965); *Correspondance de Maurice Blondel et Joannès Wehrlé.* Annotated by Henri de Lubac (Paris: Aubier Montagne, 1969).

[25.] Ignace de la Potterie, "Spiritual sense of Scripture," 749.

vation is no doubt correct but tells only half of the story.[26] Blondel was a critic not only of a "historicism" that reduces the past to a harmless museum piece, but also of an extrinsicism that champions "Truth" as a reality disclosed on a plane free of historical development. In an influential essay dedicated to de Lubac, Blondel states that "tradition anticipates and illuminates the future and is disposed to do so by the effort which it makes to remain faithful to the past."[27]

Thus, the word "tradition" in the title of the present volume does not refer to an object of historical study. For both thinkers one does not study the tradition to demonstrate causal links or rearrange deeds and facts. Whereas historicism defines the alienation of the past from fundamental questions of human existence, history pushes forward to the core definition of who we are as persons. No less worrisome are those who maintain that we can simply re-insert our contemporary selves into the mindset of the Fathers without acknowledging the prejudices and historical factors that accompany us. The vitality of the tradition lies as much in what it presents to us as utterly strange and different as in its lucid antitheses to the one-sided spirit of critical inquiry. "Scripture in the tradition" therefore describes an outlook on the past that can shape the future without jettisoning every new advance made by modern Biblical criticism.

How does this dynamic account of tradition translate into a program for Biblical exegesis? De Lubac asserted that history—precisely *qua* history—was already pregnant with a spiritual force. The spiritual significance of history lies within history; it is not an ideological superstructure added to closed temporal realities.

*There is "a spiritual force to history."* By reason of their finality, the facts themselves have an inner significance; they are already, in time, charged with eternity. On the other hand, the reality of which the Old and even the

---

[26.] See also Henri de Lubac, *L'Écriture dans la tradition* (Paris: Aubier-Montaigne, 1966), 57 and Antonio Russo, *Henri de Lubac: teologia e dogma nella storia:. L'influsso di Blondel* (Rome: Edizioni Studium, 1990).

[27.] Maurice Blondel, *The Letter on Apologetics and History and Dogma* (Grand Rapids, Mich.: Eerdmans, 1994), 268.

New Testament contain "types" is not only spiritual, but is also incarnate. It is not only eternal, but is historical as well. For the Word was made flesh and sets his tabernacle among us. *The spiritual meaning*, then, is everywhere, not only or especially in a book, but *first and foremost in reality itself.*[28]

This passage gives evidence of de Lubac's support for Blondel's so-called "method of immanence." The fleshly incarnation of the Word calls us to look to the very forces that determine historical development in order to discern the activity of God's Spirit.

When applied to the Scriptures, this meant that spiritual exegesis can never stray too far from the literal sense. De Lubac insisted that the spiritual meaning of Scripture is not found above or even alongside the plain sense of the Biblical narrative. The literal sense has an expansiveness that is seldom recognized even by its modern proponents.[29] "Honey is more pleasing," writes Hugh of St. Victor, "when taken directly from the comb."[30]

Whereas Blondel helped de Lubac articulate the reality of organic, historical development, de Lubac's collaboration on the drafting of *Dei Verbum* may have shaped his thinking on the relation of theology, and especially christology, to exegesis. In his preface he says that *Scripture in the Tradition* will help assimilate the teaching contained in *Dei Verbum*.[31] The conciliar document, he notes, also speaks to the unity of history and spirit, the need to determine the human author's "intention" on the basis of scientific study, and the paramount notion that the highest achievement of God's self-revelation is the Word made flesh. De Lubac furthermore underscores the teaching of *Dei Verbum* on the faith of Abraham, Moses, and the prophets.[32] Spiritual exegesis is thus a resource for defending the

[28] Henri de Lubac, *Catholicisme: Les aspects sociaux du dogme* (Paris: Cerf, 1947), 136, citing Maximus Confessor, *Quaestiones ad Thalassium,* q. 17 (PG 90, 304).

[29] See Hans Frei, "The 'Literal Reading' of Biblical Narrative in the Christian Tradition: Does It Stretch or Will It Break?" in *The Bible and the Narrative Tradition*, Frank McConnell, ed. (New York: Oxford Univ. Press, 1986), 36-77.

[30] Hugh of St. Victor, *Didascalicon*, Book V, 2.

[31] Henri de Lubac, *L'Écriture dans la tradition*, 7-10.

[32] *Dei Verbum*, ch. IV, pars. 14-16.

integrity of the Old Covenant's witnesses to faith rather than a means of circumventing Israel's inherent wisdom.

The lengthy commentary published in 1968 by de Lubac on the prologue and first chapter of *Dei Verbum* is also elucidating.[33] He highlights the conciliar teaching regarding Christ as "both the mediator and sum total of revelation" and focuses on the Word of God (the document's own title) not as a concept, not as a teacher, not as a doctrine but as a person.[34] No principles of exegesis make sense without the encounter with the herald of salvation who speaks the language of women and men. The difference between this sapiential approach and a fundamentalist reading lies in the personal dimensions of the Word itself:

Christianity is not, properly speaking, a 'religion of the book.' It is a religion of 'the Word,' but not uniquely or principally of the Word in either its written or even oral form. It is the religion of the Word, "not of a mute, written word," says St. Bernard, "but of a Word incarnated and living."[35]

The Word takes on flesh in the words of Scripture and bears a spiritual sense within it. By itself, no technology of criticism can grasp this sense. Furthermore, uninformed piety—a naked faith devoid of a proper knowledge of Biblical languages and literary forms—will fail to penetrate the full spiritual meaning of the books. The Bible is the condescension of the Word par excellence, and as such commands both a spiritual humbling of philology and a patient attentiveness of the faithful to the objective manifestation of the letter.[36]

## 3. The Newness of Incarnate Wisdom

In this volume as elsewhere de Lubac returns to the theme of the Christian newness. Twice he repeats Augustine's words: "The new

---

[33.] Henri de Lubac, "Commentaire du préamble et du chapitre I," *La révélation divine*, I, 157-302.

[34.] *Dei Verbum* 2.

[35.] Henri de Lubac, "Commentaire du préamble et du chapitre I," *La révélation divine*, I, 296, citing Saint Bernard, *Super missus est*, hom. 4, n. 11. Cf. idem, *Catholicisme*, 136-8.

[36.] *Dei Verbum,* 11.

lies hidden in the old; the old is made manifest in the new."[37] Herein lies the key, de Lubac says, to the whole of spiritual exegesis. He is not saying that Christ taught new ideas that render ancient philosophy or the Old Covenant meaningless. Nor is he highlighting the event of the Incarnation *qua* historical fact. "Newness" here means the total disclosure of what is real and genuine, of what will endure and be transfigured through the revelation of Jesus Christ. Newness is not a novelty. It is the single purpose and one covenant that binds the testament of Israel with Christian beginnings. For Bernard of Clairvaux, the New Testament deserved to be called "always new, because it always renews minds, and not ever old because it does not cease bearing fruit and fade into perpetuity."[38]

When eternity dwells among us in time, we face this newness. This involves communion with the sacramental Christ.[39] For de Lubac the Eucharist is our path to the indwelling of God's eternal Word in human hearts. By examining Scripture in the tradition, de Lubac is breaking and offering up spiritual bread to those who yearn for genuine wisdom.[40] The patristic and medieval practitioners of sapiential exegesis speak to an age saturated with the means of acquiring new information but spiritually famished. De Lubac was certain that the religious and moral indifference of our times could be addressed by pondering the newness of incarnate wisdom. *Sapientia* is not to be discovered in the privacy of an individual's interiority, in the security of rigid literalism, or in the well-meaning social projects that undervalue the radical novelty of the Word. Wisdom appears without warning, in unexpected places. Wisdom cries out in the streets, engages us as persons with particular roots

[37] Henri de Lubac, *L'Écriture dans la tradition*, 10, 109-9.

[38] Bernard of Clairvaux, *In vig. Nat. Dom.*, s. 6, n. 6 (PL 183; 112A).

[39] Cf. Wood, *Spiritual Exegesis and the Church*, 62: "Communion with the sacramental Christ in turn signifies and effects the union of Christ with his Church, for it is by partaking of the one bread that we become one body, namely the body of Christ which is his Church...Within spiritual exegesis, then, the "figure" or "type" functions as a sacrament which both reveals and conceals a spiritual reality. Consequently we can conclude that *the spiritual interpretation of Scripture is in fact a sacramental theology*, but one which situates sacraments within the entire historical economy of salvation." Italics added.

[40] Ibid., 153.

in families, towns, communities, and the Church, and demands an immediate response, a complete change in one's mentality.

De Lubac's research on the exegesis of the past was prodigious, and this volume represents only the tip of that very sturdy iceberg. De Lubac released *Scripture in the Tradition* to provide solid food and lasting encouragement for those on a precarious journey that will be complete only "when God may be all things in all things."[41] This collection provides a unique glimpse of a relatively small portion of the exegetical material assembled by de Lubac, but it is also complete in that one can find in each chapter not just shards of information but the recapitulation of wisdom.

A final word of caution is necessary. Faced with such a wealth of new information, the reader needs to proceed slowly if only to avoid the inevitable sourness that accompanies taking in more than one can digest at one sitting. One is well advised to read slowly and to "test everything, and hold fast to what is good!"[42] De Lubac found in the ancient texts on "the abridged Word" a Marian basis for exegesis.[43] Accordingly, the immense salvific scope of God's self-communication is compressed like a single utterance into the womb of the Virgin. Spiritual exegesis consists in unfolding the meaning of that word. As with Mary's *fiat*, we must ponder in our hearts and with great care the implications of the words presented to us. Only after a thorough meditation on what has been read can we expect to see the fruits of this new diet in our daily lives.

---

[41.] 1 Cor. 15:28.
[42.] 1 Thessalonians 5:21.
[43] Henri de Lubac, *l'Écriture dans la tradition*, 234ff.

# ABBREVIATIONS

| | |
|---|---|
| *AHDLMA* | *Archives d'histoire doctrinale et littéraire du moyen âge.* |
| *An. mar.* | Germain Morin, O.S.B., *Anecdota maredsolana,* Maredsous, 1893–1903. |
| *ASS* | *Acta Sanctorum* (Bollandists). |
| *BLE* | *Bulletin de littérature ecclésiastique.* |
| *BTAM* | *Bulletin de théologie ancienne et médiévale.* |
| *CCL* | *Corpus Christianorum,* Series Latina. |
| *ETL* | *Ephemerides Theologicae Lovanienses.* |
| Gautier | Léon Gautier, *Oeuvres poétiques d'Adam de Saint-Victor,* 3d ed., 1894. |
| *JTS* | *Journal of Theological Studies.* |
| *L. de lite* | *Monumenta Germaniae historica, Libelli de lite Imperatorum et Pontificum saec. XI et XII,* 3 vols., Hannover, 1891–1897. |
| Mai | Cardinal Angelo Mai, *Nova Patrum Bibliotheca,* 10 vols., Rome, 1852–1905. |
| Manitius | Max Manitius, *Geschichte der Lateinischen Literatur des Mittelalters,* 3 vols., Munich, 1911–1913. |
| *MBVP* | Margarin de la Bigne, *Maxima Bibliotheca veterum Patrum et antiquorum scriptorum ecclesiasticorum,* 27 vols., Lyons, 1677. |
| *MGH* | *Monumenta Germaniae historica,* Hannover-Leipzig. |
| *M.W.* | *Misset et Weale, Thesaurus hymnologicus,* vol. 1, 1888. |
| *NRT* | *Nouvelle Revue Théologique.* |

| | |
|---|---|
| Pez | Bernard Pez, O.S.B., *Thesaurus anecdotum novissimus,* Vienna, 1721–1728. |
| *PG* | Migne, *Patrologia Graeca.* |
| Pitra | Cardinal J. B. Pitra, *Spicilegium solesmense,* 4 vols., Paris, 1852–1858. |
| *PL* | Migne, *Patrologia Latina.* |
| *RB* | *Revue bénédictine.* |
| *R.bibl.* | *Revue biblique.* |
| *RevScPhTh* | *Revue des sciences philosophiques et théologiques.* |
| *RHEF* | *Revue de l'histoire de l'Eglise de France.* |
| *RMAL* | *Revue du moyen âge latin.* |
| *RSR* | *Recherches de science religieuse.* |
| *RTAM* | *Recherches de théologie ancienne et médiévale.* |
| *SC* | *Sources Chrétiennes,* Paris. |
| *Sp. casin* | *Spicilegium casinense.* |

Citations to Clement and Origen are principally to the editions of the Leipzig-Berlin Corpus: *Die Griechischen Christlichen Schriftsteller der ersten drei Jahrhunderte;* in such instances, the citation is to the page of the volume containing the cited work. Some Latin authors are quoted according to the Vienna Corpus: *Corpus scriptorum ecclesiasticorum latinorum.* The letters of Jerome, numbers 1 to 120, are quoted from the edition of the *Lettres* by J. Labourt, Paris, 1949–1958.

# 1. SPIRITUAL UNDERSTANDING

## 1. Introduction

An archeologist might lovingly labor to make Minoan civiliza-
tion live again in our mind's eye, or he might derive intense
delight from reconstructing the religious life of the cities of
Upper Asia during the era of the great Buddhist pilgrims. Yet
he has probably no real desire to take us back either to the
mores of Minos or to the beliefs of the Monks of Khotan. Even
so, he is convinced that his motivation is something other than
idle curiosity. Surely no one can doubt that such investigations
into man's past are fruitful; they enrich the human spirit and
bestow upon it a new fertility. Research becomes a kind of rich
and bountiful humus. As man explores and increases his appreciation of the varied creations of the human genius, he acquires
greater insight into his own potential. Each sounding into ancient
cultures seems to tap another spring which nourishes his own
culture.

Could it be, though, that what we so readily acknowledge
when we are dealing with distant eras or far-off societies should
be questioned when we are dealing with the rather fragile forms
which the Christian genius has elaborated? While it is certain
that not everything about these forms possesses the permanent
value which flows from truth, we cannot say that even their
ephemeral aspects should be without interest for us; *a fortiori,*
that we can ignore their earlier importance without falling into
error. Actually, we must in all seriousness beware of an inability
to appreciate the human significance of precisely those things
which are most mingled with illusion. Faced with the exegetical

1

constructs of the Fathers of the Church, we can easily be tempted to object: This was, of course, a great and lovely dream, but critical research has long since discredited it—and faith can get along perfectly well without it. Even though the historian lavishes his professional admiration on it, today's Christian has no need of it. This kind of reaction, though at least in part disputable, is readily understandable. "When we say that Greek tragedy is a thing of the past, this does not impair in the least its immortal beauty." [1] But if we were to say: "There is nothing great, nothing really new in the Christian past—those early happenings were just an aberration and are quite undeserving of an historian's sympathetic curiosity or of any effort to rediscover their essence," we would be making a false historical judgment, and this would be detrimental to the preservation and to the renewal of Christian culture.

We would be just as mistaken—and, here again, we are overstating the case, without suggesting that the opinion can actually be supported—if we admired the ancient constructs so much that we longed to make them our permanent dwelling; or if we canonized such doctrines so as to become unconscious of their weak or outdated aspects; or if we believed that fidelity to an author meant that we had to copy him or imitate him slavishly. In doing so, we would be abandoning the present without being able to find refuge in the past. Today's "primitives" simply do not give us an accurate notion of the true character of primitive humanity, which was brimming with creative energy and an openness to further and unforeseeable developments. Nor can a modern "figurist" reproduce for us the spirit of the great founders of spiritual exegesis. If the desire for servile imitation were to be accompanied by a contempt, even though only on the practical side, for the scientific methods which, painstakingly applied, have renewed our historical understanding of the sacred books, then our infidelity to the spirit of an Origen, a Jerome, or even an Augustine, would be still more evident. There is no point in wondering what one of the ancients would do if he were

1. M. J. Lagrange, *Eclaircissements sur la méthode historique,* p. 91.

alive today, in totally different conditions, and discovered all sorts of curious things unknown in his own day, enjoyed a more advanced stage of scientific development, could use the new tools of scholarship, was enlightened by an experience of the world whose very orientation could not have been foreseen by him. There is simply no answer to such questions. Still in all, the clearest history adequately demonstrates Origen's high regard for science, and his ardor and trail-blazing zeal in research. Consequently, we cannot, at least in this area, question Origen's authority, nor can we fault him with even the slightest negligence. It remains true, however, that his brand of Alexandrian Platonism created a rather dangerous climate of thought, where neither the world of natures nor the world of history possessed any real solidity. This lies behind the hasty flight, from the one as from the other, towards spiritual significance, and accounts for the tendency to pause over literal exegesis no longer than one would in the natural sciences. Thus, historical data are frequently given short shrift, and serve as springboards rather than as terms for thought. This can be observed in Augustinianism as well as in Origenism, but it obviously did not prevent St. Augustine—whose openness to scientific problems was not as great as Origen's—from having, like Origen, a profoundly historical view of life. Furthermore, as we glance over the history of Christian exegesis during the last few centuries, we see that the persistent obstacle—it was still with us, only yesterday—to critical research was not (a few significant exceptions aside) spiritual interpretation at all. It was false science; it was a pernicious literalism, "which took everything literally, out of a desire to follow the literal meaning alone";[2] it was a mania for harmonization, and false notions of biblical inerrancy or tradition. The marvellous thing is that the mind is freed from this sort of approach by regular recourse to our ancient authors.

A still more subtle misconception is possible. This concedes the tribute of admiration to the "allegorism" of the Fathers, but considers it basically as a game. The criticism may well be de-

---

[2.] M. J. Lagrange, *La Méthode historique* (2d ed.), p. 120.

served by some of the later authors.[3] Such a case could even be made against an Origen, at least *prima facie*. Origen's thought developed with such a profusion and wealth of symbols that a note of the gratuitous appears. He discovers a role for classical aesthetics in expressing the Christian history of salvation. Yet these findings, however important they might be in themselves, should not mask what is essential. Critical effort would be at fault if it stopped at them. Origen is consistently sober and respectful towards the text he has chosen to comment upon. Of course it is possible to play with Scripture as one would with a toy, or to play on "spiritual meanings." But if we are looking for this kind of amusement, we shall have to knock on another door than Origen's. For Origen, as for his equals, Scripture is always the Word of God, and not merely in general but here and now. In the hands of these commentators (or, rather, in the divine hands), Scripture is the Arm of battle against the enemy Powers, the Sword whose sharpened point reaches to the division of soul and spirit.

Moreover, their exegesis answered to the needs of a Christianity which was still being born. We find it difficult today to appreciate this sufficiently. It is not because it was unimportant that the role of this exegesis escapes us, but because the need for it has been perfectly satisfied. We who are in peaceful possession and enjoyment of its permanent achievements can no longer imagine the situation which made it necessary. The mystical interpretation of Scripture, Möhler has written, "stands as one of the most remarkable phenomena of the early Church; it has never been appreciated as much as it deserves, nor has it ever been fully understood. It would be impossible to calculate the amount of good accomplished by this method in the spread of Christianity among pagans and Jews. This mystical interpretation is also, and by its very essence, tied in with the birth of a

---

[3.] See Henri Davenson, in *Esprit,* June 1936, p. 457: "Allegorical exegesis . . . was not only a weapon in the hands of the theologians. It was also a noble game for literate Christians in early antiquity, a game which their parents had taught them to practise on Homer and Virgil." See also H. I. Marrou, *Saint Augustin et la fin de la culture antique,* II *Retractatio* (1949), pp. 646–651.

very pure conception of the Christian life." [4] During his brief career, Möhler clearly established his penetrating grasp of the spirit of Christianity, and his observations are accurate and undeniably significant. Even so, we think they are inadequate. We are dealing with something which not only is of capital importance for our understanding of primitive Christianity but also touches upon the permanent foundation of Christian thought, as Möhler himself seems to suggest at the end of the passage quoted. So we have good reason to rejoice that it has reappeared in our own day, although naturally in quite new forms, as one of the prime concerns of exegesis and theology. The process has been accompanied by much trial and error, by many obscure arguments, indeed by many mistakes. But who can be surprised by this? We shall now make an effort to see just what is at issue here—without in the least undertaking the development of all the viewpoints which can be held on a subject of such extraordinary complexity, a subject which is notoriously difficult to grasp at its vital center. [5]

\* \* \*

For a long time now, each new generation has received from its predecessors in the faith a Christianity which, objectively, was "ready-made," from the most elementary dogmatic formulation to the most sophisticated expression of spirituality. Somehow the task seems to have been done once for all, and to have won for us this universe of perfect expressions. Without troubling ourselves about the tree, we have only to gather the fruits. For this reason, among others, we can behave like pure literalists in our exegesis without any great harm. We find it perfectly natural to view purely as historians—and, in doing this, we have incomparably richer resources at our disposal than our prede-

4. *L'unité dans l'Eglise,* appendix VII (French tr., collection "Unam Sanctam," 1939, pp. 260–261).
5. Thus we shall not explicitly consider the relationship of spiritual understanding with the idea of Tradition, even though this is one of the problem's principal aspects. And we shall have nothing to say on the subject of biblical symbolism.

cessors did—everything which is to be found in the books of the Old Testament. Its figurative substance has, so to speak, already been extracted and put at our disposal.[6] But at the very beginning, and even two or three centuries afterwards, we could not have afforded the luxury of a disinterestedness of this sort. The very reading of the holy books then put into question, and in a very immediate way, the whole idea of the new faith. During that period, the spiritual interpretation of the Bible was in no sense a practice of supererogation. And it was certainly not a game. Before it was acknowledged as something well established, it had first made a contribution to the very establishment of the faith, or at least to the translating of it. It did not constitute what might be called a surplus vis-à-vis an already-existent religious capital. Rather, it entered into the constitution of that very capital, and as an essential part of it. In other words, it played an indispensable role in getting Christianity out of its diapers without breaking it off from its roots. Christianity had to acquire complete self-awareness and it had to be assured of its independence of Judaism, while still being preserved from the crude interpretations by which it was also menaced by the pagan spirit. Still more importantly, the objective expression of Christianity had to be hammered out. And while with Christ everything—absolutely everything—had, of course, been already given, the very fact of Christ still had to be expressed.

Let us give some careful thought to the question. Christian truth did not burst upon empty minds, nor was it interpreted from a purely neutral point of view. It received its embodiment and its capacity to be grasped principally from biblical realities. Indeed, we can say that the formulation of Christian truth was a prolongation of those realities. Thanks to the dual law of

6. We are not referring to Old Testament teachings or laws which can be found as such in the New Testament. This is self-evident. See, for example, Ambrose's distinction between the *mystica legis* and the *moralia probitatis: In Lucam,* 1. 8, n. 2 (*PL,* 15, 1792D). Or Augustine's distinction of *sacramenta, promissa, praecepta* in the Law: *In Psalmum 73,* n. 2 (*PL,* 36, 930). On the precepts of the Law which must still be accomplished literally: Origen, *Num.,* h. 11, 1 (p. 75). See Irenaeus, *Adv. Haer.,* 4, 12–13 (*PG,* 7, 1004–1010).

analogy and contrast, studious reflection on the Old Testament in the light of Christ made possible a better grasp of the New Testament and also a better appreciation of its newness. While this reflection served the exposition of the faith, its primary fruit was an increased understanding, even perception, of the object of faith.

In this way, the former Economy's traditional pedagogic role was carried on at the very heart of the new Economy and, in a fashion unique in religious history, the former Economy lived on in a mysterious way. The Christian mystery, because of the magnificent providential Economy which embraces both Testaments and links them together, has not been handed down to us as a collection of timeless definitions, unrelated to any historical situation and demanding only to be clothed, according to our fancy, with biblical images as with just so many illustrations. The intimate links between the two Testaments are of quite another kind. Within the very consciousness of Jesus— if we may cast a human glance into that sanctuary—the Old Testament was seen as the matrix of the New or as the instrument of its creation.[7] This meant something much more than extrinsic preparation. Even the categories used by Jesus to tell us about himself are ancient biblical categories. Jesus causes them to burst forth or, if you prefer, sublimates them and unifies them by making them converge upon himself.[8] But he somehow needs them. Furthermore, in this new employment, they are neither abstract categories nor accidental images. They retain all of their original value and flavor as allusions to precise facts, unique realities. These realities, in the context of which

7. Consider the example suggested by Père Augustin George: "Did not the old story of Moriah help him to think about his death? The Fathers, in their later comparisons between the sacrifice of Abraham and that of Jesus, frequently emphasize purely accidental analogies, but they are basically correct in seeing the profound kinship of the two sacrifices." *Le sacrifice d'Abraham, essai sur les diverses intentions de ses narrateurs*, in *Etudes de critique et d'histoire religieuse*, Lyon, 1948, p. 109.

8. See the word of which Origen was so fond: $\alpha\dot{\upsilon}\tau o\beta\alpha\sigma\iota\lambda\epsilon\dot{\iota}\alpha$. Similarly, Pseudo-Barnabas, ch. 6, and Hippolytus. *The Apostolic Tradition*, ch. 23, likened the Promised Land to the flesh of Jesus, and so forth.

Jesus places himself and which he thereby transforms, are sown all through the history of Israel and constitute the very object of Israel's expectation. We could make the same kind of statement about everything, or almost everything, which his first witnesses teach us about his person and his work. Thus, "biblical images," and the concrete facts behind them, furnish the thread, both historical and noetic, from which is woven the Christian mystery in all its newness and transcendence.

"Although it is always profitable," as Père Spicq points out, "to illuminate the New Testament teachings on baptism, for example, through recourse to the typology of the Red Sea, much more fruit can be obtained from a biblical theology which is derived from a study of St. Paul and St. John according to the literal meaning. The fulfillment of revelation affords more clarity than do its beginnings; in point of fact, the beginnings are illuminated by their fulfillment." [9] There can be no argument about the last statement, which is expressive of a reality always useful to recall. The real question, however, is to determine whether the beginning of revelation played a role, and perhaps a significant one, in the final formulation of revelation itself. Put in another way, may not the New Testament teaching be formulated and, in its literal meaning, become intelligible through some spiritual signification bestowed by Christ upon the facts of the Old Law? In the example considered here, it seems clear that "the typology of the Red Sea" or that of the Cloud is not merely a comparison which is added on to the Pauline theology: it is an explicit part of it.[10] There can be no doubt that the Apostle viewed the comparison as something more than a means of illuminating from without a doctrine on baptism which had already been put in final form. The comparison was more than a casual spiritual fruit.

It has very rightly been said that "our fathers in the faith knew of the first Adam only in relation to the Second; of Melchisedech only in relation to the Eucharist; of the tree of paradise in relation to the tree of the Cross; of the passage

9. C. Spicq, *RevScPhTh*, 1948, p. 90.
10. 1 Cor. 10, 1–3. The same can be said of the deluge, 1 Pet. 3, 20–21.

8

through the Red Sea in relation to baptism; of the Psalms of David in relation to Christ; and of the temple in relation to the Church." [11] But even that must be considered as the other side of a truth which, in all essential aspects, has first to be stated in inverse terms.[12] Baptism, Eucharist, Church, and so forth, were first thought of, at least when they were seriously reflected upon, only as "functions of" Melchisedech, the Pasch under the Law, the passage through the Red Sea, the manna, the Assembly in the desert, the Temple at Jerusalem. All the basic biblical themes: Covenant, Election, People of God, Word, Messiah, Kingdom, Day of the Lord, and so forth, enter into the Christian idea of salvation. The mystery of the Redemption, purifying us and tearing us away from servitude to sin, occupies the central role in our faith. But the truth is that if it obtained admittance into the minds of the first generations of believers, it did so by reason of a transposition, prepared for by the Prophets, of the Law's ideas of sacrifice and expiation as well as by reason of the stories about the two captivities (in Egypt and Babylon) and about the double liberation of his people which the God of Israel effected through a ransom.[13] And did not the entire New Covenant appear to be sealed by the blood of Christ just as the

11. Dom Olivier Rousseau. *Histoire du mouvement liturgique;* ET *The Progress of the Liturgy,* Westminster, 1951, pp. 146–147.

12. It may be that the mental operations of the New Testament authors transcend any such duality: simultaneously, they express the New Testament by the Old and spiritualize the Old by the New. As we reflect on an already constituted New Testament, we, in our historical exegesis, must comment on the New Testament through the Old, and then on the Old through the New. Our operation is a dual one, as is our movement—we are conscious of a rhythm whose alternating beats become distinguishable only in terms of one another.

13. See Jacques Guillet, "Le Thème de la marche au désert dans l'Ancien Testament," in *RSR,* 1948. St. Augustine, following St. Paul, will say, for example: *"Qui eduxi te de terra Aegypti. Non illi tantum populo dicitur. Omnes enim educti sumus de terra Aegypti, omnes per mare rubrum transivimus, inimici nostri persequentes nos in aqua perierunt."* (*In Psalmum 80,* 15 [*PL,* 37, 1042]). St. Irenaeus had written in like vein (*Adv. Haereses,* 1. 4, 30, 4): *"Universa enim quae ex Aegypto profectio fiebat populi, a Deo typus et imago fuit profectionis Ecclesiae, quae erat futura de Gentibus"* (*PG,* 7, 1067C). See Deut. 7, 10 and Is. 41, 14.

9

Old Covenant had been sealed by the blood of victims? [14] Thus "the rock of Golgotha was intelligible to humanity because it stood out against the background of ancient Judaism, its beliefs, its aspirations, its worship." [15] The Jewish people prefigured the Church while preparing for it, and prepared for it while prefiguring it, and the earthly kingdom which seemed promised to them was the image of the kingdom of heaven which Jesus was to announce. Ultimately, "the most specifically new themes of the Gospel: adoption by the Father, gift of the Spirit, as well as revelation of the Son, take on all their meaning, and actually possess meaning, only when they are seen as the common ground of the great themes of the prophetic Word." [16] Furthermore, is it not sufficient to read with a little attention the stories which make up our "New Testament" to see that, regardless of the special genius of individual authors or of the diversity of genres, all are basically presented as a perpetual interpretation of the Scriptures, that is to say, of what we know as the "Old Testament?" [17] In the majority of cases, this interpretation is a

[14.] I Cor. 11, 25 and Ex. 24, 8, and so forth. Bernard, *In Octava Paschae,* sermo 1, n. 5 (*PL,* 183, 294C).

[15.] Jean Levie, S.J., "La crise de l'Ancien Testament," in *NRT,* 1929, p. 835. See Louis Bouyer, "La première Eucharistie dans la dernière Cène," in *La Maison-Dieu,* 18, p. 47: "It is only through the avenues which were opened up to the mind and heart of man by the events of the Exodus, the passage of the Red Sea, the settling in Palestine that we shall ever be able to understand our deliverance from the Evil One, our passage, by baptism, 'from the kingdom of darkness into the kingdom of the Son.'"

[16.] Augustine, *De vera religione,* c. 27, n. 50: ". . . series populi uni Deo dediti . . ., cujus historia Vetus Testamentum vocatur, quasi terrenum pollicens regnum; quae tota nihil aliud est quam imago novi populi, et Novi Testamenti pollicentis regnum caelorum"* (*PL,* 34, 144). *In Psalmum 75,* n. 1: "Judaea vera, Christi Ecclesia" (*PL,* 36, 958). Louis Bouyer, in *La Vie spirituelle,* vol. 80 (1949), p. 580.

[17.] See Jean Levie, S.J., "Les limites de la preuve d'Ecriture sainte," in *NRT,* 1949, pp. 1012–1013: The dogmatic efforts of St. Paul are "efforts to express as well as possible, using yesterday's words, using old formulas inherited from the Old Testament, the new revelation which was made to humanity, or to the Apostle in particular, about Christ. To speak about Christ and about the dramatic newness of his message, he has nothing at his disposal but traditional Jewish concepts and words,

spiritual transposition and, as such, is effected through a symbolic utilization. But, again, in the majority of cases, whether the interpretation is immediate or reflective, it must not be compared to some tacked-on embroidery; it lies within the very texture of the fabric. Were we to view Christianity as a body of doctrine, the interpretation would not be a garment thrown over it after the event but a part of the body itself, whose unifying spirit is the present reality of the Saviour.[18]

## 2. "Spiritual Meaning"

The word which was first used by St. Paul, and which was generally used thereafter in the Latin tradition, to express this sym-

---

which he took, just as they were, from his environment and education, and which formed the point of departure for his thought; and yet this new reality, communicated by God, is infinitely richer than traditional concepts and words; nonetheless, it must be understood with those concepts as a starting point, . . ."; see also p. 1028.

[18.] These remarks could probably be made more general. In order to be actualized, every thought requires an expression which, by analogy or contrast, relates it to some previously expressed thought. Thus allusion is essential to it. This is even more strictly true for the period when the particular thought is being formed, prior to being transmitted, for the period of invention and creation, when something new must fill man's mind so as to transform him, "open" him to some area which was unexplored, unsuspected, until then. Thus it is true in the highest degree when the mind must humanly translate the Object of divine revelation, so as to acquire a reflective awareness of it and somehow "grasp" it. Thus there will be still more reason, in this second logical moment, to speak of invention and creation, inasmuch as revelation, and thereby welcome and reception, is so much more basically involved. Consequently, there will be more room for symbolism. We might add that, even when a thought can readily be formulated in the abstract, without any need for explicit recourse to an earlier thought which serves as impulse or symbol, such recourse can still be useful, and even necessary for all practical purposes, if we are to take better account of it and to grasp it in a more living way. In this case, the operation will be less spontaneous and will have less independent ontological significance: thus "thought comments upon itself" (J. Baruzi). A third logical moment could be found in the pedagogical use of the image or system of images.

bolic transposition was *allegory*.[1] For a long time, allegory was
taken by theology to mean, and often in the broadest sense, the
mysteries of Christ and of the Church as they appeared in
Scripture. Hence, the allegorical meaning was the dogmatic
meaning par excellence, and it was firmly rooted in history.[2] Far
from compromising the historical foundations of the faith, it
actually insured for all Christian thought the essentially historical
character which is so perfectly in keeping with the Christian
faith, but which has so often been disturbingly blurred. The
word lost favor, however, for reasons which are readily understandable. The word's etymology suggests that allegory is a
meaning *other* than the letter, or auxiliary to it, lacking organic
relationship with it. Its modern usage contrasts it either to
ontological sign or to parable, but in both instances this is false
to the ancient acceptation: actually, it evokes the idea of an
analogy which is artificial, elaborately detailed, or the idea of an
exploitation of image to develop an idea which is already
formed.[3] Such an evocation corresponds only too well to what
has in fact become the usage of scriptural "allegory." It can even
suggest certain fatal negations.[4] Moreover, even among the

---

[1.] There are a hundred examples. Here are a few: Gregory, *In
Ezechielem,* l. 2, hom. 3, n. 18: "*Scriptura . . . in litteram dividitur et
allegoriam*" (*PL,* 76, 968); l. 1, hom. 3, n. 4 (*PL* 807C). Jerome, *In
Amos,* l. 2, c. 4: "*allegoriam, id est, intelligentiam spiritualem*" (*PL,*
25, 1027D). Thomas, *Ia,* q. 1, a. 10.

[2.] See "Sur un vieux distique, La doctrine du 'quadruple sens' " in
*Mélanges Cavallera* (1948), pp. 347–366.

[3.] One of the best explanations of the difference between symbol and
allegory in their structure and noetic importance is given by Jean Baruzi
in *Saint Jean de la Croix et le problème de l'expérience mystique* (2d
ed.), pp. 323–329. It would be wrong to speak uniformly ill of allegory,
even where it seems to be at its most artificial, for in certain cases it
can be the vehicle in which a great and authentic symbolism is itself
symbolized in a hundred different ways. We sometimes find in certain
authors, and generally among the Fathers, a hint of the allegorical which
should not throw us off, lest we thereby forfeit the opportunity of penetrating its spirit. But we also must be wary of indulging in an "atomistic"
exegesis of the writings of the Fathers, no less than of Scripture itself.

[4.] See Spinoza, *Epist. 25:* "*Christi passionem, mortem et sepulturam
tecum litteraliter accipio, ejus autem resurrectionem allegorice.*" In his
Latin commentary on the Song of Songs, Luis de Leon well distinguished

Ancients themselves, the banner of Christian allegory often flew over foreign wares, and this accounts for the ambivalences and the variations in acceptance and rejection which can be found in the work of a single author. As a consequence, there has been a preference for other terms in modern times.

Certain writers, noting that the early Fathers sought "the deep Christian significance of the Scriptures in the hollow of the literal meaning," propose to restrict themselves to an expression of that meaning. As they see it, this sort of expression adequately delimits—provided it is "perceived by faith" in all its fullness—"the one true meaning of the Bible." In approaching the matter in this way, they show an admirable concern for unity, while at the same time avoiding the confusion of the authentic exegesis of the Fathers, which "consists in drawing forth the profound and objective significance of a text, in the light of the entire economy of salvation," [5] with an "allegorizing exegesis," in the manner of Philo or of the Greeks. They properly desire to get rid of the "allegorizing stucco" which is thrown over "the living architecture of the Bible." [6]

---

the two acceptations of the word: *"Tota hujus libri oratio figurata est et allegorica. Allegoricam dico, non ea allegoria quam, sancto Paulo auctore, inducunt Theologi, cum in sacris Litteris a litterae, quem vocant, sensu allegoricum sensum distinguunt; sed quam tradunt rhetores efficiex perpetua metaphora"* (*Opera*, vol. II, Salamanca, n.d., p. 15). According to Oscar Cullmann, "for allegorical exegesis, history is only a symbol behind which something else is to be sought"; this exegesis takes as point of departure "a completely formulated idea so as to find it again in the text at any price." *La necessité et la fonction de l'exégèse philologique et historique de la Bible*, in *Verbum Caro*, vol. III, 1949, p. 6. For Abbé Jean Vilnet, the allegorical meaning "consists in using facts or words from the Bible, which have a literal value, as pure symbols of other realities to which they appear to be totally unconnected" (*Bible et mystique chez saint Jean de la Croix*, 1949, p. 84, n.) This, however, is not the true traditional acceptation, which is all we are concerned with here.

[5]. See Dom Célestin Charlier in a fine study, filled with traditional vigor and packed with excellent suggestions, *La lecture sapientielle de la Bible*, in *La Maison-Dieu;* ET *The Christian Approach to the Bible*, Westminster, 1958, pp. 255–263. See Charlier's "Exégèse partistique et exégèse scientifique," in *Esprit et Vie*, 1949, p. 62.

[6]. "Typologie ou Evolution. Problèmes d'exégèse spirituelle," in *Esprit et Vie*, 1949, p. 594.

Now it is true that everything *is,* in some sense, contained
within the letter, for that which lacks foundation in the letter
must be something which has been added to the text, and is
therefore arbitrary. "We must never seek the spiritual meaning
behind the letter, but always within it, just as we do not find
the Father behind the Son but in him and through him." [7] Even
so, it seems to us that this terminology,[8] though it might have
the advantage of simplicity, is just too much at odds with universal usage to be fully acceptable. It also conflicts with the
traditional distinction according to which the inspired Scriptures
are set apart from other books, in that the things signified by
its words possess a signification willed by God, a signification
which relates to salvation. How is it possible for the meaning of
the thing to be, without more, the meaning of the letter, thus of
the word, since the proper function of the word, thus of the
letter, is to signify that thing? Whatever is true of the practice
we find the distinction in unity well expressed in a formula of
St. Gregory the Great: *"Aliquando in historia litteram suscipiunt,
aliquando vero per significationem litterae spiritum requirunt"*
(We sometimes receive the letter in history, but sometimes we
also seek the spirit through the meaning of the letter).[9] For the
letter is "the sacrament of the spirit." [10] Moreover, the termi-

[7.] Hans Urs von Balthasar, "Die Schrift als Gottes Wort," in *Schweizer
Rundschau,* 1949, p. 10. See Maurice Pontet, *L'exégèse de saint Augustin
prédicateur,* 1946, p. 586.

[8.] As a matter of fact, this is the terminology which was proposed by
the great Arnauld, "Remarques sur 'l'ancienne nouveauté de l'Ecriture
sainte'," (*Oeuvres,* vol. V, p. 346): "We must remain in agreement that
the true literal meaning of Scripture is the meaning which the Holy
Spirit intended to point out to us. . . . Thus we are interpreting the
Prophets very literally when we apply what God promised the Jews at
the time of the Messiah to Christians throughout the history of the
Church; the other interpretations, however, are not literal but Judaic."
It is true that Arnauld, as can be seen, applies his principle only to
prophecies properly so called. He also adds that those who understand
them in another fashion deserve to be told: *"Nescitis cujus spiritus estis,*
you do not know what the spirit of Christianity is."

[9.] *In Ezechielem,* l. 1, h. 3, n. 4 (*PL,* 76, 807C).

[10.] Dom Charlier, *op. cit.,* p. 279. See Jerome, *In Amos,* l. 2, c. 5:
*"medulla spiritus"* (*PL,* 25, 1036B). Gregory, *In Ezechielem,* l. 2, h. 10,
n. 2: *"latens in littera spiritualis medulla"* (*PL,* 76, 1058). Hesychius,

nology which we are discussing does not seem to be particularly
precise; just because something is within the letter, or under the
letter, it does not follow that it is literal.[11] Finally, though the
terminology might avoid one kind of confusion, does it not
court another by implying that the entire meaning of Scripture
should be reduced to what the sacred writer could explicitly
perceive of it? [12]

Thus it is that we are more likely today to speak of *typology*.
The word is a neologism and has been barely a century in use.[13]
But it was very happily coined. Since the time of St. Paul, traditional exegesis has always been concerned with "types," figures, and we can occasionally find "typical meaning" used

---

*In Leviticum* (*PG*, 93, 780B). It is also true that, taking the terms very
precisely, it is not Scripture as text, but sacred history as contained
in Scripture, which offers a spiritual meaning, since spiritual meaning is
not the meaning of words but the meaning of things: it is δια τύπου
προφητεία because δια πραγμάτων προφητεία; see John Chrysostom,
*De Paenitentia*, h. 6, n. 4 (*PG*, 49, 320); 1. 17, c. 5, n. 2, (*PL*, 41, 313).
The paradox which is here the object of our faith makes it impossible,
as in every analogous case, for us to express it in language which is
perfectly adequate and coherent.

11. Similarly, if it is true that "there is no divine content in the Bible
outside of its historical signification" (Charlier, in *Esprit et Vie*, 1949,
p. 590), we should beware of the inference that there is no divine meaning in the Bible other than the historical meaning.

12. *Règles pour l'intelligence des saintes Ecritures* (1716), p. 10: "I
call the first the immediate meaning, and the second the prophetic. . . .
The second is almost always more literal than the first because it is the
meaning which the prophet had principally in mind." On the other
hand, as Thomas says, *IIaIIae*, q. 173, a. 4, the sacred writer is an *instrumentum deficiens* in the hands of God, and he never sees what he is
writing about except *cum aliquo cognitionis defectu;* also, *etiam veri
prophetae non omnia cognoscunt quae in eorum visis et verbis aut etiam
factis Spiritus sanctus intendit.* See F. Ogara, "De typica apud Chry-
sostomum prophetia," in *Gregorianum*, 1943, p. 71: "(*Spiritus Sanctus*)
*Veteris rudibus saepe figuris Novi mysteria significare voluit, quidquid
tandem de illis mysteriis futuris scriptor humanus intellexerit.*" Newman
also thought that "the sacred authors did not always know or even suspect the spiritual and profound meaning" of what they wrote. J. Seynaeve,
"La doctrine de Newman sur l'inspiration," in *ETL,* 1949, p. 366.

13. The word seems to be of Lutheran origin, but this is certainly no
reason to find it objectionable, any more than we object to the words
"patristic" or "patrology."

synonymously with mystical or allegorical meaning, or even with figurative meaning, as in Pascal.[14] "Typology" also has the virtue of doing away, at least in intention, with all the old straw in the grain of Christian exegesis, something which could not be accomplished by the word "allegory" alone. But it has the drawback of referring solely to a result, without alluding to the spirit or basic thrust of the process which produces that result. Its connotations may also be too narrow, for, strictly speaking, it corresponds solely to the first of the three meanings spelled out in the classical division after the literal sense, "history." Typology thus puts narrow limitations on its object. In any event, it does not include within its scope the most properly spiritual explanations. This is a serious shortcoming, and it is perfectly possible that it may sometimes be intended. Although "typology" as an original suggestion was on solid ground, it was much too circumscribed. We should not place exclusive dependence upon it unless we are prepared to reduce the bold and pregnant teaching of a St. Paul to a game of figures, no matter how completely they may be authenticated.

In the final analysis, is it not preferable to revert to the most traditional [15] and the most general expression of all, and—without ruling out other terms or later refinements—to speak once again, quite simply, of "spiritual meaning," "spiritual understanding"? Some find the word intimidating, and it can, of course, lend itself to abuse.[16] But the mere possibility of abuse should

[14.] But even if we use the term "typological exegesis," we shall be careful to avoid using "typological meaning": the latter is pure jargon, for which there is neither need nor excuse. See Thomas, *Quodl. 7,* q. 6, a. 15: *"allegoricus sensus vel typicus."* On the words "type," "figure," "mystery," and "mystical meaning" as used in Christian antiquity, see our *Corpus mysticum* (2d ed.), 1949, chs. 2 and 3.

[15.] Thomas, *Quodl. 7,* q. 6, a. 15: *"Sensus iste qui ex figuris accipitur, spiritualis vocatur."*

[16.] It was against the pretense of a completely "spiritual" (that is to say, falsely spiritual) Christianity that Newman delivered at Littlemore his two sermons: "The Christian Church, a Continuation of the Jewish," and "The Principle of Continuity between the Jewish and Christian Churches," collected in *Sermons Bearing on Subjects of the Day* (new ed.), 1879, pp. 181–217. In these sermons, he stresses the literal and not merely "spiritual" fulfillment of the prophecies.

16

not force us to "dim the flame." It should not rob us of one of the essential words in the Christian language, a word which Scripture formally countenances. There is no good reason for brushing it aside. Actually, we cannot do without it if we are to obtain a relatively complete view of the reality described by it. With unique forcefulness, it expresses a characteristic note of the whole new Economy, in which the ancient people of Israel become, in the Church, Israel according to the spirit. The Old Law in its entirety becomes the Law of the spirit. As St. Augustine teaches, the sole aim of all the pedagogy, both historical and prophetic, in the Old Testament is to lead us to perceive the spiritual realities which, no longer past or future, eternally perdure.[17] And is there not a consistently spiritualizing quality about the typology of the liturgy? And is this not also true of the biblical symbolism of early Christian art? [18]

Now this spiritualization is simultaneously an interiorization: in saying "spiritual," we are also saying "interior." [19] The New Law is no longer engraved on tablets of stone, but on hearts, and the visible bonds which unite Christians in the "Body of Christ" simply express or minister to bonds in the mystical order. What we have here is a dual transposition, a dual passage (something which cannot be finally achieved in any one of us as long as the present age has not achieved its course) from the first Testament to the second. The fruit of the interpretation of Scripture

17. *De vera religione*, c. 7, n. 13 (*PL*, 34, 128). See *Epist. 196:* It is by reason of "the spiritual and apostolic understanding" of the Old Testament that the Christian can be called "a Jew according to the spirit," a son of Abraham according to the spirit (*PL*, 33, 891–899). Florus of Lyons, *In Epistulam ad Romanos* (*PL*, 119, 294A.).

18. The sacrifice of Isaac, for example, signifies not merely the exterior fact of Christ's death, but also man's salvation by Jesus. Jonah, vomited out by the whale, is not only Jesus leaving the tomb, but the Christian being reborn to eternal life. See A. Pérate, *L'archéologie chrétienne*, Paris, 1892, pp. 69, 74, 102, 112; O. Marucchi, *Manual of Christian Archeology*, Paterson, 1935, pp. 302–308. P. Perdrizet, who refers to these examples in his *Etude sur le speculum humanae salvationis*, Paris, 1908, p. 114, wrongly concludes that this symbolism is "purely moral."

19. See Thomas, *In Joannem*, c. 6, lect. 4, n. 8: *"Quanto aliquid est magis spirituale, tanto magis est intrinsecum."*

17

which takes account of this dual passage is, therefore, appropriately called "spiritual meaning." [20]

The expression proves its appropriateness in other ways as well. In the language of Christian tradition, "spirit" is naturally allied with "truth," taken in the vigorous, substantial sense possessed by that word when expressing the reality of Christ as contrasted with the shadows and figures which had gone before. From another point of view, it also allows us to exploit the Pauline antithesis of letter, or flesh, and spirit. Obviously, we must remember that the letter is by no means equivalent to the literal meaning, and the flesh still less. It is a sort of sterilized literal meaning, stripped of the spiritual potencies which lie, like seeds, within it; a materialized meaning, rigid, exclusive, and thereby falsified; as such, it is in opposition, now that the fullness of time has arrived, to the dual passage we have just spoken of. As Origen pointed out, it is a figure which, unwilling to acknowledge itself as such, refuses to yield to the reality. This was the temptation of the beneficiaries of the Old Covenant, once the Message of Christ was proclaimed. But let us not delude ourselves that all analogous temptations have disappeared from within Christianity itself. The Lord must constantly renew the changing of water into wine, lest we fall back into "Judaic" interpretations. The latter were to be detected even in an apparently totally Christian "typology." Nor have the strong warnings of St. Paul lost their timeliness—nor will they ever lose it. To give but one example, mild enough to begin with and much too old to offend anyone, can anyone seriously doubt that the great Bossuet's *Politique tirée de l'Ecriture sainte* would have been quite different if he had pondered over them more deeply?

Besides, why should we resist calling the meaning which comes in a special way from the Holy Spirit the "spiritual meaning?" [21] This, most probably, is far too obvious to need elabora-

[20]. See Alcuin, *In Joannem: "interiorem intelligentiam spiritualis sensus"* (*PL*, 100, 821C). Bernard, *Sermo 67 de diversis* (*PL*, 183, 690A-B).

[21]. See Bernard, *In Cantica*, sermo 45, n. 7: *"Sed attende Spiritum loqui, et spiritualiter oportere intelligi quae dicuntur"* (*PL*, 183, 1002D). Rupert of Deutz, *In Nahum*, l. 2 (*PL*, 168, 555B). Thomassin, *Dogmata*

tion. It cannot be doubted that the literal meaning also comes from the Holy Spirit; every true scriptural meaning is inspired, and inspiration is unique. Still in all, we have not completely perceived the intention of the Spirit as long as we have failed to penetrate to the deepest level. And if we deliberately stop short of that intention, we have been unfaithful to it. Thus we see that the spiritual meaning bears a special relationship to the Spirit, and this is further evidence that it is well-named. Since the spiritual meaning, as the meaning of things, is not bestowed upon them by the human author of a book, it stems totally from the Spirit. In it we find the *Spiritus Sancti sacramenta*.[22] Through it we enjoy the *Spiritus Sancti consortium*.[23] Furthermore—and is this not its essential characteristic?—it is the meaning of the New Testament,[24] that is to say, the meaning taught by the Spirit of Truth [25] who is the Spirit of Christ. There is no resource of the human mind, no method, no scientific procedure which will ever be enough to make us hear "the music written on the silent pages of the Holy Books." [26] Finally, and to put it still more simply, it is the meaning which is related to Christ, to the Lord: now "the Lord is the Spirit," precisely the Spirit of the Scriptures.[27]

Even the ambiguity of the word "spiritual" can add to its

---

*Theologica*, vol. III, tr. 1, c. 8, n. 6: *"Scripturae non litteram tantum sed Spiritum maxime sugere insuescant, cum ille Spiritus sanctus sit, qui has nobis Scripturas modulatus est."* Scheeben, *Dogmatik*, 237: "The divine origin of Scripture implies besides that its words do not only have the literal meaning intended by the human authors . . . ; they also have . . . a spiritual meaning proper to the Holy Spirit."

22. Jerome, *In Ezechielem*, l. 1, c. 1 (*PL*, 25, 26D).

23. *Ibid.*, l. 12, c. 41 (*PL*, 25, 399D).

24. See *In Apocalypsin expositio, visio tertia: "Spiritualis intelligentia in Veteri Testamento, nihil est aliud, quam Novum Testamentum"* (*PL*, 17, 807D).

25. Didymus, *Liber de Spiritu Sancto*, n. 33 (*PG*, 39, 1063C).

26. Louis Massignon, "L'expérience mystique et les modes de stylisation littéraire," in *Le Roseau d'or*, no. 20 (1927), *Chroniques*.

27. 2 Cor. 3, 17. See the commentary of Père Allo, *in loc.*, p. 95 and p. 107. The meaning of this expression of St. Paul is by no means exhausted by this presentation. See J. Lebreton, *Histoire du dogme de la Trinité*, vol. I, (6th ed.), pp. 611–615.

value. The word "allegory," on the other hand, could be danger-
ously ambiguous, and there surely is an interest in carefully dis-
tinguishing the imaginative literal meanings from the mystical or
"typical" meanings, which were often badly confounded by many
of the ancients. To approach the subject from another viewpoint, we see that there are excellent reasons for continuing the
use of the single expression, "spiritual understanding," for the
activity which leads to both of these meanings. In spite of objective diversity, the same basic movement of the spirit is present,
under the influence of the same Spirit [28] and towards the same
penetration of the spirit of the text, whether our purpose be to
discover an advance indication of Christ, to abandon the seemingly carnal meaning of certain prophecies, to understand a parable, or to obtain greater penetration into the teachings of Jesus
in the Sermon on the Mount. And there is the constant goal of
arriving at the *scientia spiritualis* and the *purus sensus* which,
according to St. Caesarius of Arles, are conferred upon the
Church.[29]

Finally—and here again we have an important point—the
spiritual meaning, understood as figurative or mystical meaning,
is the meaning which, objectively, leads us to the realities of the
spiritual life and which, subjectively, can only be the fruit of a
spiritual life. That is where it leads; for to the extent that we
have not arrived at it, we have not drawn a totally Christian
interpretation from the Scriptures. It is certain that the Christian
mystery is not something to be curiously contemplated like a
pure object of science, but is something which must be interiorized and lived. It finds its own fullness in being fulfilled within

[28.] Gregory, *In Ezechielem,* l. 1, hom. 3, n. 19 (*PL,* 76, 814C).
[29.] *Expositio in Apocalypsin: "In zona aurea accincta pectori, potest
etiam scientia spiritualis ac purus sensus datus Ecclesiae intellegi" (Opera
Omnia,* Morin ed., vol. II, p. 212). See Augustine, *In Psalmum 67,* n. 9
(*PL,* 36, 817). It is also legitimate to say that the figures of David or
Joshua, like the characters in the *Song of Songs,* have a spiritual
signification. On the "spiritual" meaning in St. John of the Cross, see
Jean Vilnet, *Bible et mystique chez saint Jean de la Croix* (1949), pp.
85–86, 91, 184–187.

souls.[30] *Ad haec etiam omnis Testamenti Veteris historia per-
tinet, quae carnaliter gesta ita denuntiat, ut in eis spiritualis
vitae intelligentiam exquirendam edoceat* (The whole history of
the Old Testament is also concerned with the facts reported as
having physically taken place, but in such a way as to teach us
to seek in them the understanding of the spiritual life).[31] But
the converse is just as true: the spiritual meaning of a mystery
is the meaning we discover—or, rather, into which we penetrate
—by living that mystery. Still more fundamentally, the entire
process of spiritual understanding is, in its principle, identical to
the process of conversion. It is its luminous aspect. *Intellectus
spiritualis credentem salvum facit* (Spiritual understanding saves
the believer).[32] The Word of God, a living and effective word,
acquires true fulfillment and total significance only by the transformation which it effects in the one who receives it. This is why
the expression "passing on to spiritual understanding" is equivalent to "turning to Christ"—a conversion which can never be
said to have been fully achieved. Reciprocal causality also
exists between this conversion to Christ, or this "passage to
Christ," and the understanding of the Scriptures.[33] *Cum autem*

30. For one example, see Jean Daniélou, "Les repas de la Bible et leur
signification," in *La Maison-Dieu*, 18, pp. 28–30; ET "The Banquet of
the Poor" in *The Lord of History*, Chicago, 1958, pp. 235–238, with
reference to the Passover meal. See Hilary, *Tractatus Mysteriorum*, I,
22: *"Numquid non corporaliter gestis spiritualiter gerenda succedunt?";*
2, 9 (Brisson ed.), pp. 112, 144. Gregory, *In Ezechielem*, l. 1, hom. 7,
n. 16–17, commenting on *"spiritus vitae erat in rotis"* (*PL*, 76, 848).

31. Othloh of St. Emmeran, *Dialogus de tribus quaestionibus*, c. 33
(*PL*, 146, 102).

32. Augustine, *In Psalmum 33*, sermo 1, n. 7 (*PL*, 36, 305).

33. See Augustine, *Contra adversarium Legis et Prophetarum*, l. 2,
c. 7, n. 29 (*PL*, 42, 655). Gregory of Nyssa, *Contra Eunomium*, l. 7
(*PG*, 45, 741–745). This is true of the perception of prophetic signs,
in the most narrow sense of the word prophetic (*prophetia in verbis*).
But spiritual understanding only expands within that faith which has
already been received. This is also one of the sources (the other is
liturgical) of the idea of "understanding in faith." See *Evagrii altercatio
legis inter Simonem Judaeum et Theophilum Christianum*, 1. 2; answer
of Theophilus to Simon's quotations of texts from Deuteronomy and
Isaiah: *"Sacratissima Christi vox est, quam, si tu volueris cognoscere,
oportet te primum credere. Tunc demum poteris intelligere. Esaias enim
redarguit te dicens: nisi credideritis, non intelligetis"* (Bratke ed., p. 3).

*conversus fuerit ad Dominum, auferetur velamen* (But when a man turns to the Lord the veil is removed).[34]

If we want to get to the root of the problem of spiritual understanding, which is being more and more widely discussed today, it seems advisable to refer to the act of conversion. We should look into the Church's conversion to her Lord, the Church viewed especially as made up of the first generations of the faithful. Nothing is better calculated to make us aware of the *seriousness* of a problem like this, the same sort of seriousness which we found so impressive in an Origen, for example, but which may well be masked from us by exuberance of image or subtlety of analysis. All Scripture is perceived in a new light by the soul which is open to the Gospel and adheres to Christ. All Scripture is transfigured by Christ. *Accedite ad eum, et illuminamini* (Come to him, and you will be enlightened). As can be seen, a unique activity is involved, and it implies a global interpretation which remains indeterminate as to many points, just as it is obscure to many individuals (each one of us is not the whole Church, in whose faith and understanding and hope of glory we participate only as members of the whole body). A unique movement is involved; beginning with initial incredulity, it ascends by faith to the very summits of a spiritual life which does not have its term here below.[35] Its unfolding is coextensive with the gift of the Spirit, with the progress of charity.[36] All Christian experience, in all its phases, is, in principle, comprehended therein. Newness of understanding is correlative with "newness of life."

[34.] 2 Cor. 3, 16; see Ex. 34, 34. Augustine, *In Psalmum 64*, n. 6 (*PL*, 36, 778). Here we are taking St. Paul's words in the sense which tradition has regularly given them (a meaning which is, moreover, completely in line with Pauline thought). For the immediate meaning of the text, see Dom Jacques Dupont, "Le Chrétien, miroir de la gloire divine," in *R.bibl.*, 1949, p. 399. See also the beautiful passage in Clement of Alexandria, *Stromata*, 6, c. 12 (Stählin ed.), vol. II, p. 484. See Othloh of St. Emmeran, once again applying the symbolism of the miracle of Cana to our subject (*PL*, 146, 212C, 213A).

[35.] In other words, God who reveals himself in Scripture always remains *"magis significatus quam demonstratus."* Augustine, *Contra Maximinum arianum*, l. 2, c. 10 (*PL*, 42, 811).

[36.] Augustine, *De catechizandis rudibus*, n. 35 (*PL*, 40, 336).

To pass on to spiritual understanding [37] is, therefore, to pass on to the "new man," who never ceases to be renewed *de claritate in claritatem.*

This amounts to saying that this understanding cannot lead to results which are completely controllable by a particular method or which are apt to be gathered together into a definitive canon. It amounts to saying that it can never be made completely objective. It always envelops and transcends what has been grasped, and is, at the same time, enveloped and transcended by what it has as yet been unable to grasp: *dicta igitur sacri eloquii, cum legentium spiritu excrescunt* (the utterances of sacred language thus grow with the spirit of those who read it).[38] For, "to penetrate into the spirit of Scripture means, in the final analysis, to learn to recognize the inner nature of God, to appropriate to oneself God's thoughts about the world." [39] But is it possible to conceive that we can ever have learned this? The dialectic is endless, analogous to that of mysticism and mystery. We can really speak of it only in the singular, as single act. We would never be able to understand it if we tried to judge it from a purely objective viewpoint, or to reduce it to a scientific discipline.[40] On this point, some of its partisans are in agreement

---

37. See Bernard, *In Epiphania Domini sermo 2*, n. 2 (*PL*, 183, 148B).

38. Gregory, *In Ezechielem*, l. 1, hom. 7, n. 10 (*PL*, 76, 846A); see no. 9 (844C). See Stanislas Fumet, *L'impatience des limites*, Fribourg, 1942, pp. 106–107: "Advancing like the figure of Ezekiel with those four animals, each moving forward in all directions, it [Scripture] goes beyond all things." The thought is analogous also to that of St. Gregory in Paul Claudel's *Les cinq premières plaies d'Égypte:* "The word of God is not like a projector designed to throw light in advance on particular points but is like a hand-held torch, shedding light around us as we move forward."

39. Hans Urs von Balthasar, *loc. cit.*, p. 11. Thus we must say about the understanding of Scripture what St. Augustine said about the knowledge of God: *"Si finisti, Deus non est"* (sermo 53, n. 12 [*PL*, 38, 370]). Also, *"Si quasi comprehendere potuisti, cognitione tua te decepisti; hoc ergo non est, si comprehendisti; si autem hoc est, non comprehendisti"* (sermo 52, n. 16 [*PL*, 38, 360]).

40. Assuredly, this is not to say that there are some explanations with objective validity and others which are solely derived from individual fancy. As for the reasons for believing: only those which are valid make of the act of faith a reasonable act. But it should be added that the

23

with some of its adversaries. The practice of spiritual understanding, once it is no longer carried forward by the movement
which initiated it, soon becomes nothing but idle fancy, barely
respectful of the divine Word—unless, in its desire for perfect
objectivity, it limits itself to the recording of a series of symbols,
whose respective values are determined by the dual criterion of
greater or lesser resemblance to the object signified and frequency
of affirmation in tradition. A good dictionary could dispose of the
problem once for all. Furthermore, even though there be a
legitimate interest in them, it is inevitably a limited one. Then
too we can see that the two criteria do not belong to the same
order nor do they always overlap: certain symbolisms, very well
supported in tradition, still have about them an air of the artificial or the tenuous. It remains an open question whether we can
aim for something else today, whether we even have the right
to do so. But, limiting ourselves for the moment solely to the
historical aspect, we must approach matters in greater depth and
with greater freedom if we hope to recapture anything of the
spiritual interpretation of Scripture as it existed during the first
centuries of the Church. We must, above all else, reproduce a
spiritual movement, often through completely different methods,
while avoiding a retreat into the archaic or into slavish imitation.
And this is the struggle of Jacob with the Angel of God, a struggle which we must begin again and again.[41]

\* \* \*

But there is another misunderstanding which must also be
eliminated. We sometimes demand of the "spiritual meaning"
something which it cannot give us. And sometimes we reject it
as lacking importance or even as detrimental to the true understanding of the Bible, because we have misunderstood both its

---

more these reasons approach the character of a personal sign, the less
capable they are of being directly universalized. This, *mutatis mutandis,*
is what happens here, where the role of personal opinion can be legitimate—always, of course, within the "analogy of faith."

[41.] Rupert of Deutz, *De Trinitate et operibus ejus, In Genesim,* 1. 8,
c. 9 (*PL*, 167, 498).

nature and its proper sphere of influence. The misunderstanding is, moreover, enhanced by a number of faulty distinctions which are to be found throughout the history of exegesis, the most ancient as well as the most recent. At the risk of somewhat over-stating the case, we can sum it all up antithetically by saying that we must make a careful distinction between the spiritual meaning of Scripture, as it has been understood by an unbroken tradi-tion, and the religious meaning of the Bible.[42]

The acceptations which we shall distinguish are mutually ex-clusive and do not have the same ends. They can hardly be compared without being contrasted. The religious meaning of the Bible is also an historical meaning. We can study the history of religion—including the religion of Israel—like any other col-lection of facts, but we cannot do it in any serious fashion with-out carefully educing, by means of an effort which goes further than mere critical erudition, the religious meaning of the texts which express it. In doing this, the historian somehow becomes contemporary with the facts he must describe and explain. In-tent upon avoiding both an overestimation of the texts and a superficial interpretation of them, he seeks to reconstruct the religious consciousness of men in the biblical past, just as he would do for any other past. He studies carefully the spirit of an Abraham, a Moses, a David; the spirit of an Elijah, an Isaiah, a Jeremiah. He strives to understand the religious insti-tutions of the people of Israel precisely as understood by them, not only in general but also in particular. He restructures his own view of the universe, and he discovers in ancient documents the wellsprings for his own prayer. He certainly does not deny himself the advantages which are his by reason of his having been born in a later generation and of his ability to encompass a long series of events in a single glance. While preserving him-self from the facile ultimate explanations and the extremely arbitrary views sheltered under the name of "philosophy of his-tory," he is skilled in sorting out the interplay of causality and influence, and in discovering what promise existed, even though

42. This "equivocation" has been attacked by Père Spicq in *RevScPhTh*, 1948, pp. 90–91.

unknown to its subject, in a particular institution, a particular light, a particular new attitude. For, in the history of the human mind, whether religious or secular thought is involved, certain moments possess a special density, a special fertility, and these can be properly evaluated only by taking account of their antecedents, their "sources," and especially the progression originating in them. Even the least profound religious experience, however crude its first expression, contains spiritual seeds which will only bear fruit in the tradition issuing from it. The "inevitable refraction" stemming from the glance backwards created by perspective thus becomes a legitimate and illuminating "elaboration." [43]

Nevertheless, the historian will always be attentive to differences in historical situations. He will, for example, highlight the abyss which separates "the religious level of Yahweh's Covenant with a few tribes of looting nomads whose only aim is to assure themselves of the conquest of a long-coveted territory and the transcendent level on which the Spirit of Jesus consecrates the love-union of the elect with the father for eternal life in his Son." [44] All his attention is directed towards recon-

[43]. These expressions are to be found in H. I. Marrou, *Saint Augustin et la fin de la culture antique, Retractatio* (1949), p. 644, n. 12. See the study, cited above, by Louis Massignon, "L'Expérience mystique et les modes de stylisation littéraire." These remarks have greater significance where the Bible is concerned, because "the Hebrew mind, unlike the Greek mind, never cultivated the tendency to give precise definition to notions. Its mode of thought was dynamic; it uses terms and concepts more for the purpose of suggesting that it transcends them than for the purpose of signifying that it stops at them; all the elements of vocabuluary are somehow reflective of the tendency to become symbolic and thereby acquire a 'plusvalue'." J. Coppens, *Les harmonies des deux Testaments*, p. 53, summarizing J. DeZwaan, *Hermeneutical Plus-Value*, in *Conjectanea Neotestamentica in honorem A. Fridrichsen* (1947), pp. 242–250. This is basically what Massignon finds to be true of all Semitic languages. A similar observation can be found as early as Luis de Leon: "The Hebrew language, in which this book [The Song of Songs] was written, is, in its constitution and even in its particulars, a language of a few words and short expressions, and the latter are filled with a multitude of meanings" (quoted by Alain Guy, *La pensée de Fray Luis de Leon*, p. 270).

[44]. Dom Célestin Charlier, "Les Thèmes bibliques et leurs transpositions successives," in *Esprit et Vie*, 1948, p. 153.

stituting the past. This is not devoid of interest for the believer, not by any means. Since we are dealing with a unique history, it is important that the historian who recounts that history do so as a believer—but he will still be a believer.

The "spiritual meaning" strikes us as quite another thing altogether, particularly when it is considered in the pure form usually found in tradition. It does not derive from any backward-oriented curiosity. Even though it is, in its own way, or at least in one respect, an interpretation of the Jewish past, it interprets the Jewish past solely from the viewpoint of the Christian present. It is the Old Testament understood in the spirit of the New. Far from having to be wary of an ultimate view, it presupposes such a view, and this is completely legitimate since the ultimate view is based on a definitive Event,[45] which in certain respects is already "the end of history." But this ultimate view is of necessity a view in faith. The meaning which stems from it is only perceived in the light of Christ [46] and under the action of his Spirit, within his Church. One who takes up the study of the history of Israel's religion in this fashion gives all its historical importance to it, because he understands it as the salvation history of the Church. Strictly speaking, though, he does not study this salvation history as a historian, whose goal is to see the spectacle of events unfold before him; he meditates on it as a believer—and not as a Jewish believer, but as a Christian believer—in order to live by it. This is his own history, from which he cannot remove himself. This history interests him personally. It is a mystery which is also his own mystery, identically. Consequently, he does not question the Bible as he would any other document or series of documents about the past, but he "searches the Scriptures" to discover God's thoughts and

---

[45]. On the incomplete character of history outside of this perspective, see Origen, *Jos.* 4, 8, 4 (pp. 339–340); h. 16, 3 (pp. 395–396).

[46]. See the extremely profound words of St. Augustine, *In Psalmum 47*, n. 1: ". . . *ut intelligas Deum fecisse lucem, cum Christus a mortuis resurrexit*" (*PL*, 36, 532). Only the Christian knows this spiritual meaning, because he has received from the Lord τὴν ἀκριβαστάτην ἐκ καταβολῆς κόσμυ εἰς τέλος ἀλήθειαν (Clement, *Stromata,* 6, 9; vol. II, p. 470).

designs on him. He is not attracted by the psychology of the Old Testament believers. Besides, he knows that they could not have been explicitly aware of everything which he discovers in their writings; the seals of the Book had to be broken by the Lion of the Tribe of Judah.[47]

The antithesis which we have set out is, to be sure, a formal one. We can even admit that it is somewhat artificial. Its precise importance can be measured by what will follow. Concretely, the spiritual meaning of Scripture and the religious meaning of the Bible coincide at many points. The ideal is for them to continue each other and interpenetrate. They somehow need one another: the former must have a permanent basis, and the latter must not be truncated. We might express this fact by saying that, before we can undertake any spiritual interpretation of the Old Testament through the New, we must first have historically understood the New Testament through the Old. It is of equally great importance—and the formula itself indicates it—that we avoid confusing the disciplines.[48] Their union is desirable, and even necessary, but it is a delicate one. Spiritual interpretation, even though it is, in an eminent way, historical interpretation, must not imprudently or prematurely interfere with historical study. Still more certainly, it should not be confused with history, even religious history, or be substituted for it. Left to its own devices, it would be somewhat hostile to history. Its use, even in the most authentic tradition, while it might be easily complemented by historical criticism, is not always in line with the religious understanding of the ancient texts. The more religiously beautiful and powerful a text is, the more is it stripped of its beauty and power by too ready or rigid an attempt to find a

[47.] See Jerome, *In Isaiam* (*PL,* 24, 332). Gregory, *In Ezechielem,* 1. 2, hom. 4, n. 19 (*PL,* 76, 983–984). Caesarius of Arles, *Expositio in Apocalypsin* (*Opera Omnia,* vol. II, pp. 221–222).

[48.] Père Lagrange suggested an analogous distinction, which stemmed from the same concern, when he distinguished in prophecy a "literal meaning considered under its religious aspect" from a "spiritual meaning." "Pascal et les prophéties messianiques,' 'in *R.bibl.,* vol. 15 (1906), p. 541. Here, however, we think that the two meanings tend to come together.

"spiritual meaning" in it. Yet if we were to combine the dual exclusivism of the critical and the allegorical methods, the process would be just as sterilizing. We must, therefore, reject too all-embracing or too automatic a practice of spiritual interpretation, so as to preserve the religious value of the Old Testament, considered both literally and in its historical situations.[49]

This is not to say that there is no tendency to disparage the Jewish Scriptures in the doctrine of the spiritual meaning (not as it can be reconstructed in idea, but as historically given, as apparent from traditional usage). Generally speaking, the *modus judaicus intelliqendi* is referred to in the doctrine only to be rejected with disdain. Let us not forget its Pauline origins.[50] It results, principally, from the Apostle's polemic stance. Paul pits one Testament against the other. He pits the letter which kills against the Spirit which gives life.[51] He pits vain shadows against the fullness of Christ. He argues against Jewish Law. The danger in following him would, therefore, be that we would underestimate historical fact, not that we would overestimate it by going beyond the letter.

The danger can, however, be rather easily avoided. We must not take the Pauline opposition solely from the historical point

[49.] Abbé Jean Steinmann is perfectly correct when he writes: "The allegorists are mistaken in pretending, through their game of facile appearances, to draw the true religious meaning from the inspired text"; he is also correct in thinking that "the historian's entire effort should allow him to become an intimate of God's witness, to know his particular language, the style which expresses his soul, to know his habits and his interior life, the rites which he observed, his tastes, and the flavor of his meditation." And yet we are still inclined to believe that, properly understood and properly limited, the spiritual understanding of Scripture is immune to his criticism and fails to bear out his fears. See "Apologie du Littéralisme," in *La Vie intellectuelle,* May 1948.

[50.] They are quite Johannine as well, and perhaps more so. But we do find in St. Paul a number of strongly phrased theoretical formulas which had a decisive influence on Christian tradition.

[51.] 2 Cor. 3, 6 See, on this text, P. Benoît, "La Loi et la Croix d'après saint Paul," in *R.bibl.,* 1938, p. 491. It is commonly acknowledged that the Apostle's thought is often punctuated by antithesis: see Jean Nelis, "Les antithèses littéraires dans les épîtres de saint Paul, in *NRT,* vol. 70 (1948).

29

of view. It was not set up between two different ways of evaluating Israel's ancient religion. When Paul looked towards the past, he magnified the privileges of his race and exalted the religion of his ancestors.[52] The entire point of his polemic was directed against "Israel according to the flesh," with its pretensions about perpetuating itself after its rejection of the Messiah, or against unstable Christians who still placed their hope in abrogated practices. It was not the Old Covenant as such which was the object of his scorn, but the Old Covenant as superannuated, the Old Covenant become aged, the Covenant whose role in history had come to an end. He holds no brief against "Jewish antiquities," only against Jewish decay—and this implies, in tacit antithesis, the Christian newness.[53] Paul takes aim at "the letter," not at the literal meaning.

After Paul, we shall again see this opposition concentrated exclusively on the Law of Moses. St. Augustine, for example, will speak of those Judaizers who, *"exstinguentes prophetiae spiritum vivum, ad carnalia opera sine vita, hoc est, sine intellectu spirituali remanserant"* (killers of the living spirit of prophecy, abide in the works of the flesh without life, that is, without spiritual understanding).[54] From this standpoint, it is a legal system, a cult, and not a history which is at the core of the problem. And in the later tradition spiritual interpretation will almost always find its chosen ground in the Pentateuch. It is, in fact, on the most thoroughly material data of Mosaism that it prefers to dwell. In any event, it will always be the search for the meaning of *things*. Spiritual interpretation will, therefore, offer us an analysis of extrinsic facts and objective institutions

---

[52.] See Rom. 3, 21; 9, 4–5. But Paul exalts it precisely as the religion of the Promise, and to the extent that it must end in Christ.

[53.] We can find this expressed in Père Merlin, for example, in his *Dissertations sur la nature de la Loi de Moïse,* First Part, appealing to the authority of St. Paul: "You may be wondering where all these arguments of St. Paul are leading. They are leading to the proclamation to the Jews that, if they refuse to answer the call of Jesus Christ, they can never again hope to share in grace and in justification, which they could until then have received by an outpouring of the riches of the Gospel on the ages which preceded . . ." (*PL,* 47, 1058–1059).

[54.] Sermo 10, n. 3 (*PL,* 38, 94).

rather than an elucidation of feelings or thought, and, generally speaking, will not undertake to fill the gap between the primary meaning of those institutions or facts, as understood and lived by the majority of ancient Jews, and the Christian meaning received, in sign, by them.[55]

## 3. The Spirit of the New Testament

From all we have seen up to now, it quite clearly follows that the spiritual meaning of Scripture, strictly understood, is none other than that of the New Testament. It is the New Testament itself: [*Lex*] *spiritualiter intellecta, Evangelium est* (The Law, spiritually understood, is the Gospel).[1] It would not exist without Christ and would not be perceived without conversion to Christ. Consequently, if the fact of Christ had not occurred, and if it had not been continued in the fact of the Church, all the exegesis which "spiritual understanding" or related terms suggest within Christianity would be pure phantasmagoria. There would be willfulness not only in a particular objective detail or in a particular practical process, but in the root itself.[2] For the "newness" which is the foundation for such exegesis would then be as "vain" and as hollow as the "decay" which it does away with. The Christian revolution was necessary for the passage over from Israel to the Church. It was no less necessary for the generation of the Christian meaning of the Jewish Scriptures. For this to occur, a new element had to be introduced, one which could not be reduced to anything which went before. A discontinuity was implied, a breach, a crossing of a threshold, some-

55. See Eusebius, *Ecclesiastical History,* l. 1, c. 3, n. 4, on the συμβολικὴ λατρεία established by Moses. This would be no less true of a St. John of the Cross, for example, whose primary interest was in the soul of Prophet or Psalmist and who discovers all his own experience in theirs: See J. Vilnet, *op. cit.,* pp. 130, 138–143, 161. It is not possible to reduce to a single formula everything which Christian tradition has actually incorporated into its understanding of Scripture.

1. Augustine, Sermo 25, n. 2 (*PL,* 38, 168). See above, *PL,* 5, p. 1, n. 3.
2. See Augustine, *Contra Faustum,* l. 12, c. 39 (*PL,* 42, 274–275).

thing which could not be accounted for in a purely historical exegesis, however complete it sought to be or however religious its inspiration. Just because we have acquired a thorough knowledge of the men and events of the Old Testament in their being and in their historical becoming, it does not follow that we have "understood" them from their Christian viewpoint. *Si vis ista intelligere, non potes nisi per Evangelium* (If you want to understand these things, the only way to do so is through the Gospel).[3]

One author, reacting against the atomism and myopia of a certain type of exegesis, has properly reminded us "that the Old Testament forms a unity, that fractionation, pushed to extremes, is disastrous because it is anti-critical, that the prophetic texts constitute a living tradition, that these documents themselves have never ceased to be revived, rethought, commented upon and enriched." Subsequently, and with no less justification, he added: "There is no prohibition against reading the ancient texts in the perspective of more recent texts, by which the former have been fertilized and deepened . . . Something which cannot be understood by a purely verbal and philological interpretation can sometimes be grasped by means of a more historical and comparative exegesis, which looks at the texts through the eyes of tradition." [4]

We do, in fact, see an almost constant process of spiritualization at work in biblical history. "The great remembrances of the past are carried on by the religious thought of Israel, which, while being purified and deepened, slowly gets closer to their meaning." [5] It never stops reflecting on the events of Exodus: the departure from Egypt, the sojourn and march in the desert, the conquest of the Promised Land. It finds in them something more than "a living portrait of divine goodness and justice, of

---

[3.] Origen, *In Exodum,* hom. 7, n. 7 (p. 213). See Bernard, *Sermo 57 de diversis,* n. 2: *"Resurgendo autem et in caelum ascendendo, librum aperuit"* (*PL,* 183, 681C); Bonaventure. *Breviloquium,* prologus (Quaracchi ed.), vol. V, p. 201.

[4.] Joseph Coppens, *Les harmonies des deux Testaments* (1949), II, *Les apports du sens plénier,* p. 61.

[5.] A. George, *loc. cit.,* p. 10.

the fervor and faults of Israel." [6] The Prophets see in them a perfect type of the great exodus which is to come, of the final liberation, and of the glory of the chosen people. The psalmists discover in them the drama of the interior life, which is every day renewed in every Israelite.[7] Indeed, the texts of a number of Psalms "were carried down by the Jewish community," which read the texts in an increasingly spiritual way; we can, as a matter of fact, use the history of such readings to obtain "a kind of sketch of the history of the tradition of Israel." [8] Through the course of centuries, the process becomes more general. It was intensified by the Babylonian Exile and by the Diaspora. The Apostle Paul had undoubtedly conceived of a "spiritual worship" simply from his reading of Jeremiah—it did not depend on his conversion to Christ.[9] The Sabbath had been spiritualized by Isaiah. In certain circles, the basic ideas of Kingdom, Messiah, Sacrifice [10] became the objects of an ever-increasing allegorization, whose final flowering was to make up the New Testament. This was not a matter of a few more or less aberrant phenomena of minor importance such as the processes of accommodation which have been noted, for example, in Ezekiel [11] or in the Book of Wisdom.[12] "The re-use and reinterpretation of ancient

6. L. Desnoyers, *Les Psaumes,* introduction, p. 24.

7. See Jacques Guillet, *art. cit.* Here, prefigured, we have the eschatological (anagogic) and spiritual (moral) meanings of later Christian tradition. In the expectation of the Jews, the former occupied the role of our mystical (allegorical, dogmatic) meaning, which could not have had a distinct object at that time. That object actually results from the gap which separates the two comings of Christ.

8. This is emphasized in the commentary by M. E. Podechard, *Le Psautier, traduction littérale et explication historique,* and *Notes Critiques* (Bibliothèque de la Faculté de Théologie de Lyon, vols. 3, 4).

9. See Jer. 29, 10–14.

10. Compare Ps. 50, 14 and 1 Pet. 2, 5. Tertullian, *Adversus Judaeos,* c. 5 (Kroymann ed.), p. 268; Minucius Felix, *Octavius,* c. 32 (Halm ed.), pp. 45–47.

11. Ezek. 28, 13–16 (applying the story of fallen man to the King of Tyre); 47, 1–12 (the heavenly Jerusalem described with characteristics taken from paradise). Ezekiel, though, does not use only canonical sources.

12. Wis. 10, 17; 16, 5–7; 17, 20, and so forth. Both methods and spirit are, at least in part, similar to those of Philo.

33

tales, tending towards transpositions which are real metamorphoses, seem to be the secret of the composition of the Old Testament writings in their final form." [13]

These facts, which are by no means insignificant, have led some to conclude that spiritual understanding, as practised by the Fathers and by the Middle Ages, did not date back only to the Gospels, but to the Old Testament itself. Thus there has been talk of a "prehistory of typology." The expression, while supportable from a literary standpoint, seems somewhat extreme to us. Surely it is necessary to point out that a "prehistory" of this kind is still quite different from the first phase of a history. Even though the Old Testament as a whole might manifest "the uninterrupted continuity of homogeneous historical development," [14] this development does not, in and of itself, lead to the New Testament. While "organic becoming" is unquestionably present, it stops at the threshold of Christian reality, whose flowering results from the appearance of a new principle. Before that occurs, all intermediate innovations and metamorphoses are still part of the *Old* Testament. The Christian transposition, although it is at the close of the successive "transpositions" which mark the religious history of Israel, belongs to a completely different order and constitutes, "under the impulse of the Spirit," a radical transfiguration. Without it, an impressive unity, derived from unceasing repetitions along an ascending scale, can be discerned in the biblical literature, but it is by no means "the Word once more become complete," [15]

13. Louis Bouyer, "Liturgie et exégèse spirituelle," in *La Maison-Dieu,* no. 7 (1946), p. 35. Of the many studies which have appeared on this subject in recent years, this article strikes us as one of the most remarkable. There are similar observations to be found in Newman, *op. cit.,* pp. 189–190.

14. Joseph Coppens, *op. cit.,* p. 61.

15. Paul Claudel, "L'Ecriture sainte," in *La Vie intellectuelle,* May 1948, p. 10. W. Vischer, "Le sens de l'Ancien Testament," in *Cahiers bibliques de Foi et Vie,* III, no. 4, p 86: "For the New Testament witnesses, Holy Scripture constitutes a whole: When it is touched at any point, it reverberates throughout, just as, in a living body, the slightest contact is transmitted by the nervous system to all its parts." See Hugh of St. Victor, *De Arca Noe morali,* l. 2, c. 8. *"Omnis Scriptura unus liber est, et ille unus liber Christus est, quia omnis Scriptura divino in Christo impletur"* (*PL,* 176, 642C-D).

which is what Scripture must be for us, what it can be only for us. Without this transposition, before it, and especially independently of it, *a spiritualized meaning* could be obtained from the biblical facts, but it was impossible to obtain *the spiritual meaning* [16] in the full and proper sense of the term. Before the spirit was "given"—though the Spirit had been at work from the very beginning of "sacred history"—this meaning could not appear. And the gift of the Spirit assumed the accomplishment of the fact of Christ. Thereupon, the veil was immediately sundered.

It was a radical innovation, prepared for, foretold, but not initiated. There is, in the very progression of Revelation, a transcendence which is proper to the New Testament in relation to the Old, and here we have an aspect of it. We must not permit it to become obscure, *ne evacuetur Crux Christi*. It is true that all the ancient Scriptures "reveal the mystery of the Cross," [17] but they in turn are revealed by it, and by it alone.[18] It is the only key which can make us grasp their meaning.[19]

[16.] Spiritual worship, as conceived in the Diaspora, for example, is quite different from the Christian, whose entire essence and value depend on the unique sacrifice of Jesus Christ. See Heb. 13, 10–16. The legislation found in Deuteronomy is a reinterpretation "in a humanitarian way of a collection of Mosaic (or even pre-Mosaic) prescriptions whose purely sacral original significance cannot be doubted in the least" (Bouyer, *art, cit.,* p. 36); but it is something completely different which brings about the sudden displacement of carnal circumcision by what St. Paul calls "spiritual circumcision" (Rom. 2, 29). See Jer. 4, 4; Tertullian, *Adversus Judaeos,* c. 3 (Kroymann ed.), p. 260.

[17.] See Ambrose, *In Lucam,* l. 6, n. 33: *"Crucis aperire mysterium"* (*PL,* 15, 1677A). Pseudo-Hesychius, *In Leviticum,* 1. 1 (*PG,* 93, 825D). Rupert of Deutz, *In Reg.,* l. 2, c. 6 (*PL,* 167, 1102D).

[18.] Let us cite a rather late text, which summarized a unanimous tradition: *"Sacrarum Scripturarum intelligentiam pertingere non valet qui Crucis mysterium non recipit, et Christi passione non credit esse salvatum. . . . In Christi namque passione velum templi scissum est, et revelata sunt sancta sanctorum"* (Bruno of Segni, *Tractatus de sacramentis Ecclesiae, PL,* 165, 1095B-C). See Jerome, *Adversus Jovinianum: "Neque enim Evangelium ante Crucem Christi est"* (*PL,* 23, 245A).

[19.] Augustine, *In Psalm. 45,* n. 1 (*PL,* 36, 514); Sermo 300, n. 3 (*PL,* 38, 1378); *De spiritu et littera,* n. 27 (*PL,* 44, 218). Peter Damian, Sermo 46: *"Hujus vineae ille vindemiator exstitit qui in torculari passionis suae pressus, mysticos nobis divini eloquii sensus aperuit, et vinum nobis evangelicae gratiae propinavit"* (*PL,* 144, 756B). Arnold of

35

From then on they are bathed in its light. The Old Testament is definitively recaptured, reread, and reinterpreted *in the spirit* of the New.

It is not that there is any lack of continuity between the two. But the continuity is in God, not in man. It is the continuity of the divine Plan, something to be admired after the event. *Unus idemque Veteris ac Novi Testamenti Deus, . . . uno scopo sibi proposito* (The one same God of the Old Testament and the New . . . with a single purpose).[20] The same Deed which saved Israel from the land of Egypt is carried on for the benefit of the Church, to save her from the world.[21] The Church is "the Israel of God." [22] The Church is always that people whom God, in his mercy, has chosen for himself. Although national Israel has become universal Church, it is always the same People of God. The Promised Land has become the *consortium sanctorum* in the eternity of the blessed, but it is always the Kingdom of God. For Yahweh, the "rock of Israel," is faithful. There is only one same God, who is the Author of two Testaments. Perhaps we should vary the traditional formula a bit so as to better express its spirit and say that there are several covenants but only one Testament which, as covenant follows covenant, becomes more clearly defined and grows even deeper.[23] *Redemp-*

Bonneval, *De verbis Domini in Cruce,* tract. 7: "*Extensa in Cruce pelle corporis sui, in psalterio decachordo, veteris et novi Instrumenti concutit consonantiam*" (*PL,* 189, 1701). Bonaventure, *In Hexaëmeron,* cols. 13, 5: "*Qui sine isto ligno (Crucis) vult intrare mare Scripturae, submergitur*" (Quaracchi ed.), vol. V, p. 388.

[20.] Theodore of Mopsuestia, *Introduction to the Commentary on Jonah (PG,* 66, 318). J. Touzard, *Juif (Peuple):* "The study of the Messianic idea and its realization helps us to see in the old order and in the new order two parts of an organic whole which is perfect in its unity, . . ." (*Dictionnaire apologétique de la foi catholique,* vol. II (1915), col. 1648).

[21.] See Pascal, *Pensées,* no. 674: "God has then shown by the deliverance from Egypt, and from the sea, by the defeat of Kings, by the Manna, by the whole genealogy of Abraham, that He was able to save, to send down bread from heaven, . . . so that the people hostile to Him are the type and the representation of the very Messiah whom they know not, . . ." (Modern Library ed., 1941, pp. 225–226).

[22.] Gal. 6, 16.

[23.] See Rom. 9, 4, and Lucien Cerfaux, *The Church in the Theology of St. Paul,* New York, 1959, pp. 30–33.

*tionem misit Dominus populo suo, mandavit in aeternum testamentum suum* (The Lord has sent redemption to his people, he has promulgated his testament for eternity). To go into a little detail: if, for example, the manna is really the figure of the Eucharist, or if the sacrifice of the paschal Lamb really prefigures the redemptive death, the reason for this is not extrinsic resemblance alone, no matter how striking this might be. There is actually an "inherent continuity" and "ontological bond" between the two facts, and this is due to the same divine will which is active in both situations and which, from stage to stage, is pursuing a single Design—the Design which is the real object of the Bible.[24] And if St. Paul, looking back on "the events which occurred in the desert and the 'spiritual' rock at which the Israelites quenched their thirst," can add: *"Petra autem erat Christus,"* it is because "the event which took place in the desert was itself part of the forward movement, driven on by a force which surpasses time and for which 'a thousand years are as a day,' towards the Easter event, and was destined to find, in that event, its own true meaning." [25] It is therefore correct to speak, with Père Bouyer, of the real "genetics of ideas and themes of the final revelation, the Christian revelation," and this is what distinguishes it from "organic allegory," which is wholly based on "imaginary symbolism." [26]

But how was God's Plan to be achieved? In the final analysis, what would the manna or the paschal Lamb mean? What reality was prepared and prefigured by the things of which we read in the Bible? The Israelites themselves could not know. No doubt,

[24.] See Yves Congar, "L'ancien Testament témoin du Christ," in *La Vie intellectuelle,* October 1949, p. 337.

[25.] T. G. Chifflot, *Water in the Wilderness,* New York, 1967, pp. 56–57.

[26.] *Art. cit.,* pp. 44–45. We thus come back to the thought of Origen, or even Augustine, who both saw prefiguration in the very preparation. See Chifflot, *op. cit.,* p. 42: "Correlations, 'figures,' are to be found as between the Old Testament and the New, Christ's New Testament and Christians, and the 'whole' Christ in His present condition and in that of the age to come. And the reason for this is that a causality, a 'preparation' exists." Augustine also saw each stage of history as preparing the later stages, with the final stage having to integrate them all in its definitive truth. *De vera religione,* c. 26–28 (*PL,* 34, 143–145).

when they looked back on the great events of far-distant Exodus: deliverance from Egypt, march in the desert, conquest of the Promised Land, they were conscious of seeing "real laws of nature" in those events, laws which should properly have governed the destiny of the chosen people throughout its history. Their conviction was a perfectly legitimate one.[27] When they celebrated their Passover, they rightly evoked the memory of a great historical fact, the word of the God of their fathers, while looking forward to a great eschatological fact, in which that work would be consummated.[28] But they could have no idea of what this consummation would be, how it would occur, what perspectives it would open up, what new existence and new dimension of being it would create for the beneficiaries of the divine kindness. Judged from the standpoint of objective knowledge, their very expectation proved that they were still men of the Old Testament.

There were undoubtedly, as St. Augustine says, a few among them who, in the depths of their hearts, were already men of the New Testament, who, though preceding their Head as did the hand which came first from Rebekah's womb, were members of Christ.[29] Men like this, living out the first phases of the one history of salvation with an extremely pure faith, possessed an orientation of soul or spiritual dynamism which spontaneously carried them beyond Jewish perspectives, though they might not have been aware of it. As they fulfilled the figurative rites, there was a deeper purpose at work which could make them cling mysteriously to the Reality figured by those rites.[30] As they held on to the promises which had been made to their race, their greater attention to divine faithfulness than to love of earthly

[27]. H. M. Féret, O.P., "La Messe, rassemblement de la communauté," in *La Messe et sa Catéchèse*, 1947, p. 219.

[28]. See F.-J. Leenhardt, *La Sainte Cène*, pp. 18–21, 73.

[29]. Augustine, *In Psalmum 61*, n. 4 (*PL*, 36, 731).

[30]. See Thomas, *Ia-IIae*, q. 101, a. 2, ad 1; q. 103, a. 5, ad 4; *IIIa*, q. 8, a. 3, ad 3. These texts are quoted and commented on by Dom J. Gribomont, "Le lien des deux Testaments selon la théologie de saint Thomas; Notes sur le sens spirituel et implicite des saintes Ecritures," in *ETL*, vol. XXII (1946), pp. 70–89.

goods proved that they were already open to the real meaning of those promises. To put it more precisely, their belief in the Promise made them rise to what, in the Law, surpassed the Law. We can explain this without historical improbability if we have recourse to a philosophy of knowledge like St. Thomas's,[31] or, better still, like Maurice Blondel's. Historicism, which reconstructs the past without paying any attention to what the past was pregnant with, is unable to perceive these things. Yet the historian, instructed by the actual event, can discern earlier hints of it. Without succumbing to the temptation of forcing the texts, he still keeps clear of a narrowness of method which would lead him to underestimate such hints. By drawing out all the religious meaning of the Bible, he opens the way to spiritual understanding for the meditation of the Christian, or at least retrospectively justifies this understanding in his own fashion. One of the most beautiful examples which could be mentioned, and also one of the best known, is the contemplative tradition associated with the great figure of Elijah.

But let us not exaggerate.[32] The mystery which God was to reveal to the saints, once the fullness of time had come, remained

31. Inasmuch as it allows for the study of the sign. This is developed by Dom Gribomont in the article referred to. It will be noted that the "implicit" knowledge of which Thomas speaks in several passages is not exactly the same as Dom Charlier's "implicit awareness" in a passage soon to be quoted. The former deals only with implications which can be called logical, though the logic be a spiritual one.

32. Dom Gribomont carefully avoids exaggeration. After saying that the "master lines" of Thomas's thought on the question seemed to him "to retain considerable theological value," he adds (pp. 79–80): "But when St. Thomas, true to his time, assumes that the Prophets had a much clearer (though still imperfect) revelation of the typological value of their surroundings, we do not see that this requires us to admit *a priori* that the hagiographers had so clear a view of the future; on the contrary, if the texts show an extremely vital perception of the transcendental religious value of the Israelite world, their continued concern with it, even with its material, earthly and transitory aspects, leads us to believe that the authors of such texts did not always perceive the relativity of that world. The very least we can say is that the historical notions of the theologians of the middle ages are not binding upon us, and we have no hesitation in taking a more modern position on this question."

39

hidden from all prior generations.[33] The expectation of Israel could find its term only in Jesus Christ. In fact, he had already polarized all that expectation. Still in all, this is not to say that the Christian innovation was completely unforeseeable. As Dom Charlier [34] has very well written: "When we look for the prefiguration of Christ in the Bible, we should look less on the subjective level and more in the objective realm of realities in living development. It was only rarely that the authors, even the prophets, had so much as an 'implicit' awareness of the individuality of Christ. That was not the essential element of his presence in the Bible. Christ's presence in the Bible transcends both awareness and men and lies in the profound logic of idea and event. It is infused by God into the living flesh of his People."

Nevertheless, the objective continuity of figure and reality is well-translated, on earth, by continuity of awareness. If we want the fullness of that awareness, though, the only place to look for it is in the messianic awareness of Jesus. In that sacred spot, everything comes together and finds its unity. It is there that the whole takes on its definitive meaning. It is there that the passage from one Testament to the other is effected with perfect clarity, as is the alchemy which transforms the one into the other. It is there that the entire dialectic of the two Testaments is drawn tightly together: the New Testament in its entirety is brought forth by the Old, while at the same time the Old Testament in its entirety is interpreted by the New. It is there that all things appear new, because they have actually been made new: *ecce nova facio omnia.* Jesus is aware that he is fulfilling the religion of Israel, and that it then becomes completely spiritual in him. He is aware both of fulfilling and of transfiguring, of fulfilling while transfiguring. As he brings to fruition the oracles of the Prophets, he knows that he is doing much more: he brings a wholly prophetic religion to the summit of its activity and he lays bare the absolute essence of the great

33. Eph. 9, 10; Col. 1, 26.
34. "Les thèmes bibliques et leurs transpositions progressives," in *Esprit et Vie,* 1948.

divine Deed which had until then been totally symbolic—in point of fact, he fulfills the great divine Deed in all its reality. The scene of the transfiguration, on which Origen commented with so much love, is like a glimpse into this mystery.[35] Christian Tradition was to take this intuition of Jesus, identical to the awareness of his role as Saviour, and coin it in a thousand ways, finding signs of it everywhere in the Old Scriptures. Christian Tradition also did its best to share this intuition by spiritualizing through an analogous process all the visible data of the work of the Saviour and of his establishment of salvation. For in the awareness which serves him as guide, the two comings coincide. The visible has suddenly become linked with the invisible, and the temporal with the eternal. The Father has glorified his Son. For Jesus, then, the work which the Father had given him is already done. For us alone, and not for its Author, the New Testament means still another spiritual deepening and development, from the time of its appearance on earth until the eschatological era.

But is this to say that, under the Old Law, no ray of the light which was to shine forth in Jesus had ever filtered through, other than the wholly implicit knowledge which we have just defined? Certainly not. But these rays, like the rays of the dawn, came from the Sun which was still to rise. They could just as well be called shadows, which is what Origen called them.[36] They did not constitute a stage which was, in itself, independent of the stages which were to follow. There is one important fact in this order, and it allows us to say that the Old Testament somehow anticipated the New. That fact, however, is not the present spiritualization of an earlier history or of the institutions of

[35.] See also Augustine, Sermo 78, n. 2: *"Moyses et Elias, id est, Lex et Prophetae, quid valent, nisi cum Domino colloquantur?"* (*PL*, 38, 491). When the scene of the transfiguration was placed at the very bottom of the apse in the old church which was built at Sinai, an accurate and profound emotion found expression. See G. Millet, in *Histoire de l'Art*, ed. Michel, vol. I, p. 182. Note also the significance of the detail which is found in St. Luke, 9, 31: *"Et dicebant excessum ejus, quem completurus erat in Hierusalem."*

[36.] See *L'Entretien avec Héraclite*, commenting on Lam. 4, 20 (Schérer, pp. 173–175).

41

Israel. Nor is it even, in any absolute sense, the eschatological orientation of Israel's reflection on the great memories of its past. The important fact is the announcement of a future spiritualization due to the insertion of a Principle given from above, the announcement of a total and definitive renewal.[37] *Sicut locutus est ad Abraham patrem nostrum, daturum se nobis.* It remains inscribed in several features of fire, particularly in the book of Jeremiah,[38] in Deutero-Isaiah,[39] in certain texts of Ezekiel.[40] In these summits of Jewish prophecy, though merely as fleeting anticipations, the religious meaning and the spiritual meaning, as we have distinguished them, come together completely. It is not enough to say that they are in continuity. They actually coincide.

## 4. From the Beginnings to the Middle Ages

The problem which faces us is an exceedingly complex one. We have not attempted to resolve it in a practical way, nor have we tried to define all its terms or to determine all its nuances.[1] We have merely tried to "situate" the problem by going back to the very beginnings. The next step would be to trace the subsequent development of these beginnings. We would note in detail the transformations which, one after the other, occurred during twenty centuries of history and reflected the recurrence of the essential problems of the Church or the impact of new

[37.] Augustine, *In Psalmum 72,* n. 1 (*PL,* 36, 914).

[38.] Jer. 38, 31; 39, 32, 33. See Bernard, *Super Missus est,* hom. 2, n. 8: "*Audiamus et Hieremiam, nova Veteribus vaticinantem . . .*" (*PL,* 183, 64D).

[39.] Is. 55, 3; 56, 8; 65, 15–17; 66, 22. See Jn. 12, 41. Pascal, *Pensées,* no. 729.

[40.] Ezek. 36, 26–27; see 1 Jn. 3, 24; 4, 13; 5, 18. See M. E. Boismard, "La connaissance de Dieu dans l'Alliance Nouvelle d'après la première lettre de saint Jean, in *R.bibl.,* 1949, p. 389.

[1.] To do so, it would principally be necessary to distinguish it from the question of the prophecies. As will readily be seen, the two questions are connected, but they are by no means identical. A detailed examination of their relationship would call for an entire additional study.

requirements or new circumstances on scriptural meditation. There is a secret logic which presides over this process, something which has often been remarked about the development of dogma. All we are able to do here, however, is to retrace, in rather a general way, certain stages of that history.

As we have seen, the spiritual interpretation of the ancient Scriptures—the only Scriptures which then bore the name of Scripture—played a role of the first importance in Christianity's self-awakening. One of the masterly intuitions of the early Church was that, like her founder, she was both completely old and completely new. *Et in veteribus novam, et in novis veterem.*[2] As we have also seen, St. Paul reflected upon this intuition and drew from it a weapon of battle. In his dialectic of the two testaments, he first shows their mutual exclusiveness rather than their inclusiveness. This powerful but essentially ambiguous thought is summed up in three pairs of words. In the first, γράμμα-πνεῦμα, contrariety dominates. In the second, ὁ τύπος-ὁ μέλλων, the dominant note is positive signification. In the third, σκία-σῶμα, continuity regains the favored position, for darkness is opposed to body as vain appearance to reality or vacuum to fullness, while at the same time suggesting a relationship of exemplarity.[3] We should also observe that, in the first of the three pairs, a positive relationship is, in a certain fashion, immediately reestablished, when St. Paul adds that "the Law is spiritual." The signification emphasized in the second pair is there only because of an "allegorization" of the fact which serves as "type," or, following the etymology, because of an explanation dependent on a meaning other than the immediate meaning.[4]

---

2. See Tertullian, *Adversus Marcionem*, l. IV, c. 21 (Kroymann ed.), p. 489.

3. See Augustine, *In Joannem*, tract. 28, n. 9 (*PL*, 35, 1626–1628). Or Tertullian, *Adversus Marcionem*, l. V, c. 19 (p. 646). See also J. B. Lightfoot, *The Epistles of St. Paul*, vol. III, Grand Rapids, 1957, pp. 192–193.

4. Similarly, though the two ministries, those of Moses and of Jesus, are "glorious," one is τὸ καταργούμενον, while the other is τὸ μένον; what is more, the first is called the "dispensation of death . . . dispensation of condemnation," while the second is called the "dispensation of the Spirit . . . dispensation of righteousness": 2 Cor. 3, 7–11.

43

Thus, St. Paul never sets up an antithesis without also affirming a symbolic relationship, and vice versa.[5]

The Letter to the Hebrews shows the same alternation, or, rather, the same alloy, of figuration and contrast. We know that Origen, who never stopped commenting on it, considered it Pauline, even though not from the Apostle's hand. This is a proof of his perspicacity. It is, of course, true that Paul saw the New Testament mostly as "the destruction of the Old," whereas the Letter to the Hebrews views it rather as the fulfillment and, so to speak, "idealization" of the Old.[6] In this vast fresco, completely biblical in color and aspect, the tragic sense of breach is far less pronounced. Polemic argumentation is secondary to actual use. Even so, the Old Covenant, while it might be retained, is allegorized. As for the New Covenant, it is not only declared to be "superior" and its mediator, Jesus, "greater" than Moses and Aaron, but it is also contrasted to the Old like heaven to earth, like worship in the spirit to material worship. The Covenant codified on stone has become "obsolete"; the Covenant which is today inscribed on the heart is forever "new."[7]

These ambivalent reflections laid the foundation on which the Fathers of the Church were to construct their teaching. In doing so, they would have basically the same resources at their disposal. Exemplaric thought and allegoric methods will be borrowed from the prevailing culture and will be profoundly transformed.

The daily use of the Book in worship, as well as unending controversy, soon created an entire system of figures. This, really, was something less than consubstantial with the faith, for the

---

[5.] See P. Benoît, "La loi et la croix d'après saint Paul," in *R.bibl.*, 1938, pp. 508–509. Edouard Reuss, *Les épîtres pauliniennes*, vol. II (1878), p. 52. Auguste Sabatier, *L'apôtre Paul* (1896), pp. 73–74. But note also that the very allegory of Sarah and Hagar (Gal. 4, 21–31) is entirely devoted to the establishment of a contrast: a "great and profound mystery," which is well-explained by St. Augustine, *Epist. 196*, n. 9 (*PL*, 33, 896–897).

[6.] E. Ménégoz, *La théologie de l'Épître aux Hébreux* (1894), p. 196.

[7.] Heb. 3, 2–6; 5, 22; 8, 6; 9, 19; 12, 25; 13, 20. Compare, for example, Heb. 10, 9 and 2 Cor. 5, 17.

primary task was not to find an initial expression for the faith, but to sanction it, to defend it, to explain it. Apologetics and pedagogy acquired an increasingly more important role in this use of Scripture. But by no means is this to say that the exercise was not a serious one. Indeed, even when "allegory" can produce no new discoveries, properly speaking, it can still retain an important role, for there is no more apt way "to bring an idea to its complete development." [8] During the early centuries, it dominated the doctrinal development of the "economy." Moreover, it served as a weapon in a bitter combat. Circumcision, Sabbath, manifold observances—these were not simply things that were read about, allusions to the past, memories, or symbols, but present realities which did not allow for a non-committal attitude. Judaism, with all the force of its Scriptures, refused to die and mounted a vigorous counterattack. Within the new Faith itself, the Pauline approach had not been everywhere triumphant, and there was a certain amount of backsliding. The fight was a stiff one indeed, and this accounts for the harshness expressed in the Letter to the Galatians. After Christ, was there still to be sacrifice to the letter which kills, or was confidence to be placed in the life-giving Spirit, by those who would practise the true Law of God? [9] In the third century, this aspect of the problem still had to be faced.

And the other aspect had to be faced as well. It was also necessary to preserve Scripture from the anti-Jewish gnosis. In doing this, the authors of the New Testament always remained the models. What was needed was the exploitation of their idea of positive figuration, just as their idea of contrast had been followed out. The spirit was opposed to the letter, but, once it had become the spiritual meaning, it was added to the literal meaning. This second aspect becomes increasingly predominant, while remaining inseparable from the first. A hierarchy of mean-

8. Auguste Sabatier, *L'Apôtre Paul*, p. 74. This is what a writer like J. Denis, *La philosophie d'Origène*, p. 33 and pp. 52–53, fails to understand.

9. See Origen, *In Matthaeum*, vol. XII, 5, p. 76. *In Rom.*, l. 6, n. 12 (*PG*, 14, 1093–1097).

ings begins to take shape. Dichotomic contrast yields to trichotomic progression. There soon rings out everywhere the triumphal hymn, whose first notes we heard in St. Irenaeus, then in Clement and Origen, in Hilary and in Ambrose. Now-opened eyes saw the Gospel everywhere in the Law, and the Church everywhere in Israel. The "symphony" of the two Testaments was renowned in Christian antiquity long before the Middle Ages performed it in poems in stone. The golden age of Patristics is saturated with it:

What is better established, what more solid than this word? To proclaim it, the double trumpet of the Old and New Testaments ring forth in perfect harmony and everything which bears it witness in ages past is to be found in the teaching of the Gospel. The pages of each covenant actually strengthen one another, and he who had been promised in ancient symbols under the veil of mystery is now shown clearly and certainly in the brilliance of his present glory.[10]

But after a short time, something else took place. Origen is rightly considered as the founder of biblical science.[11] Yet he did not found exegesis as an independent and specialized discipline. His "scholions" were little more than brief notes, with no pretense of being sufficient. His exegetical work, considered either in the great commentaries or in the homilies, was in no sense an activity pursued on the periphery of the Church's life or of the most current Christian reflection. Such problems and concerns are not merely reflected in his work, but are an inherent part of it. This great man of the Church never studied the Holy Books as a pure scholar or disinterested intellectual. He is less intent on explaining Scripture than on illuminating everything by it. This is why we must not judge his work as that of an exegete, in the narrow sense which the word has

[10.] Leo, *Sermon 38* (51), c. 4 (*PL*, 54, 311BC); see *Sermon 60*, c. 1 (342–343). The theme of harmony thus becomes the theme of Christian antiquity, of the *"magnum sacramentum spei ac salutis nostrae a saeculis antiquis dispositum"* (Gregory of Elvira, *Tractatus 3*, p. 23). The Old Testament is no more *past* than the New is *recent*. See Caesarius of Arles, *Sermon 104. De comparatione Ecclesiae vel Synagogae* (Morin ed., p. 412).
[11.] See, for example, *R.bibl.*, vol. XIII, 1904, p. 298.

acquired in our language. Origin's work is a theological meditation on sacred history. It is not, to speak very precisely, the
scientific study of a text.

Now the same thing simply cannot be said of the Antiochians
of the following century. To be sure, they did not cut themselves
off from the Church in any of their activities. And they were
fully aware of the "ecclesiastical canon" of the harmony of the
two Testaments,[12] even though they understood it more modestly,
and they certainly did not reject all typology. But it is beginning
with them that the exegesis of the Bible starts to lead a life of
its own. Their attitude of mind and their form of work entitle
them to be considered as the real founders of biblical exegesis,
and explain why so many modern scholars have a predilection
for them. It has often been noted that the famous distinction
between Antioch and Alexandria (if such generalizations be allowed) "is pretty much the distinction between exegetes and
theologians"—we could just as well say, between exegetes and
men of the Spirit—"the former being particularly aware of the
originality of the Old Testament, of the special character of the
Jewish religion and prophets, and fervent followers of Abraham
and Jeremiah; while the latter are particularly concerned with
spiritual constants, and with discovering everywhere the features
of the Word of God." [13]

But we should add, lest we fall into error on the significance
of this polarity, that it is not, as is occasionally said, the polarity
of letter and spirit. Broadly speaking, the whole of Orthodoxy,
whether Alexandrian or Antiochian, is on the same side in this
regard. The "partisans of the letter," the "friends of the letter,"
against whom Origen struggled, were not the forebears of the
scholars of Antioch. These scholars were also absent from the
ranks of Judaizers, naïve literalists, false gnostics, and even from
the school which had some relationship with Hippolytus and
paid attention only to extrinsic resemblances between the facts

12. See Clement of Alexandria, *Stromata,* 6, 15 (Stählin ed.), vol. II,
p. 495.

13. Jacques Guillet, "Les exégèses d'Alexandrie et d'Antioche," in
*RSR,* vol. 34, 1947, p. 297.

of both Testaments.[14] It would not even be an exaggeration to say that the whole exegetical tradition in the Church, in the East as well as in the West, is the heir of the Alexandrian master.[15] In actual fact, even if not in Antiochian prejudice, there was much less opposition than succession and overlapping. The work of Diodorus of Tarsus and his school belongs to another moment in Christian history; [16] it became possible only after certain stages had already been passed and certain results obtained. Their exegesis is a kind of refinement within a doctrine which had acquired stability.

As always, this implied both progress and a risk of loss. Between Origen and them, the primary difference was in historical situations and the problems involved therein. The difference is less rooted in space than in time. Diodorus came a century after Origen, and this fact is of greater significance than the contrast between the genius of Antioch and the genius of Alexandria. The unfairness and violence of certain critical remarks can be partially explained by the secular rivalry of the two cities.[17] They are probably even more indicative of the lack of understanding which usually marks the attitude of the young towards their elders. Once problems have changed, the forcefulness and sometimes even the interest of old solutions are no longer grasped. The exegesis of Origen had its weak spots, but the principal reason for the attack on it was that the spiritual understanding—

14. We find a good example of this crude typology in the Gospel of Pseudo-Matthew, c. 23. C. de Tischendorf, *Evangelia Apocrypha* (2d ed.), 1876, p. 91: *"Factum est autem cum beatissima Maria cum infantulo templum fuisset ingressa, universa idola prostrata sunt in terram, ita ut omnia convulsa jacerent penitus et confracta in faciem suam; et sic se nihil esse evidenter docuerunt. Tunc adimpletum est quod dictum est per prophetam Isaiam: Ecce dominus veniet super nubem levem et ingredietur Egyptum, et movebuntur a facie ejus omnia manufacta Egyptiorum."*

15. See F. Prat, *Origène,* p. xx: "Was the exegetical growth of Antioch and of Cappadocia possible without the vigorous impetus given by Origen?"

16. It was prepared for by the teaching of Lucian of Antioch, who is still enveloped in a "thick veil." G. Bardy, *Lucien d'Antioche,* p. 188.

17. See H. Lietzmann, *Histoire de l'Eglise ancienne* (Fr. tr.), vol. 3, p. 93.

48

in all its fullness—of Scripture could no longer enter into the framework of exegesis, as it had newly been conceived.

Another kind of specialization was slowly taking place within spiritual interpretation itself. Historians of exegesis and supporters of the "spiritual meaning" readily distinguish the literal interpretation of the Bible, which alone has dogmatic import, from its mystical interpretation, which has the more modest and more personal aim of edifying. On the one hand, then, we have scientific, objective study, which is the foundation for theology, while, on the other, we have pious meditation, sound enough in its general principles but which the theologian can and should disregard. After a certain date and for certain authors, this distinction corresponds to reality—or at least to one aspect of reality. Abbé Jean Châtillon, writing about several twelfth-century mystics, is quite right in saying that, for them, "Scripture is no longer the *locus theologicus* from which the scholar gathers his premises, but is now the *hortus conclusus* where the soul meets the Spouse, listens to his voice and inhales the fragrance of his perfumes." [18]

But for the early centuries, this would be an anachronism. After what has already been said, there would be no point in going into a lengthy explanation of how the mystical understanding of Scripture became an essential component of theology; more precisely, of the branch of theology which was called in Patristic times "the economy." The so-called mystical or allegorical meaning was always considered as the doctrinal meaning par excellence, as the meaning which disclosed the mysteries relating to Christ and the Church. We also know how often it was that moral and spiritual applications were made of that meaning, which found its fulfillment in them. Even in the work of Origen, we sometimes find these applications taking up all the space, while the exposition of the mystery remains implicit. In the fourth century, St. Gregory of Nyssa's commentary on the life of Moses is almost uniquely from the viewpoint of the individual soul. [19] Cassian, in his *Conferences,* is something of a

18. *RMAL*, vol. IV (1948), p. 439.
19. See Gregory of Nyssa, *Vie de Moïse* (Daniélou tr.), *SC,* vol. 1.

49

codifier of the usages of the Desert Fathers, who were principally interested in the practical. We also see that the meaning which relates to the spiritual life acquires a kind of independence in the measure that the doctrine becomes more firmly established in its least details. There is a much more rapid progress through the obscurity of "allegories" towards a penetration of the "secret delights" promised by them.[20] Mystical exegesis is no longer much of an aid in reflecting on mystery; in this respect, it no longer has an active role; but it is still a marvellous springboard for interior *élan*. The spiritual meaning of Scripture becomes the special preserve of the contemplative.

It would be arbitrary of us to fix a date for this development. If we had to choose a name which would be evocative of it, though, the choice would probably be St. Gregory the Great. In his era, the great flowering of doctrine had already passed, but not the mystical flowering. After supporting and nourishing the former, "rumination" on Scripture [21] continues to aid the latter. Gregory is a monk, and his is a monastic exegesis. He popularizes the conception of the Bible as a mirror of human activity or of the inner man.[22] But above and beyond the tropology which he zealously cultivates, as a conscientious shepherd of souls, he still searches for the "spiritual allegory" which will allow him to unfold the "wing of contemplation." [23] For *notitia* is not enough for him; what he wants is *volatus*. In other words, even though he first expects Scripture to ground his faith in the mysteries of the incarnate Word, he then looks for something to raise him above himself, to the higher regions, where the divinity of the Word can be contemplated. What the divinity communicates to him, however, cannot be reduced to distinct knowledge;

20. See Bernard, *In Cantica*, sermo, 80, n. 1 (*PL*, 183, 1166D).

21. See Gregory, *In Ezechielem*, l. 1, hom. 5, n. 1 (*PL*, 76, 821C).

22. *Moralia in Job*, l. 2, c. 1 (*PL*, 75, 553D). See Augustine, *In Psalmum 103*, sermo 1, n. 4 (*PL*, 37, 1938); following Jas. 1, 23.

23. *In Ezechielem*, l. 1, hom. 3, n. 4 (*PL*, 76, 807C); nn. 1 and 2 (806A-C). After history and figure, Gregory looks for the *"intelligentia contemplativa"* as related to the *"vita contemplativa"*: l. 1, hom. 7, nn. 8–10 (*PL*, 76, 845–846). See *Moralia in Job*, l. 16, c. 19, n. 24 (*PL*, 75, 432C).

it is more a question of seeds which are sown in the heart, of an *élan* which nourishes the "contemplative life" in spiritual freedom.[24]

Gregory will have many imitators, who, like him, will drink at scriptural sources so as to find in them the *"gustus contemplationis internae."* [25] The passage from Old Testament to New, or from letter to spirit, will naturally be understood by them as the passage from the external world, with its forms and affairs, to the *"festivitas contemplationis in mente."* [26] By reason of a standard transposition, *"conversio"* no longer means for them entry into the Church but, within the Church itself, the flight from the "world" through entry into religion.[27] Monks need a different spiritual nourishment than do those who remained in the world.[28] Let us take another typical example. With its double movement of angels descending and ascending, Jacob's Ladder had seemed to refer to the historical mystery of the Word's long descending among us, and then the long ascending of humanity towards God over the course of history. For a Gerhoh of Reichersberg, it becomes symbolic of the saints who are raised to the knowledge of God so as to descend again to the knowledge of themselves.[29] The quest for spiritual meaning becomes the quest for a "spiritual fruit." [30] The "honey in the

[24.] *In Ezechielem,* l. 1, hom. 3, n. 1 (*PL,* 76, 806A-B); n. 6 (808B); n. 11: *"Ad contemplativae vitae libertatem transit"* (810C). See n. 14, 15 (812B-C). See also the lovely passage in the *Moralia in Job,* l. 4, c. 1 (*PL,* 75, 633–634).

[25.] Gilbert of Stanford (Dom Jean Leclercq, "Le commentaire de Gilbert de Stanford sur le Cantique," in *Studia Anselmiana,* 20, p. 229; see p. 225, on the *"spiritualium sensuum gurgites abundantes"* which flow from Scripture). See Peter Damian, *Opusculum 60,* c. 26 (*PL,* 145, 854B-C).

[26.] Rupert of Deutz, *In Nahum,* l. 2 (*PL,* 168, 551B).

[27.] See Bernard, *In Annuntiatione,* sermo 1, n. 5 (*PL,* 183, 384D). Likewise, in this "optics," the struggle between the two cities of Babylon and Jerusalem is no longer exactly the struggle betewen the pagan world and Christ's Church, but between the world and the cloister. Bernard, *In Cantica,* sermo 55, n. 2 (*PL,* 183, 1045C).

[28.] Bernard, *In Cantica,* sermo 1, n. 1 (*PL,* 183, 785A).

[29.] *In Psalmum 38* (*PL,* 193, 1382–1383).

[30.] Bernard, *In Cantica,* sermo 51, n. 2 (*PL,* 183, 1025B-C).

SCRIPTURE IN THE TRADITION

honeycomb" which, for Origen, was the spirit in the letter, becomes, though it still remains spirit, "devotion." [31] In this completely interiorized reading, there is always a concern with "unction," "taste," "savor," "delights" [32]—and this is probably the reason why there is so much talk today about the savory quality of early spiritual exegesis, even though this is far from enough to explain its importance. We know what masterpieces can be produced in this genre. Actually, they are extremely diverse in character.[33] But if we keep to the viewpoint of exegesis and its doctrinal orientation, we soon realize that there is another side to this success. In the offing, there are two even more serious hazards.

To begin with, we have a darkening of social and eschatological perspective. Within the classical differentiation of four meanings, the fourth had to do with realities which were both heavenly and future, *mysteria futuri saeculi*. In the works of Origen, and for a long time thereafter, these two characteristics found their union in anagogy, which bore within it all the expectations of the pilgrim Church. An exegesis which, in essence, concentrated on the interior life was, however, worlds apart from

[31]. Bernard, *In Cantica*, sermo 7, n. 5 (*PL*, 183, 809B); see sermo 14, n. 8 (843A-B). The two biblical expressions, *"mel de petra"* and *"oleum de saxo,"* suggest to Bernard the two ideas of sweetness and unction, which are dear to him. See Guerric of Igny, *Sermo in verba Cant., quae habitas in hortis*, n. 2 (*PL*, 185, 211B-C).

[32]. Gregory, *In Ezechielem*, l. 1, hom. 3, n. 19 (*PL*, 76, 814C); *Moralia in Job*, l. 16, c. 19, n. 24 (*PL*, 75, 1132D). Thomas, *In Joannem*, c. 9, lect. 1, n. 1, will write of the *"sapor intimae contemplationis,"* following Gregory (with respect to the spittle applied to the man born blind). Bernard, *In Cantica*, sermo 1, n. 5 (*PL*, 183, 787B-C); sermo 39, n. 1 (977D); sermo 54, n. 5 (1035C); sermo 73, n. 2 (1134D). See Teresa of Avila, "Conceptions of the Love of God," in *Minor Works of St. Teresa*, London, 1952, pp. 92ff.

[33]. See, for example, some of the sermons of Gilbert of Holland on the Song of Songs, particularly the wonderful fourth sermon (*PL*, 184, 26–32). (Gilbert, certainly much less personal than his inimitable predecessor, has sometimes been greatly underrated.) Certain texts from the old school of Carmel, commenting on the history of Elijah, are totally different, but no less beautiful. See the small collection assembled by Père François de Sainte-Marie, O.C.D., *Les plus vieux textes du Carmel* (1944).

52

what we call today "the end of history." Centered as it was on the individual soul, it really could tell us no more about the triumphant Church than about the militant Church. As long as the resultant mysticism retained its foundation in mystery, the specialization was legitimate. Eventually, though, habitual neglect of other aspects most probably led to a narrowing of the dimensions of Christian expectation. As spiritual individualism gained ground, the great dogmatic vision became blurred. This, in any event, seems to be borne out by a number of medieval definitions of the anagogical meaning.[34] The etymology given during that period, *"quasi sursum ductio,"* could have sustained the dogmatic vision. But it is revealing to note how a St. Bonaventure, for example, in his *ex professo* treatments of the meanings of Scripture, maintains that anagogy is the object of the *"studium contemplativorum"* and instructs us *"qualiter est Deo adhaerendum,"* [35] or how he speaks of anagogy as that sort of understanding *"quae perficit per excessus mentales et sapientiae perceptiones suavissimas."* [36] From evidence such as this, we can see the progress which mysticism was making, but we can also see that the historical and social character of the Christian synthesis, which had stood out so dramatically in the exegesis of the Fathers, was in immediate danger of being compromised. For all practical purposes, morality and spirituality, though still referred to as tropology and anagogy, split into two,[37] and this

---

34. In the *Glossa ordinaria,* for example: *"Anagogia, id est, spiritualis intellectus per quem de summis et caelestibus tractatur et ad superiora ducimur."* In St. Teresa's commentary on the Song of Songs, no trace of the ecclesial meaning, which had been so much emphasized by a St. Bernard, a Gilbert of Holland, and even a Luis de Leon, will remain.

35. *De reductione artium ad theologiam,* n. 5 (Quaracchi ed. vol. V, p. 321); *ibid.: "Dei et animae unionem."*

36. *Itinerarium mentis in Deum,* c. 4, n. 6 (Quaracchi ed., vol. V, p. 307). But *ibid.,* n. 5: *"Sponsam, scilicet totam Ecclesiam et quamlibet animam sanctam."* As early as Augustine, *In Joannem,* tract. 120, n. 8: *"Sanctae deliciae"* (*PL,* 35, 1955).

37. Bernard, *In Cantica,* sermo 23, n. 2, drawing a distinction between the *moralis sensus* and the *arcanum theoriae contemplationis* (*PL,* 183, 885D). Note, however, that Bernard does not succumb to the tendency of which we are speaking; see, for one example, the beautiful passage, *In Cantica,* sermo 68, n. 4 (*PL,* 183, 1110A-C). Hugh of St. Victor, *De arca Noe morali,* l. 4, c. 9 (*PL,* 176, 679C).

was at the expense of eschatology. The Jerusalem of the Book of Revelation becomes more or less assimilated to the contemplative soul.

The second hazard is sophistication and eccentricity. Is it really possible to refer to certain commentaries on the Song of Songs as "exegesis"? "Rather than an ecclesiastical and moral explanation of the text," they are "equivalent to a treatise *De amore;* the verses of the Song of Songs are little more than a pretext for the expression of a personal experience." The author of such works "has no desire to instruct, but simply to release his fervor and occupy his moments of leisure by ministering to his own edification."[38] The sacred text still furnishes the basis for thought, but is no longer what inspires it, at least in any direct way.[39] To use the Augustinian expression, which is totally meaningful here, the text is merely the "occasion"[40] for thought. Often, too, there is an effective breaking away from all ties with the doctrinal meaning which had formerly, even though implicitly, always dominated spiritual developments. Or the Bible might provide nothing more than a framework, as when Ruysbroeck, like so many others, constructs piece by piece and with great ingenuity his *Spiritual Tabernacle*[41] on the model given by Moses. These shortcomings are not particularly serious, at least as long as the experience thus expressed remains linked to an

[38.] Dom Jean Leclercq, *Le commentaire de Gilbert de Stanford, loc. cit.,* pp. 208 and 212. See the same author's *Saint Bernard Mystique,* p. 136.

[39.] This explains how a St. Hildegard (to take an extreme case) could ascribe to the understanding of Scripture the visions of which she writes: see *Scivias,* l. 1, *praefatio* (*PL,* 197, 381–384). See Lazzarino of Pisa, telling St. Catherine of Siena: "I have heard tell how the Lord reveals to you the meaning of the Scriptures," in Laurent and Valli, *Fontes vitae S. Catharinae Senensis historici,* vol. LX, *Il processo Castellano* (1942), p. 332.

[40.] Bernard says so, very candidly, in the *Excusatio* which follows the homilies *Super Missus est: "Noverint tamen qui me tanquam de otiosa et non necessaria explanatione sugillant, non tam intendisse exponere evangelium, quam de evangelio sumere occasionem loquendi quod loqui delectabat"* (*PL,* 183, 86D). See Guerric of Igny, *In Natali Ap. Petri et Pauli,* sermo 3, n. 1 (*PL,* 185, 183D).

[41.] Among his precursors, we can note St. Cyril of Alexandria (*De adoratione,* 1. 9, 10 (*PG,* 68, 587–726).

authentic meditation on the Bible.[42] Actually, we have to admire in many of these writers a quality which had been admirable in Origen also, and was admirable in St. Bernard as well: the incredible familiarity which they had acquired with the sacred text, "so that the spontaneous play of associations brings constantly to their minds . . . biblical images and words"; here we have "the overflow of a powerful imagination wholly fashioned by the Bible and of a memory wholly nourished by the Bible." [43] And no matter how hard we try to establish the eccentricity of individualized explanations by judging them according to our own rules, can anyone dare to break the long-standing and powerful bond which exists between biblical exegesis and the development of Christian spirituality? Who, with any reading, experience, or reflection behind him, does not sense how much would be lost, not only in form but also in substance, by the works of a St. Bernard, a St. John of the Cross, a hundred others, if we were to suppose that all biblical references and allusions could be extracted from them, when each was judged as of little value? And yet, what a world of difference there is between such works and the passages from St. Paul in which they originate! What a long road has been travelled since the time when Christian liberty was affirmed and vindicated through a renewed understanding of ancient Scripture!

## 5. Declines and Renewals

The mark which was made on medieval exegesis by the monastic mind did not prove to be an impediment to the continuation of the tradition handed down by the Fathers. There was, in fact, a remarkably fruitful spontaneity about the way in which the

42. See Bernard again, *In Cantica,* sermo 84, n. 7: *"Verba Domini sunt: non est fas suspendere fidem. Credant quod non experiuntur, ut fructum quandoque experientiae fidei merito consequantur"* (*PL,* 183, 1187C).

43. Dom Jean Leclercq, *"La 'lecture divine',"* in *La Maison-Dieu,* 5, p. 29.

tradition was preserved. Medieval exegesis also made some fortunate discoveries, such as the applicability to the Virgin Mary—*prioris Ecclesiae pars optima, exemplar junioris Ecclesiae* (the better part of the former Church, the exemplar of the youngest Church)[1]—of texts which had already been understood of the Church and of the individual soul.[2] For the most part, though, it repeats, amplifies, and adds complexity to that tradition. It produces a seemingly endless number of florilegia, catalogues, anthologies of allegories. On the other hand, medieval exegesis embarks upon a system of universal symbolism whose fruits are sometimes exceptionally beautiful, even though the mind's initial delight in them might later turn gradually into numbness. It is also inclined towards organizing and codifying. Certain texts of St. Augustine and of Cassian, among others, are at the root of a classification of scriptural meanings which will later be adopted by the great thirteenth-century theologians and subsequently transmitted by them to our own era. There are many medieval commentaries which remind us of very subtle patchworks. In this respect, the advent of Scholasticism brought with it no perceptible change. The formulas of a St. Thomas summarize and distill the tradition in a most successful fashion. Through Nicholas of Lyra the tradition is still everywhere diffused towards the end of the Middle Ages. In theory, then, the spiritual interpretation of Scripture is continued. But, practised or not—and, actually, it was practised more and more[3]—the majority will find it more and more a dead letter, as is perfectly apparent.

It had had its weaknesses from the very beginning. After a long life, it had eventually grown old. The problems had changed, and so had the needs of Christian thought. Once the period of intense effervescence in which it had originated had passed,

[1]. Rupert of Deutz, *De operibus Spiritus Sancti,* l. 1, c. 8 (*PL,* 167, 1577D).

[2]. See Guerric of Igny, *In Assumptione b. Mariae,* sermo 3, n. 3 (*PL,* 185, 195A).

[3]. Note, for example, the enormous success, which continued for more than two centuries, of the *Speculum humanae salvationis* (1324). In forty-five chapters, the work develops an extremely detailed typology of the work of redemption, with a role always found for the Virgin.

56

mystical exegesis had furnished the apologists with a weapon, then the Doctors had drawn from it a unified vision of the divine Economy; and then the monks had found in it a method useful in their *"lectio divina."* Now came the intellectuals who were interested in constructing a new theology with new methods, but within the continuity of the faith. With them, reason awakes from its symbolic dream. "The Age of Proof" begins. What aid could these intellectuals find in an exegesis which was too much a part of this dream and was a victim of "hardened arteries" to boot? Mystical exegesis could only be an anachronism for an undertaking which sought to be scientific. St. Thomas very clearly says so: *"Ex solo sensu litterali potest trahi argumentum"* (From the literal sense alone can arguments be drawn).[4] This was fully perceived during the century which followed, when the papal theologians wished to base their claims on Scripture. They relied on St. Luke's text about the two keys possessed by Peter. But a John of Paris, who spoke for all the royal theologians, cut their claims short: *"Mystica Theologia non est argumentativa."* And it was certainly more valuable for argumentative theology to hold fast to the letter rather than to distort spiritual understanding by diverting it from its proper end and to introduce questionable doctrines or individual fancies in the guise of allegorical meanings.[5]

Beginning with the sixteenth century, the development was to become more pronounced. We then find an effort to escape from the old "set patterns" and to rediscover, "far from all scholastic conventions," an exegesis which would be both truly scientific and truly spiritual.[6] The symbolism of the Renaissance, however, was far too muddled in its inspiration to be able to revivify the

[4.] *Ia.* q. 1, a. 10. See *Quodlib. 7*, a. 15; a. 14, ad 4m. Also, Augustine, *Epist.* 93, 8, 24 (*PL*, 33, 334). See Melchior Cano, *De locis theologicis*, 1. 2, cc. 4, 11; 1. 5, c. 6; 1. 12, c. 11.

[5.] See Joseph Lecler, "L'argument des deux glaives dans les controverses politiques du moyen age," in *RSR*, vol. 21 (1931), pp. 299–339. J. Huizinga, *The Waning of the Middle Ages*, London, 1924, pp. 182–194. There are a number of details about these abuses in R. Guelluy, "L'évolution des méthodes théologiques à Louvain," in *Revue d'histoire ecclésiastique*, vol. 38 (1941), pp. 45–46, 61.

[6] Jean Baruzi, "Les diverses interpretations de saint Paul au XVIe siècle," in *Revue de Theologie et de philosophie*, 1929, pp. 89–91.

early patristic exegesis. The onslaught of Protestantism soon required a concentration of effort on the establishment of the literal meaning.[7] The obscurity of certain passages, which had given the Fathers an opportunity to extol the profundities of Scripture, was better exploited in demonstrating the insufficiency of the Book and the need for a Tradition.[8] Then the onslaught of rationalism and the necessity of examining the biblical accounts in the light of the documents discovered by modern scholarship again brought apologetical considerations to the fore. The problem of inerrancy received the major share of attention, and the spiritual interpretation of the sacred texts, along with the earlier method of understanding the faith, were henceforth almost completely abandoned.[9] Before very long,

---

[7.] With respect to the Psalms, see Mersch, *Le Corps mystique du Christ*, vol. 2, p. 139; ET *The Whole Christ*, Milwaukee, 1938.

[8.] Thus Melchior Cano, *De locis theologicis*, l. 7, c. 3. On this problem, See Edmond Ortigues, "Ecritures et Traditions Apostoliques au Concile de Trente," in *RSR*, vol. 36 (1949), pp. 271–299.

[9.] Beginning with this situation, the fact is that "many contemporary exegetes . . . viewed spiritual exegesis as alien to scriptural science." Are such exegetes to be criticized, as having thereby "totally neglected the second part of their job"? In our opinion, this would be excessive. "Science" is, after all, an ambiguous term, which can denote, in the ancient acceptation, knowledge of Scripture in all its aspects, and can also be restricted, in the modern acceptation, to the disciplines of "positive science." By definition, "scientific exegetes" are concerned with "positive science." They are primarily specialists, and their function has become both very necessary and very important during the last few centuries. They must realize (and this realization is something they have occasionally lacked) that their very specialization imposes limitations on them; that their "science" thus cannot be the whole of scriptural science; but they are not required, in their role as scientific exegetes, to give us the whole of scriptural science; and they should not even aspire to do so. As Oscar Cullmann points out, *art. cit.*, p. 13: "the great and unique responsibility of the biblical exegete is to be faithful to the text in radical fashion, even if the exegetical result thereby obtained is a modest one and possibly seems, at first glance, useless for dogmatics or for the practical life of the Church." We have discussed the question in *Mélanges Cavallera* (1948), pp. 347–366, "Sur un vieux distique, la doctrine du 'quadruple sens'," especially pp. 363–366; also see Luis de Leon, *Les noms du Christ*, text cited by Alain Guy, *op. cit.*, p. 234. We might add that, if exegesis is not always sufficiently spiritual, it

neither their importance [10] nor their principle was understood, and only their defects or their minor details were considered.[11] From that point on, spiritual interpretation was viewed by many

should also be admitted that spirituality is not always careful about being sufficiently scriptural.

It is still eminently desirable, of course, for the talents of the scientific exegete and of the theologian, just as those of the historian and of the spiritual man, to be combined in the same scholar. In any event, the scientific exegete has to be enough of a theologian to be able to mark out his own field of work, and the theologian has to be sufficiently up-to-date on scientific activity to assure a solid foundation for his teaching. The required distinction between the disciplines is not a dogmatic separation inherent in the object. But the fullness of gifts is something rare, and cannot be demanded of anyone. Undoubtedly, too strict a division of labor can really be "a hindrance to the *interior dialogue* which must constantly be taking place between the historian and the theologian" (Oscar Cullmann, *art. cit.,* p. 11). But the laws of this division are nevertheless imposed in practice, and they produce or reveal differences in mentality or point of view which need not be hardened into doctrinal opposition. The history of theology teaches us that the supporters of the Council of Ephesus were sometimes too quickly accused of monophysitism, and the supporters of the Council of Chalcedon, of Nestorianism. There is no "God or Man?" dilemma about the one who is both God and Man. Neither is there an "Either Scripture is a human work, or else it is a divine work" dilemma about the book which is both human and divine.

10. A comparison will make this clear. Accordingly to Origen, the blessed will receive, after this life, the understanding of the Scriptures. This is to say that they will have new lights on the mysteries of salvation, God's conduct in human history, the depths of the Logos. But this is what Lessius in the seventeenth century has to say when describing the knowledge of the blessed: *"Denique . . . cognoscunt clare omnia Scripturarum arcana, omnes prophetias, omnes figuras, omnes symbolicas adumbrationes, omnes mysticos sensus"* (*De Summo Bono et aeterna beatitudine hominis,* l. 2, c. 9). *Quaenam videantur a beatis in Deo vel cum Deo?* (Hürter ed.), 1869, p. 168; see p. 174. But in the thought of Lessius, this is little more than a kind of particular object, supplementary, intended to satisfy some remnant of unsatisfied curiosity. For Lessius has just finished listing all the mysteries of the faith, and he is already preparing to speak of the entire course of history and of the events of providence. One cannot help wondering what "the secrets of Scripture" could suggest for him.

11. See, for example, Cardinal du Perron, *Traité de l'Eucharistie,* p. 40, on Augustine: "His was a mind which, in order to express the graciousness of its inventions and to whet the appetites of its listeners, took pleasure in enlivening them with allegorical games and meditations." It would be impossible to be more superficial.

as an idle amusement, an "agreeable pastime,"[12] or even as a "disastrous illness" of the mind.

On the other hand, theology, to the extent that it became specialized and rejected the sovereign role which it had occupied during the period of its greatness, readily assumed an anti-mystical bias. Outdoing the Cartesian spirit, the prosaic pragmatism of the eighteenth century (which all churchmen did not escape) accentuated this bias. Richard Simon, who was good enough an historian to recognize that "allegory" was not Origen's gift to the Church (Simon found it everywhere, beginning with the first Christian generation),[13] viewed it nevertheless as little more than "witticism," "ingenious ornamentation," "mystification," all without interest, and which, he added, "cannot be appreciated by people with any judgement."[14] A similar myopia was to contribute, along with the much more regrettable attacks by Bossuet, to the compromising of the cause of the nascent criticism in the eyes of many. Duguet, not without reason, then complained of many who showed "a secret hostility to everything mystical and everything which goes deeper than the surface of history."[15] Underneath their subtle exteriors, certain commentaries of St. Gregory the Great conceal pure wonders, but "this is not their most useful feature" is Fleury's disdainful verdict.[16] And Dupin, writing about St. Cyril's treatises, has this to say: "Commentaries of this sort are of little use, for they are no help whatever in explaining the letter. They teach little in the way of morality, and they demonstrate no dogma. It is all a question of metaphysics and abstract relationships which cannot be used either to convince unbelievers nor to edify the faithful."[17] Leonard thinks that he must pardon

---

12. See Dom Charlier, in *Esprit et Vie* (1949), p. 594.

13. *Historie critique du Vieux Testament* (1685), 1. 3, c. 8 (p. 386). *Histoire critique des principaux commentateurs du Nouveau Testament* (1693), preface; ch. 1 (pp. 6–7).

14. These remarks are put into strong relief by Père Baltus in his *Défense des prophéties de la religion chrétienne*, vol. III (1737), p. 10 and pp. 56ff. See the comments of Dom Pitra, *loc. cit.*, p. 79.

15. Duguet and d'Asfeld, *Explication de l'ouvrage des six jours* (new ed.), 1740, p. 34. Dom Cellier will also make a few timid protests.

16. *Histoire ecclésiastique*, 5th discourse, n. 11.

17. *Bibliothèque ecclésiastique*, vol. 3, p. 100.

the Fathers for aberrations like these because of the difficulties they encountered; but, he adds, completely contrary to the evidence, "they rarely escaped them."[18]

Just as a vanquished cult, despised by the conqueror, finishes by debasing itself and by producing a caricature of itself, the few remnants of the old school of exegesis seemed intent upon providing support for such judgments. The last adherents of allegorism never rest from exaggerating its failings. They do not grasp its innermost nature any better than its detractors do. This is an ecclesiastical aspect of the quarrel between ancient and modern. It is much easier, though, to side with the ancient than to recapture his spirit. There are some narrow-minded "figurists" who think they have to take certain expressions of the Fathers literally and want to discover mysteries behind every word in the Bible. They insist beyond all proportion on "the multiplicity of meanings which it contains."[19] Making oracles of the Holy Spirit out of their wild imaginations and putting exegesis at the service of the passions of their sect, they discover in the history of Israel a figure for everything which happens to them in the history of the Church.[20] If everything in the Law

18. *Traité du sens littéral et du sens mystique des saintes Ecritures selon la doctrine des Pères* . . . (1727), ch. 6, p. 189. In his *Réfutation du livre des Règles* . . ., (1727), he says, with no greater objectivity, that the Fathers "unanimously condemn" the exegesis of Origen (pp. 399–400; see pp. 23, 29). De la Rue is another example.

19. *Les Principes* . . ., beginning. This work, which remained in manuscript form, is cited by Leonard in his *Réfutation* . . ., p. 393.

20. *Parallèle abrégé de l'histoire du Peuple d'Israel et de l'histoire de l'Eglise* (1723), by the author of *Les Principes*. Page 21, for example: "The change which took place in the government of the people of Israel, to whom God gave a King, is a figure of the change which took place in the discipline of the Church, when the papal power took on new accretions." Or page 35: "By the young men who give bad counsel to Roboam are painted, in the most vivid colors, the sycophants of the Court of Rome." Similarly, Nicolas le Gros, a famous advocate, in his biblical "Meditations" (1735–1754). Though the explanations are different, the system is imitated by the Protestants, Cocceius (Koch) and Jurieu (the latter's *L'accomplissement des prophéties ou la délivrance prochaine de l'Église* (1686), had a huge success). The system was also employed in the work which Arnauld had combatted not long before, *L'ancienne nouveauté de l'Ecriture sainte ou l'Eglise triomphante en terre* (see *Oeuvres,* vol. 5, pp. 321–362). This was the complete antithesis of a real system of spiritual interpretation.

is not immediately clear, the reason for this, they think, is that Moses was not allowed to "speak except in enigmas to a people which had no love for the truth."[21] In all these respects, which prove that they perceive neither *history* nor *spirit,* they are completely different from the great patristic exegetes.[22] They are no less so when, like the Abbé d'Asfeld [23] or the Protestant mystic, Poiret, they go out of their way to criticize the first exponents of critical exegesis, or become indignant at such efforts as if they were sacrilegious pretensions.[24] Still others, taking routine for tradition and mental laziness for fidelity, endlessly repeat mystical explanations; but these have by now become nothing but formulas, lacking any power whatever. The general atmosphere is hostile to symbolism. Only the "conservatory" of the liturgy offers it some kind of haven and affords it a precarious continued existence.

When we look at the situation which prevailed only yesterday, we have to agree with Père de Ghellinck[25] that the mystical exegesis of the ancients and of the men of the Middle Ages "is shocking to the modern reader." Some understanding of it was preserved by a few first-class writers, such as a Drey,[26] a Möhler, a Newman, a Scheeben; a Keble did all he could to rehabilitate it by restoring its true significance; but the thought of men like these seems to have been largely disregarded by most theologians. Even in treatises on hermeneutics (where there is much more discussion about the inspiration of the sacred writers than

---

[21]. *Explication de cinq chapîtres du Deutéronome* (1734), p. 221.

[22]. Leonard is mistaken when he writes, intending to characterize figurism: "In a word, it restores the system of Origen" (*Réfutation . . .,* p. 29).

[23]. In his *Règles pour l'intelligence des Ecritures saintes* (1717), he censures Christians, "accustomed to a bold criticism, full of secular ideas," who "amuse" their readers "by guessing at the relationship of the prophecies to the history of the era in which the prophets lived." The work was written with the collaboration of the Abbé d'Etremare and under the inspiration of Duguet.

[24]. Poiret, *L' Economie divine,* Amsterdam, 1687, vol. 3, p. 343; vol. 4, p. 312. Texts cited by A. Monod, *De Pascal à Chateaubriand,* Paris, 1916, p. 143.

[25]. *L'essor de la littérature latine au XIIIe siècle* (1946), vol. 2, p. 306.

[26]. See Drey, *Introduction à l'étude de la théologie,* Tübingen, 1819.

about the inspiration of Scripture), questions relating to it are
either passed over in silence,[27] or are the subject of a few rapid
definitions and distinctions, which are immediately forgotten. It
is admitted that "spiritual meanings" exist, though few in number
and hidden away in odd corners of the sacred text. But they are
never linked up to anything organic; and it is almost invariably
added that these meanings, being "proper to God" and depending "on his free arrangement," can only be recognized by a
positive revelation—which for all practical purposes is to say
that they can be recognized by the fact that they are referred to
specifically in the books of the New Testament. Outside of that,
"to look for spiritual explanations is to go astray."[28] This was
Fourmont's opinion, as early as the eighteenth century.[29] According to him, it was nothing but "rashness and blindness to
apply to Jesus Christ any text from the Old Testament, other
than those which the Apostles themselves had applied to him."
The *Mémoires de Trévoux* have the following to say about that
opinion: "We know not the Theology from which the Author
has derived so curious a Doctrine. It is certain that it was totally
unknown to the Fathers of the Church, and that it was unheard
of before now . . . .[30] The Author is not to be admired for a

27. Two examples are the treatises of Vosté, *De divina inspiratione
et veritate sacrae Scripturae* (2d ed.), 1932, and Lusseau, *Essai sur la
nature de l'inspiration scripturaire* (1930). Still in all, Père Vosté had,
in the *Xenia thomistica*, Rome, 1925, recalled the doctrine of the four
senses, following Thomas (vol. 2, pp. 45–47). Setting forth the same
doctrine in the same collection (pp. 27–29), R. P. Marcus Sales wrote:
*"Etiam in hac parte Angelicus normas tradit omnino sequendas."*
28. S. Zarb, O.P., "Sancti Isidori cultus erga sacras litteras," in *Mis-
cellanea Isidoriana,* Rome, 1936, pp. 133–134. Cornely-Hagen, *Compendium* (7th ed.), 1911, p. 135.
29. *Réfutation du livre des Règles pour l'intelligence des saintes Ecritures* (1727). The great Arnauld had written more accurately, *loc. cit.,*
p. 345: "One of the greatest principles of the Christian religion is that
the true understanding of the Old Testament depends on the New; and
that we must not only understand, as did Jesus Christ and the Apostles,
the passages of Scripture which they explained, but also take these explanations as divine rules, which must lead us to the understanding of
other similar passages, of which they said nothing."
30. The *Mémoires* go a little too far here. Calvin had shown a similar
requirement, *Institution de la religion chrétienne,* vol. 1, ch. 2 (Pannier

SCRIPTURE IN THE TRADITION

principle which would make of the Fathers nothing but Adventurers and Visionaries." [31] The rejoinder was a sound one. Even so, once the "spiritual meanings" had been envisaged as just so many atoms, and the movement of thought which had previously encouraged the search for them had been forgotten or almost completely misunderstood, Fourmont's position became the logical one, so it is not surprising to find that the modern treatises have made it their own. We should not be surprised either to see that "criticism" and "mysticism" are generally understood, either expressly or by implication, as being opposed to one another. As if it were impossible to have both, or, at the very least, to recognize that both are legitimate, and indeed necessary! [32] As if (alas!) any number of moderns had not proven themselves lacking "criticism" and "mysticism" in like degree! But, once a certain situation had occurred, this undoubtedly became a fatal presumption.

Should we grieve over such neglect, such lack of appreciation? Less, perhaps, than we might be tempted to. Spiritual exegesis accomplished an essential part of its task a long time ago. It has made its contribution to the expression of the Christian mystery

---

ed.), p. 194; as did a number of Protestant authors, following Calvin, such as Barbeyrac and Withey. Dom Cellier discusses them, *Apologie de la morale des Pères de l'Eglise* (1718), pp. 103–105. In point of fact, there seems to have been some such rule at Antioch: L. Pirot, *L'œuvre exégètique de Théodore de Mopsueste*, p. viii and pp. 274–275.

31. *Mémoires de Trévoux* (January 1728), pp. 27–28. See Dom J. Gribomont, "Le lien des deux Testaments," in *ETL*, vol. 22 (1946), pp. 86–87. Along the same line, see the prudent observation of Père Chifflot, *op. cit.,* pp. 43–45. See also Newman, *Sermons Bearing on Subjects of the Day* (new ed.), 1879, pp. 167–168.

32. The opposites of a healthy criticism are the absence of criticism and hypercriticism. The opposite of a good literal exegesis is a bad literal exegesis, not spiritual exegesis, in its proper place. Can anyone deny the fact that our libraries are overburdened with works which lack either scientific or spiritual value? Think, for example, of the huge amount of Concordist literature during the last century. The practice of spiritual exegesis is neither a token of critical spirit nor the mark of a lack of criticism. In any event, it is no more contrary to science than are, for example, the views of a certain philosopher on the ontological meaning of sensible quality to physics or chemistry. See J.-P. Sartre, *L'être et le néant*, pp. 690–696.

and to the building of the Church. It would be impossible to restore it today in all its fullness. As long as there is no repudiation of the achievements of spiritual exegesis, no mortal damage has been done. It should, however, be borne in mind that in the spiritual order it is an illusion to think that anything can be absolutely acquired, once for all. It is only by the always actual and incessantly active presence of the Holy Spirit that the Church herself preserves the faith. On the other hand, the genre had been cultivated for such a long time and had had so many ramifications that many understandably considered its sap to have been exhausted. However that may be, there are certainly better things to do today, as Père Lagrange used to say,[33] than "to wrinkle one's brow in efforts to discover new spiritual meanings" or "to index the spiritual meanings of the Fathers, so as to give the public a modern historical commentary in the style of Cornelius a Lapide."

This, however, is not to say that the exegesis of the Fathers was nothing but a temporary substitute for scientific exegesis, which would alone be considered to be the true and complete exegesis. And it is not to say that the entire function of spiritual exegesis was to "preserve the Bible within a very pure and very exalted sphere of ideas and sentiments, until minds reached sufficient maturity to be able to understand the past and to be given the direct explanation of the texts." [34] In spite of our admiration for Dom Wilmart, we must say that such statements smack of a modern self-sufficiency. The true believer will always look for more than "the understanding of the past" in the Bible. We do not see, either, that it is expedient to ask Christian exegesis, as some have done, to "get rid of the diapers of allegorism," for this could be misinterpreted. Moreover, if it is indisputable that the rules of interpretation which the Fathers followed "were quite often purely random means, long since

33. *Eclaircissements sur la méthode historique,* p. 100.
34. Dom Wilmart, "Un répertoire d'exégèse composé en Angleterre vers le début du XIIe siècle," in *Mémorial Lagrange* (1940), p. 312, n. Dom Wilmart refuses, moreover, to "treat in passing" a "subject so vast" and recognizes "the profound truth" which underlies the theory of the scriptural meanings.

obsolete, which still served to save the treasury of Scripture," [35]
and that "believing exegesis today is, in certain respects, better
employed than was theirs," [36] we can nevertheless think that the
Fathers had a kind of connaturality with Scripture which today's
faith cannot duplicate without much difficulty. Newman confirms this:

This age is a practical age: the age of the Fathers was more contemplative; their theology, consequently, had a deeper, more mystical, more subtle character about it, than we with our present habits
of thought can readily enter into. We lay greater stress than they on
proofs from definite verses of Scripture, or what are familiarly called
texts, and we build up a system upon them; they rather recognized
a certain truth lying hid under the tenor of the sacred text as a
whole, and showing itself more or less in this verse or that as it
might be. We look on the letter of Scripture more as a foundation,
they as an organ of the truth. Such a difference is quite allowable,
or rather natural or even necessary. The Fathers might have tradi-
tionary information of the general drift of the inspired text which
we have not; they are able to move more freely. Moreover, a certain
high moral state of mind, which times of persecution alone create,
may be necessary for a due exercise of mystical interpretation. To
attempt it otherwise than from the heart, would be a profanation;
better not attempt it at all.[37]

For the reasons given by Newman—the last is especially
applicable to the case of Origen—and for other reasons which
follow from what has already been discussed, we shall avoid an
excessive enthusiasm for the ancients which would lead us to
imitate their methods. We continue, of course, to believe that a
great idea came to birth through their human ingenuity, through
a respectable but contingent tradition, and that the idea is
worthy of preservation; and also that a sacred element lies at the

[35]. Möhler, *L'Unité dans l'Eglise,* appendix 7.
[36]. Dom Charlier, *Exégèse patristique et exégèse scientifique,* in
*Esprit et Vie* (1949), p. 63.
[37]. "Prospects of the Anglican Church," an article written in April
1839, collected in *Essays Critical and Historical* (1871). See also the
fair reflections of Scheeben, *Dogmatik,* no. 242.

heart of their exegesis, an element which is one of the treasures of the faith. In a matter which is so delicate and so difficult to discern, it is up to each one of us to determine for himself what is ephemeral and what is external, what is divine and what is human. It is certain that our exegesis, even our spiritual exegesis, cannot have the same outward characteristics as theirs. This applies both to our incapacities and to the progress we have already made. The Fathers bear witness to a springtime, an adolescence, and no one will ever be able to take that privilege away from them. We, on the other hand, must successfully represent the age of maturity.

"The holy doctors, despite all their commentaries and all that might be added to them, have never completely succeeded in expounding the language of the Holy Spirit; ordinarily, it is the least part of it which is expounded." [38] The Word which God addresses to each generation is always the same Word, and its fecundity cannot be defined. Consequently, it is impossible to give a precise description of the ways in which the Holy Spirit will nourish the Church on that Word in times to come. Always faithful and always consistent, the Spirit is also always unforeseen.

Even so, there are a few features which become apparent. Our spiritual exegesis, assuming a revival of it, will, of course, remain Christological, purely Christological—and will neglect none of the dimensions of Christ, just as before.[39] Unlike an unintelligent science whose ravages were often to be deplored, it will strive always to be sensitive to the "wonderful profundity" of the divine words, which inspired in St. Augustine a love mixed with fear.[40] But we shall be extremely careful to avoid giving the impression that our exegesis is built upon the weaknesses of

[38]. St. John of the Cross, *Spiritual Canticle,* prologue.

[39]. See Louis Massignon, "Soyons des Sémites spirituels," in *Dieu Vivant,* 14, p. 82.

[40]. Augustine, *Confessions,* l. 12, c. 14, n. 17: *"Mira profunditas eloquiorum tuorum, quorum ecce ante nos superficies blandiens parvulis, sed mira profunditas, Deus meus, mira profunditas! Horror est intendere in eam: horror honoris, et tremor amoris!"* (*PL,* 33, 382).

criticism.[41] Consequently, though without departing from the basic principles of the ancients, we shall often have to depart from their practice and from their imagined justification of it. We shall imitate their habitual modesty rather than their procedures.[42] No less attentive than they to the mystery as signified in history, we shall be more attentive perhaps to the historicity of the type, or, at the very least, more aware of the steps demanded for an exact knowledge of this historicity. In this way, we shall strive to unite our modern "historical sense" to that profound "sense of history" which the ancients were able to draw forth by means of their spiritual exegesis. We shall also be better able than they "to remove the anthropomorphism of a God required to calculate subtly a design of contingent details so as to ordain in figures certain historical facts"; we shall be even more successful in seeing that, in reality, it was "from the very thread from which it was spun that he made the Old Testament an image of the New, and both Testaments a type of glory." [43] In other words, a simplified symbolism, one which is habitually more sober, will be able to receive new strength, by reason of a stronger link with history.[44] This is not to say that it should ever be replaced by a simple reflection on this providential history, but it will have its roots and its underlying unity in that reflection. Following the example of men of the spirit like Newman or St. John of the Cross, we may also succeed in taking a closer look at the eternal significance of the great bibli-

41. With his usual common sense, Isidorus of Pelusium long ago put one of his correspondents on his guard against the excesses of beautiful allegories. Very often, he told him, "those who use such methods do so out of ignorance and as a means of escaping difficulties." *Epist.*, 1. 3, ep. 84 (*PG*, 78, 789B-C). Richard Simon was not mistaken either when he wrote: "Under the pretext of giving a spiritual meaning, we can sometimes outrun ourselves, and offer our own imaginings as spirituality" (*Histoire critique du Vieux Testament*, 1. 3, c. 10).

42. See, for example, Cassian, *Conlatio 8*, c. 4 (Petschenig ed., p 221).

43. Dom J. Gribomont, "Le lien des deux Testaments," in *ETL* (1946), pp. 74–75.

44. There is an example related to the Psalms in Bouyer, "Les Psaumes, prière du peuple de Dieu," *La Vie spirituelle,* vol. 80 (1949), pp. 579–597.

cal episodes, but always in the light of the Christian Mystery,[45] and thus we shall learn "better to recognize the eternal youth of the ancient text." [46] Then, in a resurgence which is completely possible, the symbolic function of our intelligence may unfold anew and produce new fruits in the unforeseeable freedom of the Spirit [47]—with the essential and final criterion remaining always the analogy of faith, which is, we must never forget, an ecclesiastical criterion.[48]

An attempt at reconstruction pure and simple does not seem any more desirable than a bold projection. It would be sheer pretense, and is not seriously to be feared. To put it very simply, the spirit of the age is carrying us in quite another direction. If we said that our age repudiated or dissociated itself from every kind of symbolism, we would still be stopping at appearances. What it does, rather, is to institute an anti-symbolism. If we followed it, we would not, like Origen, see angels in the publicans,[49] but publicans—or some other wholly human reality— in the angels. Unlike the Christian ages, and quite like the ancient Greeks who found in the stories of their gods an allegory of the forces of nature or the faculties of the soul, we are

---

[45.] "If, as we all do, he went looking in Scripture for the science of Revelation, he went also to discover the revelation of consciences. . . . He believed that the Holy Spirit himself, who had inspired the book, concealed in it his earlier interventions and the permanent law of his operations" (J. Wehrlé, "Le doctorat de saint Jean de la Croix," in *Revue apologétique,* July 1928, p. 11). See also Jean Baruzi, *Saint Jean de la Croix . . .* (2d ed.), pp. 233–234, and "Saint Jean de la Croix et la Bible," in *Histoire générale des religions* (Quillet), vol. III, pp. 188–191. And it was Newman who, in his profound naïveté, said: "Thus did he (Jacob) foreshadow that condition of life, which is not only a lesson, but a pattern to us of our very state of life, 'if we live godly in Christ Jesus'." *Parochial and Plain Sermons,* V, 20, New York, 1907, p. 286.

[46.] A. M. Dubarle, in *RevScPhTh* (1949), p. 180.

[47.] "[Scripture] cannot, as it were, be mapped. . . . To the end of the Church, it must be an unexplored and unsubdued land." *Development of Christian Doctrine* (Harrold ed.), New York, 1949, p. 65.

[48.] See Rom. 12, 6. There are patristic texts on the subject in Thomassin, *Dogmata Theologica,* vol. 5, pp. 108–128, 134–139.

[49.] *In Lucam,* h. 23 (Rauer ed., pp. 154–155).

victims of totalitarian "terreneness" and humanism. In their various ways, psychologists, sociologists, and metaphysicians conspire to impose such views upon us.[50] To put it very briefly, our major temptation is to make of God a symbol for man, the objectified symbol of himself. As should be perfectly obvious, this frightful inversion would carry off all biblical allegory, and faith itself, in a single stroke.

But even this inverted symbolism bears witness to the symbolic function, inherent in the human mind, to which we have just alluded. For a long time, a similar function could be mistaken by a rationalistic, narrow, and superficial doctrine or mentality. At the time of the "enlightenment," it was only the "seers," such as a William Law,[51] indeed a Swedenborg,[52] who continued to exercise it. Someone like Hamann put it better at the service of traditional inspiration,[53] but he had no school. Today there is a general rediscovery of this symbolic function on all the levels of being and thought. To be strictly accurate, it had never been completely stifled, not even in the most classical philosophy. It played a role in the *Monadology* of Leibniz, in the *Critique of Practical Reason* of Kant, in the *Synthèse subjective* of Auguste Comte. Its place in the work of Hegel and his disciples was considerable, as it was in the work of Proudhon. Still closer to us, we see it emphasized from many different points of view in the works of a Freud and a Jung, a Lévy-Bruhl and an Eliade, in the analyses of a Sartre. Not long ago, Jean Lacroix wrote: "The deepest thing in the spiritual history of mankind is the

50. See the reflections of Rupert of Deutz in *De Operibus Spiritus Sancti*, l. 1, c. 7 (*PL*, 167, 157B-C).

51. For the preceding century, the *Mysterium Magnum* of Jacob Boehme deserves to be cited.

52. In April 1745, he has a vision in which he hears the Lord saying to him: "I chose you to set before men the spiritual meaning of the holy Word." From this date forward, he publishes or edits a considerable number of commentaries. See Charles Byse, *Swedenborg*, Paris, 5 vols., 1901; Martin Lamm, *Swedenborg*, Leipzig, 1922.

53. See Johann Georg Hamann, *Méditations Bibliques de Hamann* (Pierre Klossowski ed. and trans.), Paris, 1948. Hamann's hermeneutics has been studied in greater depth by X. Tilliette and by Hans Urs von Balthasar, *Herrlichkeit*, vol. 2.

comprehension of the sign, and every great philosophy is a semeiology: the discovery of the world's cipher and the consequent ability to reveal its language is the object of man's basic desire. And mysticism is undoubtedly the meaning of signs before anything else." [54]

These are only a few examples.[55] We have no intention of associating the names we have mentioned with scriptural symbolism. But they do evoke a certain climate of thought, which is far more favorable to an understanding of it than was the climate in the recent past. Since this climate is developing at a time when biblical criticism and history are at their peak and scientific methods of exegesis enjoy an undisputed "freedom of the city" within the Church, we certainly have the right to anticipate a fortunate convergence which will be of benefit to the study and meditation of the Book.[56]

We have even more reason to hope for it because of the fact that an extremely lively taste for the Bible is growing among educated Christians. Père Bouyer once wrote that "the Bible is no longer enjoyed or understood because spiritual exegesis is not appreciated and is known even less." [57] But the time may not be far off when this diagnosis will be replaced by a less pessimistic one. The Bible will be enjoyed and understood anew because a healthy spiritual exegesis will once more rise on the foundations of a tested science. We must be grateful to those who have been the precursors of this development, to Léon Bloy and to Péguy not very long ago, and especially to Claudel in our own day.

We would be wrong if we were to be cool to their message

54. *Marxisme, existentialisme, personnalisme* (1949), p. 47.

55. Among the principal influences to be cited are poets such as Baudelaire, Mallarmé, and Rimbaud, without speaking of a number of others who are closer to us.

56. Provided, however, that account is taken of the profound transformation made in this area by the revelation made to Israel and consummated in Christ, of the new rhythm substituted for the ancient rhythm by Christian thought. See *Catholicism,* ch. 6.

57. "Liturgie et exégèse spirituelle," in *La Maison-Dieu,* 7 (1946), p. 30.

on the grounds that "they are just poets," or that they sometimes fail to appreciate simple history, or even that they are less than fair towards biblical criticism. The truth of the matter is that they gave it a big push forward. They helped us to reintegrate ourselves into the most authentic tradition. It is unrealistic to expect them to speak like specialists in exegesis, any more than in theology or in spirituality. But the kind of witness they give, no matter what its weaknesses and its excesses, has the special virtue of reminding the experts that the Bible, unlike many other ancient documents, can never be their exclusive possession. And it also demonstrates the law that certain values are only discovered, or recaptured in all their power, outside the circles of the professionals. There are many professionals who are clear-sighted enough to see this, and humble enough not to be shocked in the least by it.[58]

## 6. Conclusion

Holy Scripture contains under its human garb the very Word of God. This has always been believed and will always be believed in the Church. But, exclusive of all precise theories of inspiration, there are in practice two quite different ways of understanding this belief. As he confronts the sacred Book, the believer has a choice of two possible attitudes. (We are speaking primarily of the Old Testament.) The first attitude consists in viewing the Old Testament as a document which instructs us about the past of the People of Israel, about their religion, their expectations, about the preparation made by God through them for his Christ. It is clearly understood that this document possesses a unique privilege, divine inspiration, which guarantees its perfect veracity. It is also clearly understood that the beliefs which passed from the Old Testament into the New are still

---

58. Did not as great a scholar as Père Lagrange declare that the best "Life of Christ" was still the one by Ludolph the Carthusian? *L'Evangile de Jésus-Christ;* ET *The Gospel of Jesus Christ,* London, 1938, p. xi.

imposed on our faith, and that the prayers which express those beliefs can still be on our lips.

But such an attitude inevitably remains essentially objective and impersonal. It is correct, but it is also incomplete. The second attitude, on the contrary, could actually be dangerous if it were not referred back to the first, and unless it assumed the first, at the very least, it would be positively false. And yet it completes the first through some kind of necessity. It consists in seeking in the Bible "not a dead word, imprisoned in the past, but a living word, immediately addressed to the man of to-day . . ., a word which affects him, since it is for him that it was uttered and remains uttered." [1] When we open our Bible, not merely as believing historians or even as members of the faithful who simply seek instruction, but also as believers who are accomplishing a religious activity according to the total logic of our faith, then "it is inaccurate to say that we are questioning Scripture. It would be more exact to acknowledge that it is Scripture which is questioning us, and which finds for each of us, through all time and all generations, the appropriate question." [2]

This wholly consistent attitude has always been the attitude of many men of the Spirit. It is this attitude which made St. Ambrose, for example, write: *"Et nunc deambulabat in paradiso Deus, quando divinas Scripturas lego"* (Even today, God walks in paradise, when I read the divine Scriptures).[3] It is the atti-

---

[1]. L. Bouyer, *loc. cit.*, p. 30. See Pascal, *Le Mystère de Jésus:* "I am present to you through my word in Scripture." Jean Vilnet, *Bible et mystique chez saint Jean de la Croix* (1949), p. 170: "St. John of the Cross thus used to read the Bible as the always open book of an always current teaching."

[2]. Paul Claudel, "L'Ecriture sainte" in *La Vie intellectuelle* (May 1948), p. 8. See G. van de Leeuw, *La religion dans son essence et ses manifestations* (Fr. tr.), p. 433. See also Karl Barth, "The Strange New World within the Bible," in *The Word of God and the Word of Man,* New York, 1957, p. 28. W. Vischer, *La loi ou les cinq livres de Moïse* (Fr. tr.), introduction, p. 42. Jacques Maritain, "Les chemins de la foi," in *Foi en Jésus-Christ et monde d'aujourd'hui* (1949), p. 30: "When we meditate on the Gospel, it is the Gospel which speaks to us."

[3]. *Epist. 49,* n. 3 (*PL*, 16, 1154B).

tude of the saints, it is the attitude of the Church, which never ceases to turn towards her Lord in response to the voice which he addresses to her. Undoubtedly, this attitude is not necessary at all times, either in relation to all the texts taken materially, one after the other, or as to each individual member. But the ideal remains that each one prudently conform to it, thereby realizing to the greatest possible extent the traditional idea, so powerfully experienced by Origen, of *Anima in Ecclesia*.[4] The truth of the matter is, we can repeat with Hans Urs von Balthasar,[5] that

Just as the Eucharist is not a simple remembrance of something which happened in the past, but the perpetual reactualization of the Body of the Lord and of his Sacrifice, in the same fashion is Scripture less a question of history than of the form and vehicle of God's Word uttered unceasingly, and uttered even now. If human existence, understood at the deepest level, is a dialogue with God, and if in this dialogue the Word of God to man means infinitely more than the word of man to God; if the human response can only be exact when it stems from a constant listening to the Word (contemplation would be worth more than listening in this instance); if, still more, God said once for all in Christ what he had to say to man (Heb. 1, 1), so that there is nothing more for man to do but to recognize and to take to himself the treasures of wisdom and of knowledge which are hidden in Christ (Col. 2, 3); if, finally, Holy Scripture is nothing other than this divine testimony of Christ, then the reading of Holy Scripture and meditation on it ought to be the surest way I have to discern the concrete will of God for my life, and destiny such as God conceives it.

"This is why it is a great perversion," as Père Lallemant used to say, "to read so many works of piety and so little Scripture." Far more than to persuade certain educated persons to seek the history of revelation in the Bible, his desire was to convince as many of the faithful as possible that they should seek in Scripture and draw from Scripture the nourishment for their minds. Père Lallemant's advice is always valid. But if the reading is to be truly Catholic, the need for spiritual understanding

---

4. See Augustine, *De sermone Domini in monte,* l. 1, n. 5.
5. *Loc. cit.,* p. 13.

immediately becomes apparent.[6] Indeed, the more Scripture is received in such a total spirit of faith, the greater would be the danger of the faith's being falsified, if interpretation of Scripture remained on the purely literal level. We must follow the guidance of the liturgy and grasp the letter in a new spirit, that is to say —let us repeat it—in the spirit of the New Testament, the fruit of the Spirit of Jesus. Without the unceasing transposition by which ancient Judaism is Christianized, Christianity today could very easily become Judaicized in one way or another.

From an objective point of view, this is what separates us from certain Protestant exegetes—in much the same way as we are, from a subjective point of view, separated from them by our mode of reading Scripture, whether it be individual or ecclesial (with all that is implied by the latter word).

Luther, as we know, has many sagacious criticisms to make of the abuses of allegorism. Quite early in his career he abandoned the use of the "four senses," although he had started out by using them. But he does not lose his grasp of the essential elements of spiritual interpretation and continues to follow St. Paul and St. Augustine. For Luther, Christ is really the key to all Scripture. His one-sided way of contrasting the Gospel and the Law did, however, lead this extraordinary genius to disrupt the balance of traditional thought. This may explain, at least partially, the tendency which frequently reappears in Lutheran thought to reject the ancient Scripture as a "crucifying burden."

The liberal and critical spirit enhanced this tendency, and we see it in full growth in a Harnack, for example: an inverse principle inspired Calvin to a criticism which appeared to be analogous to Luther's. The Calvinist tendency, however, was not to suppress the Old Testament, but to re-evaluate it, as the City-Church experiment shows, and as the later history of Puritanism also shows. Calvin proved to be quite harsh towards "Origen and many others," whom he accused of distorting

6. At the same time, the benefit of the teaching of the Fathers becomes apparent. Whatever be true of their excesses, it would certainly be profitable to be familiar with many of their principles and to meditate on them, so as to preserve oneself from other excesses which are more tempting today.

Scripture by their "quibbles." The object of his attacks was not some particular excess or other, but the universal practice of the Church. A recall to sobriety was certainly in order, and we can only agree with him when he writes, for example: "It is, therefore, presumptuous and almost blasphemous to turn the meaning of Scripture around without due care, as though it were some game we were playing. And yet many scholars have done this at one time." [7] But his reaction runs away with him. For Calvin, everything which is not the direct literal meaning is "fiction," and every exegesis which goes beyond the letter is "an invention of Satan." He sees only an erroneous interpretation of St. Paul in "the scholastic dogma" that the sacraments of the Old Law were types of the grace conferred by our sacraments: as if, he says, the things which happened then had only been shadows of the realities to come.[8] According to him, it is "a great insult to the Law of God" given by Moses to utter "the vulgar expression that the Law of the Gospel is much greater": in reality, Christ added nothing to the Mosaic Law, but was perfectly content to "restore" it to its initial purity.[9] One might even think that, for Calvin, the old letter still directs us, at least in spirit.[10] A Calvinist from seventeenth-century Lyons was to write: "Christians, in their belief and in their worship, should have no feelings, no practices which differ from the beliefs and practices of the Jewish Church, apart from the ceremonial and the symbolic." The great Arnauld's reply to this showed him to be a faithful interpreter of the ancient tradition: "This is rather like saying that man, apart from his reason, is the same as a

---

[7.] *Calvin's Commentaries, Romans, Thessalonians,* Edinburgh, 1961 (Torrance ed.), p. 4 ("Dedication to Simon Grynaeus").

[8.] Calvin, *In I Cor.,* X, 3, 11 (*Opera,* vol. 49, 1892, pp. 454, 460); *Cinquième sermon sur la première Epître aux Corinthiens* (*ibid.,* pp. 640–641); *In Galat.,* IV, 22–26 (vol. 50, 1893, pp. 236–237); *In Hebr.,* X, 1 (vol. 55, 1896, p. 121). On the various nuances of the "scholastic dogma" denounced by Calvin, see Dom Gribomont, *art. cit.,* pp. 80–83.

[9.] *Institution de la religion chrestienne,* c. 3, *De la Loy,* vol. I (Pannier ed.), Paris, 1961, pp. 205–207.

[10.] A. Westphal, *Les Prophètes,* vol. I, Paris, 1924, p. 13. Calvin never lost the marks of his early juridical formation or of the mentality of his age; see Pierre Mesnard, in *Foi en Jésus-Christ et monde d'aujourd'hui* (1949), p. 118.

76

beast. It is impossible to read the Letter to the Hebrews attentively without becoming aware that the substance and essence of the Jewish religion, as Jewish, were, quite simply, to be ceremonial and symbolic." [11]

We do not wish to exaggerate the disagreement. A further reason for not wishing to do so is that portions of our common heritage are returning to us today from Protestant hands. Frequently, the question is principally one of emphasis. In point of fact, the conflicting affirmations, looked at in a material way, are complementary far more often than they are really contradictory. Calvin was perfectly able to recognize in the *Institutes*[12] that the Lord's "pedagogy" with respect to the Israelites had been "to give them no clear spiritual promises, but rather to present them with some image and figure thereof under the form of earthly promises." The exegesis of a Karl Barth, a Roland de Pury, a Wilhelm Vischer, are reminiscent in many ways of the exegesis of the early Fathers. Their vehement rejection of the ancient word "allegory," though, is not uniquely attributable to the ambivalences of this word, to which we have already referred.[13] It is derived from their difficulty in recognizing a real

11. *Remarques sur une lettre de M. Spon, de la religion prétendue réformée, médecin à Lyon* (Antwerp, 1681). The authenticity of this work is not certain, but it was, nevertheless, collected in the *Oeuvres* of Arnauld, vol. 12 (1777); see pp. 467–468. See Augustine, *Contra Faustum*, l. 13, c. 15 (*PL*, 42, 290–291).

12. L. 2, c. 11, n. 2. This text is quoted by W. Vischer, *La loi ou les cing livres de Moïse* (Fr. tr.), p. 27. In chapter 7, moreover, it is well said by Calvin that "the covenant made with the Fathers of old, in its substance and truth, is so similar to our own that it can even be said to be one with it," but Calvin immediately adds that it differs "in the order of being which is dispensed" (Pannier, vol. III, p. 8). Nevertheless, throughout this chapter, he wears himself out with laborious reasonings designed to establish that the ancient Jews had received, like us, the revelation of divine grace and of Christ's mediation.

13. See Jean Bosc, in *Dieu Vivant*, 4, p. 54. We think we can see signs of a more comprehensive attitude in this respect in the following reflections of Jean Héring, commenting on 1 Cor. 10, 6: "We cannot deny that these (allegorical and typological) methods are, in principle, authorized by the use made of them by the Apostle Paul. But, on the other hand, it is appropriate to take into consideration the warnings of the reformers who feared the allegorical fantasies of the Alexandrians as they would fear fire." *La Première Epître de saint Paul aux Corinthiens* (1949), p. 80.

progress in the order of knowledge from one Economy to the other.[14] The reaction against theories of religious evolutionism was pushed to the point of paradox by some who refused to see in any notion of progressive revelation anything but a "vestige of humanism, of that incorrigible humanism which, from Erasmus's day down to our own, has never stopped blowing on theology." [15] For such critics, "it is an error to pretend that the revelation brought by Jesus Christ is superior to the revelation brought by Abraham, Moses, the Prophets, and all the other instruments used by God in the Old Covenant." [16]

It was necessary to make special mention of this position, in order to avoid any misunderstanding. And at first glance, could anything be more gratifying than Wilhelm Vischer's formula: "The Old Testament tells us *what* Christ is, while the New Testament tells us *who* he is"? [17] The formula is reminiscent of many of the traditional formulas,[18] and we can even make it

[14.] With respect to this progress, see Origen, for example, *In Cantica*, 1. 1, p. 94.

[15.] André Lamorte, *La notion de révélation et l'Ancien Testament* (1935), p. 157. But neither the Fathers nor the great scholastics were contaminated by post-Erasmian humanism! See Alexander of Hales, *Summa theologica*, I, 3, p. 2, inquis. 4. qq. 3–10 (Quaracchi ed., vol. IV, pp. 840–879); p. 866: *"Considerando Legem ad litteram, addit Evangelium Legi, sed differenter quantum ad caerimonialia, quantum ad moralia, quantum ad judicialia";* see pp. 841–842. Augustine, *De concordia evangelistarum*, 1. 1, c. 1 (*PL*, 34, 1042); *De sermone Domini in Monte*, l. 1, c. 8 (*PL*, 34, 1239). See Jean Levie, *art cit.*, p. 1016: it would be a "grave error" to "place all the affirmations [of the Bible] on the same religious level simply because they are all the 'word of God'."

[16.] *Ibid.*, p. 197. The author does, however, recognize a "moral and spiritual education of the Jewish people, the purpose of which was to lead them from a quasi-absolute incomprehension to an ever more perfect comprehension of revealed truth" (p. 277).

[17.] *La loi ou les cinq livres de Moïse*, introduction (Fr. tr.), p. 9. See Luther, *Preaching on John* (1522), cited in Vischer: "The apostles drew everything they taught or wrote from the Old Testament. . . . There is not a word in the New Testament which does not refer back to the Old, in which it was announced in advance. . . . The New Testament is nothing but a revelation of the Old, exactly as if someone first had a sealed letter and then opened it. Thus, the Old Testament is a letter from Christ which he opened after his death."

[18.] Pseudo-Dionysius, *Celestial Hierarchy*, c. 3, n. 5, has a text which is quite similar: "When we study these texts through holy eyes, we see in them the unity and the uniqueness of an agreement whose motive

our own. In our explanation of it, we would, of course, introduce
a few nuances. Vischer really—as Emil Brunner points out—
"overshoots the mark." [19] For, until we knew who Christ was,
we could not possibly obtain an adequate knowledge of what he
had to be. All the lines in the painting gave no appearance of
converging and in no way revealed their true nature. Before
they found their basis in the Gospel, the phrases of the heralds
formed no sort of concert at all.[20] Had it been otherwise, everything would have been too easy. At the decisive moment, the
ambiguity required for the discernment of hearts would have
been lacking.[21]

The light brought by Christ's very presence did not shine on
his identity alone, but also, if it can be said, on his essence: a
transfiguring light, in which Moses and Elijah appeared as one
with Jesus. Those who were faithful to him were then able to
recognize Christ, but it was with the feeling that, as they awaited
him, they had not yet known him. *"Quidquid universis retro
saeculis mystice gestum aut dictum fuit, totum verius ac plenius
impletum est in hac plenitudine temporis."* [22] This accounts for
the vivid impression of newness, the early-morning joy which
were everywhere present in the early Christian communities,
whether they were made up of those who had never stopped

---

power is the very unity of thearchic Spirit. . . . The Old Testament
foresaw the divine works of Jesus, the New describes how they came
about; one presents the truth in images, while the other demonstrates
their actual reality . . . , and it is in the operation of God ($\theta\epsilon o\upsilon\rho\gamma\iota a$)
that the Word of God ($\theta\epsilon o\lambda o\gamma\iota a$) culminates and is fulfilled" (Maurice
de Gandillac, Fr. trans.), Paris, 1943.

19. *Offenbarung und Vernunft* (1941), pp. 82–83.

20. Paschasius Radbertus, *In Matthaeum,* l. 8, c. 18 (*PL,* 120, 623–624).

21. Irenaeus, *Adversus Haereses,* l. 4, c. 16, 1 (*PG,* 7, 1052–1053).
John Chrysostom, *Second Homily on the Obscurity of the Prophecies,*
nn. 1–2 (*PG,* 56, 176–178); *Summary of Holy Scripture,* Protheoria
(*PG,* 56, 317). This is even true for the prophecies properly so-called,
which have, as a whole, "an inferior and apparent meaning," and it is
only by reason of their realization in Jesus that we can interpret them
properly. See Abbé de Broglie, *Questions bibliques* (1897), pp. 348,
374–380. M. J. Lagrange, "Pascal et les prophéties messianiques," *loc. cit.,*
pp. 550, 559.

22. Guerric of Igny, *De nativitate Domini,* sermo 4, n. 3 (*PL,* 185, 42A).

79

meditating on the Law and the Prophets or of those who had come from the darkness of the Gentiles. *Surge, illuminare, Jerusalem, quia venit lumen tuum, et gloria Domini super te orta est* (Arise, shine, Jerusalem, for your light has come, and the glory of the Lord has risen upon you). The formula which we have quoted above becomes absolutely true, therefore, only after the event, only at the moment when the event is perceived, only when the Old Testament, thanks to this recognition of Christ, begins to be read in the spirit of the New. In fact, "It was for Christ, as St. Paul saw clearly, to take his place in the tradition prepared for him—and thereby shatter that tradition to fragments. All had to be reinterpreted in the light of *Him*." [23]

And this is why "each Old Testament notion reveals its potentialities only in the New, to the eyes of faith, and by virtue of the Design of the divine Wisdom." [24] Everything which touched the Jewish people was afterwards given by God to the Gentiles as so many parables, or, as St. Ambrose explained it, *"quasi figurae egentes solutione"* (like figures which are in need of an explanation).[25] To put it another way—and here we again come across the idea which constantly crops up in every portion of this study—the correlation between the Testaments simultaneously expresses both tendencies: *Novum Testamentum in Veteri est figuratum, et Vetus in Novo est revelatum* (The New Testament is figured in the Old, and the Old is revealed in the new).[26] Or, in the maxim which has long since become classic:

[23.] Jean Guitton, *La Vierge Marie;* ET *The Virgin Mary,* New York, 1952, p. 56.

[24.] Louis Bouyer, "Les Psaumes, prière du peuple de Dieu," in *La Vie spirituelle* (1949), p. 586. Jean Steinmann, "Entretien imaginaire de Pascal et du Père Richard Simon sur le sens de l'Ecriture," in *La Vie intellectuelle* (March 1949), p. 247: "If the Law of Moses, the writings of the Prophets and of the Wisdom writers, and the Psalms can be mirrors of the Gospel, the reason is that they were undoubtedly prepared to receive its light. But they do not radiate that light by themselves. They cast back on the Gospel a light which they receive from it" (R. Simon). See Hugh of St. Victor, *Didasc.,* l. 6, c. 6 (*PL,* 176, 805–806). Certain penetrating remarks of Bergson's could be transposed here. See *La pensée et le mouvant;* ET *The Creative Mind,* New York, 1946.

[25.] Ambrose, *In Ps. 43,* n. 56 (Petschenig ed., pp. 300–303).

[26.] Augustine, *Contra adversarium legis et prophetarum,* 1. 17, n. 35 (*PL,* 42, 623).

*Novum Testamentum in Vetere latet, Vetus in Novo patet* (The New Testament is hidden in the Old, the Old is made manifest in the New).[27]

If this distinction is rejected—but surely there is no one who rejects it completely—we do not see how it is possible to escape the following dilemma. Either one will want to find Christ and the realities of the Gospel throughout the Bible, and in the very understandings of the inspired writers themselves (a view which is very much out of line with history and with textual criticism); or else one will want to be consistent with history and with criticism, and thereby condemn himself to see nothing but a witness of the past in the Bible, a few oracles aside, so that it can no longer be true that the Bible speaks wholly of Christ. And this is merely the exegetical aspect of a doctrinal dilemma which is serious for other reasons as well. For, if the New Testament is nothing more than the literal fulfillment of the Old, then there is either an exaggeration of the revelation made to Israel, and we forget that it is only in Jesus that the very idea of the Messiah attains its fullness and perfection, or the evangelical doctrine and the very idea of the Messiah becomes the object of a restrictive interpretation. In both cases, there is a compromise of the newness of Christ. Of his newness, and of his fruitfulness.

In point of fact, there is a definite relationship between the reserve which certain authors show towards the old idea of the spiritual understanding of Scripture and the suspicion in which they hold the very idea of development in the spiritual life.[28] This dual rejection frequently appears to be connected with a more general bias against mysticism, which, in the name of pure

27. Also familiar is the Suger inscription on one of the windows of Saint-Denis: *"Quod Moyses velat, Christi doctrina revelat."* See Pseudo-Chrysostom, *Hom. on Luke:* "The Old Testament anticipated ($\pi\rho o\acute{\epsilon}\lambda\alpha\beta\epsilon$) the New, and the New explained ($\acute{\eta}\rho\mu\acute{\eta}\nu\epsilon\upsilon\sigma\epsilon$) the Old" (*PG*, 50, 796). This is what Bernard in his own fashion was expressing when he commented on the verse from the Song of Songs: *"Oleum effusum nomen tuum"* (*In Cantica*, sermo 14, n. 8 [*PL*, 183, 843A-B]). See also Thomas, *In Joannem*, c. 5, lect. 1, n. 10.

28. It is, however, already in the Gospel and in Paul: see Col. 1, 10; Phil. 1, 9; 1 Cor. 2.

biblical faith, greatly devalues the teachings of a St. Paul and a St. John, and strenuously resists the Catholic dogma of sanctifying grace and its practical corollaries. Because of an excessive fear of "pagan" infiltrations or "mystical misunderstanding," [29] the Mystery of love, so magnificently prefigured in the prophecy of Hosea and in the Song of Songs, is never completely accepted. The Law of love is then no longer the proclamation of a real union between man and God. Or, at the very least, such a union does not yet exist in the present Economy. God has not yet given himself over to us. We are still waiting for him. The Spirit has not yet been bestowed. The promise of all these things is merely a bit more definite.[30] Christians remain "in the category of John the Baptist." [31] Or else, and this is strange indeed, the solemn declarations of the Sermon on the Mount, "You have heard that it was said. . . . But I say to you . . .," no longer establish a definitive order, but simply a sort of parenthesis between the two comings.[32]

Here we have the profound significance of the traditional doctrine of the spiritual meaning as it is most disputed outside of Catholicism. It maintains the notion of development in the spiritual life at the very heart of the Church. It insures an

[29.] W. Vischer, *op. cit.* The fear is similar to that shown by Anders Nygren in connection with the Platonic eros, a fear which prevents him from recognizing the thirst for the living God which fills the Old Testament itself.

[30.] *Ibid.,* pp. 31–32, quoting Karl Barth. The author is also of the opinion that if there is such a thing as spiritual understanding, it can only be the work of the Holy Spirit, who is his own exegete; thus there can be no possibility of making it into a method, since the Holy Spirit is not at man's disposal in that way (p. 41). This is more or less what Origen said, and what Catholic tradition also acknowledges. Taking the word "method" in a somewhat strict fashion, there is absolutely no "pneumatological method," no method of spiritual interpretation. Only the spirit hears the spirit. But in these excerpts, we think we can discern the same tendency which leads to the rejection of sanctifying grace, and of the institutional Church, and of the sacramental order as they are understood in Catholicism, the rejection being based on an inferred pretension of placing God at the disposal of man, and constituting a rejection of any real human-divine synthesis. See Hans Urs von Balthasar, "Deux Notes sur Karl Barth," in *RSR*, vol. 35 (1948).

[31.] Yves Congar, O.P., in *Foi et vie* (1947), pp. 61–62.

[32.] See Roland de Pury, *Le Libérateur, Notes sur l'Exode*, pp. 18–21.

eschatological mysticism which is no more an eschatology without mysticism than a mysticism without eschatology. In its delicate balance and in its fullest import, it is especially expressive
of the relationship between the two Testaments. How mysterious
a relationship, how unique,[33] how completely an object of the
constant meditation of the Church! Yes, for anyone who reflects
in faith, "the New Testament proves itself . . . to be really the
quintessence of the Old." [34]

Yes, it is "the shadow of Christ which is everywhere at play
in the history of the (chosen) people." [35] Yes, too, "all of
Scripture bears witness to Christ," and it "bears witness to the
whole Christ." [36] Yes, from one Testament to the other, just as
the God who gave both Testaments is one, "the faith is one," [37]
whether it be considered in its principle or in its practice; Abraham is truly "the father of believers," our father; "your father
Abraham rejoiced that he was to see my day; he saw it and was
glad." [38] Yes, finally, from end to end of both Testaments, it is
one single Design which is being accomplished, always the
unique Design of God.[39]

But "the Covenant of the spirit" is still a "New Covenant,"

[33.] This had already been well established by the Abbé de Broglie, in
opposition to Kuenen, *op. cit.*, pp. 355, 360–361.

[34.] Karl Barth, "Biblical Questions, Insights and Vistas" in *The Word
of God and The Word of Man*, New York, 1957, p. 79. See *ibid.*, p. 62:
"What conception of God and of the world was it which made it possible for men to refuse to accept the Old and New Testaments upon the
same basis, but to understand one in the light of the other?"

[35.] See Karl Barth, *The Knowledge of God and the Service of God*,
London, 1938, p. 65.

[36.] Roland de Pury, *op. cit.*, p. 17, Cf. W. Vischer, *op. cit.*, p. 250:
"The Jesus preached by the apostles is truly the Christ of Israel."

[37.] Luther, quoted by W. Vischer, *op. cit.*, p. 94. See Augustine,
*Epist. 187*, n. 34 (*PL*, 33, 845). Bonaventure, *Breviloquium*, p. 5, c. 7
(Quaracchi ed., vol. 5, p. 261).

[38.] Jn. 8, 56. Rom. 4, 11–12. On the former text, see M. J. Lagrange,
*Evangile selon saint Jean*, pp. 253–255. The information possessed by
Maldonatus, reported by Lagrange, was incomplete. See Guerric of Igny,
*De adventu Domini*, sermo 2, n. 2: *"Vidit, sed apud inferos . . ."* (*PL*,
185, 15D).

[39.] See Suzanne de Dietrich, *Le Dessin de Dieu;* ET *God's Unfolding
Purpose*, Philadelphia, 1960. Dietrich, *Le renouveau biblique*, Neuchâtel,
1949, pp. 55–58.

new and definitive.[40] The *Verbum abbreviatum* which gathers into the unity of his Person all the *verba* which had been uttered until he came surpasses them all as he fulfills them all.[41] Through him, "the old has passed away, behold, the new has come." [42] Let not the continuity cause us to forget the break! Let it not mask over the threshold which cannot be breached! Let not the realization of what had been foretold prevent us from seeing him who, foretold, surpasses all foretelling: [43] the opening of the pierced heart. How happy are those who, through this opening, now can explore the Mystery of Christ in all its dimensions! How happy are those who can cast their gaze upon the "unfathomable riches of Christ," which the Ancients so longed to see and yet did not see! [44] Happy are those who are invited to see, as by a boomerang, Moses and Elijah completely illuminated by the unique Light of Christ! Three times happy are those who, following the counsel of the Apostle, strive today "to know the love of Christ which surpasses knowledge"! [45] The celebrated phrase of St. Irenaeus, which is so accurately mirrored in the thought of the Fathers of the Church and their successors, must not lose any of its power: *Omnem novitatem attulit, semetipsum afferens.*[46]

---

[40.] 2 Cor. 3, 6.

[41.] For this epithet applies to him in a double sense. See Guerric of Igny, *In Nativitate Christi,* sermo 5, n. 3 (*PL,* 185, 44C-D). See Augustine, *In Ps. 61,* n. 18 (*PL,* 36, 742).

[42.] 2 Cor. 5, 17.

[43.] See Is. 43, 19.

[44.] Lk. 10, 23–24. See Eph. 3, 5–6. Bernard, *In Cantica,* sermo 61, n. 4 (*PL,* 183, 1072D); see sermo 78, n. 8 (1162C).

[45.] Eph. 3, 19. See Dom Jacques Dupont, *Gnosis, la connaissance religieuse dans les Epîtres de saint Paul* (1949). This entire work can be considered as a commentary on this verse from Ephesians.

[46.] *Adversus Haereses,* 1. 4, 34, 1 (*PG,* 7, 1083). See Guerric of Igny, *De Nativitate Christi,* sermo 1, n. 1: *"Puer natus est nobis. . . . Non tam novus, quam ipsa novitas, in se manens et innovans omnia, a quo quaeque res prout recedit, inveteratur; prout reaccedit, renovatur"* (*PL,* 185, 29B).

# 2. THE DUAL TESTAMENTS

## 1. Evolution and Alteration

Christian tradition recognizes two meanings of Scripture. The most general terminology for them is the "literal meaning" and the "spiritual meaning." These two meanings are related to each other the way the Old and New Testaments are related. It would be more exact, indeed perfectly precise, to say that these meanings constitute, that they *are* the Old and the New Testaments.

In the Book of Revelation, St. John, following Ezekiel, speaks of a scroll written within and on the back.[1] The Vulgate translates the phrase as *intus et foris,* inside and outside, and it is a good translation, since we are dealing with a roll, such as the roll we sometimes see represented, in medieval painting or sculpture, as held in the eagle's claws, whereas the other three symbolic animals are holding codexes, analogous to our own books. Tradition customarily viewed this as the book of the Scriptures. On the outside it is written according to the letter; on the inside it is written according to the spirit.[2] In order to understand it, we must pass over from the one to the other. We must acquire the spiritual understanding of the Word of God

---

[1.] Rev. 5, 1; Ezek. 2, 9–10.
[2.] Origen, *In Joannem,* 1. 5, c. 6 (103). Jerome (*PL,* 25, 35A; see 24, 517C, 631C). *In Hier.,* l. 1, n. 5 (Reiter ed., 9). Gregory, *In Ezechielem,* l. 1, h. 9, n. 30 (*PL,* 76, 883B). Ambrose Autpert, *In Apoc.,* l. 3 (469). Haimo of Auxerre, *In Apoc.* (*PL,* 117, 1013B-D). Bernard, *In Cantica,* s. 14, n. 8 (*PL,* 183, 843B). Anselm of Laon (*PL,* 162, 1520A). Rupert of Deutz (*PL,* 167, 1468A). Alcuin (*PL,* 100, 669C, 1119A, 1120A). Richard of St. Victor, *In Apoc.* (*PL,* 196, 756B).

as contained in the Bible. This understanding, which goes beneath the letter, or rises beyond the letter, is recommended or dispensed, in an *"expositio spiritualis,"* [3] by all those who are teachers within the Church, for they have received from God the *"ministratio spiritus,"* [4] as St. Paul says. There is "a higher degree of understanding," [5] a "higher" or "more profound" [6] understanding, "more absolute" than the understanding of the letter,[7] and from it there results "a nobler meaning," [8] "a more exalted meaning." [9] It is "interior" and reveals the "internal causes," [10] which will never be "grasped in their fullness" as long as the meaning of the letter remains exterior, on the surface.[11] It is a "sublime" [12] and "sacred" [13] understanding, *"sacratior quaedam intelligentia,"* [14] which we receive in order to become perfect,[15] and to which we draw near by degrees or by stages [16] under the influence of a grace from above.[17] It yields us a "sublime" and "divine" meaning by raising us up to the

[3.] Gregory (*PL,* 76, 71C). Chromatius of Aquileia, *In Matt.,* tr. 4 (*PL,* 20, 337D, 338B). Gaudentius, trs. 8, 9 (Glueck ed., 64, 79, 86). Hilary, *Tr. myst.,* 2, 2 (P. Brisson ed., *SC,* 19, 144); *In Ps. 136,* n. 13; 143, n. 3 (Zingerle ed., 733, 815). Hesychius, *In Lev.* (*PG,* 93, 930B, 1157B, 1171B, 1154B).

[4.] 2 Cor. 3, 8.

[5.] Origen, *In Gen.,* h. 4, n. 4 (54); *In Num.,* h. 17, n. 2 (155).

[6.] Origen, *In Num.,* h. 22, n. 1 (205); *In Jer.,* h. 14 (*PL,* 25, 687A). Ambrose (*PL,* 17, 344B, 375B). Jerome (*PL,* 24, 250B; see (*PL,* 25, 1391C, 1484B). Bede (*PL,* 92, 109D). Bruno of Segni, *In Deut.* (*PL,* 164, 545D). Luke of M. Corn., *In Cant.* (*PL,* 203, 506B).

[7.] Hilary, *In Ps. 134,* n. 6 (Zingerle ed., 697).

[8.] Origen, *In Gen.,* h. 17, n. 8 (*PG,* 12, 260B). Hilary, *In Ps.,* 150 (Wilmart, *RB,* 43, 281).

[9.] Jerome, *Adversus Jovinianum,* l. 1, c. 12 (*PL,* 23, 241).

[10.] Origen, *In Jos.,* h. 23, n. 3 (442); h. 7, n. 7 (334). Gregory, *In Ezechielem* (*PL,* 76, 1058C); l. 1, h. 9, n. 30 (883B).

[11.] Raoul of Argences (*PL,* 155, 2035B-C). Rupert of Deutz (*PL,* 167, 796B). Gregory, *In Ezechielem,* l. 2, h. 9, n. 1 (*PL,* 76, 1042B).

[12.] Ambrose, *In Lucam,* h. 7, n. 134 (Tissot ed., *SC,* 52, 57). Hesychius, *In Lev.,* praef. (*PG,* 93, 790B, 789A, 791B).

[13.] Jerome, *In Is.* (*PL,* 24, 171A); *In Ez.* (*PL,* 25, 148A).

[14.] Origen, *In Ez.,* h. 4, n. 1 (360); h. 6, n. 1 (378). Jerome, *In Ps. 106* (*An. mar.,* III, 1, 79).

[15.] Haimo of Auxerre, *In Ap.,* 1. 2 (*PL,* 117, 1011B).

[16.] Hilary, *In Ps. 134,* n. 1 (695).

[17.] Claudius of Turin, *In Reg.,* l. 4 (*PL,* 50, 1177D).

regions in which the heavenly mystery is exposed to our view.[18] It is in it that we find the repose of interior light,[19] and it is in it alone that we admire all the beauty [20] and relish all the savor of revelation.[21] It creates spiritual joy in each one of us, and in the whole Church.[22]

Far from being an invention, the fruit of whim or of reverie, this understanding has a structure of its own, which we must conform to. The spirit is not separate from the letter but is contained and, at least initially, hidden within it.[23] The letter is both good and necessary, for it leads to the spirit: it is the instrument and the servant of the spirit.[24] If the high priest wore two tunics in ancient Israel, this had the effect of signifying to later generations the dual acceptation of the divine Law, according to the letter and according to the spirit.[25] Spiritual understanding comes along to remove the veil from the letter, or the veil which is the letter, and thereby free the spirit from it; [26] or it may also throw over the poverty of the letter a royal mantle which completely transfigures it.[27] Without it, as we often read in the ancient Fathers, we see Scripture and yet we see it not.[28] It discloses the spirit as the sun behind the cloud,[29] like the pea under the pod,[30] like the grain underneath the straw.[31] It illumines the whole of Scripture, for everything in Scripture must be under-

18. Jerome, *In Gal.* (*PL,* 26, 390); *Ep. 119,* n. 10 (*PL,* 26, 118). Gaudentius, tr. 9; n. 1 (75).

19. Gregory, *In Ez.,* l. 2, h. 3, n. 15 (*PL,* 76, 965C).

20. Jerome, *In Amos,* II, 1 (*PL,* 25, 1003D).

21. Gregory, *In Ez.,* l. 1, h. 3, n. 19 (*PL,* 76, 814C).

22. Gregory, *Moralia,* 1. 31, c. 20, n. 47 (*PL,* 76, 778B). Absalon, *Sermo 37* (*PL,* 211, 218A).

23. Claudius of Turin, *30 Quaest. sup. 1. Regum,* 1. 4 (*PL,* 104, 753A).

24. Hesychius, *In Lev.* (*PG,* 93, 1176B).

25. *Decret. Bonizonis,* l. 3, n. 54 (Mai, 7, 3, 27), following Origen, *In Lev.,* h. 6, n. 3 (364).

26. Bruno of Segni, *In Gen.,* on the blind Isaac (*PL,* 164, 205C).

27. See Rupert of Deutz (*PL,* 167, 1473D).

28. Berengarius, *In Ap.,* v. tertia (*PL,* 17, 808B-C).

29. Alan of Lille, *Sermo 4* (*PL,* 210, 207A).

30. Gregory, *In Ez.,* h. 10, n. 2 (*PL,* 76, 1058C). Alcuin, *In Jo.* (*PL,* 100, 821C). Bernard, *In Cantica, Sermo 47,* nn. 1–2 (*PL,* 183, 1008C-D); *Sermo 86,* n. 4 (1196D).

31. Ps.-Hugh, *Sermo 27* (*PL,* 177, 957A).

stood spiritually, once "the truth of history" has been acquired; [32] everything in it is "spiritual," everything in it is "understandable" [33]—on the sole condition that we do our best to hear it, with the help of a spiritual interpretation, a spiritual contemplation, a spiritual anagogy.[34] Everything told in Scripture actually occurred in visible reality, but the account which stems from that reality does not have its end in itself: it must all yet be accomplished and it is in fact accomplished daily in us, through the mystery of spiritual understanding.[35] Then alone—but this, to be sure, is a direction which is recommended rather than an end which is ever reached—will Scripture exist for us in all its fullness; then alone will we possess its "truth."

If we take all these traditional expressions and disregard the context which determines their importance, we discover nothing, up to this point, which cannot be found (we do not say in reality, but at least in the belief of their adherents) at the heart of the various "Book religions." In every Scripture which is held to be revealed, the tradition which is its witness fancies that there is some hidden meaning, and this becomes the point of departure for any number of odd constructions and subtleties of thought. Let us now see what it is which does away with all comparisons and gives a unique significance to the "spiritual understanding" found in the Christian tradition.

For the Christian, there are two successive "Testaments," but at no point whatever are they essentially two books [36]; they are

32. Jerome, *In Is.* (*PL*, 24, 20B). Arnobius the Younger, *In Luc.* (Morin, *RB*, 1903, 72).

33. Hesychius, *In Lev.* (*PG*, 93, *passim*).

34. Hesychius, *In Lev.* (*PG*, 93, 1034B, 1036C, 1044D, 1119B, 1122C, 1123C, 1128A, 1130B, 1134B). Hugh of Rouen, *Dial.* l. 5, c. 7 (*PL*, 192, 1200D).

35. Peter Damian, *Op. 32*, c. 2 (*PL*, 145, 541D). Ps.-Anselm (Hervé), h. 13 (*PL*, 158, 660B). Jerome, *Tr. in ps.* (*An. mar.*, III, 2, 21). Gregory, *Moralia*, l. 2, c. 36, n. 59 (*PL*, 75, 585A).

36. It is in Melito of Sardes (*ob.* 175) that we first find the Old Testament mentioned as a collection of books; as for the New Testament, we must wait until the appearance of the anti-Montanist writer who was writing in 192 or 193; in point of fact, the meaning of the expression is still discussed.

two "Economies," two "Dispensations," two "Covenants," which
have given birth to two peoples, to two regimes, each of them
established by God for the ordering of man's relations with him.
The goal of the one which is first in time is to prepare for the
second. But this is still not what gives them the names of "old"
and "new." The New Testament is not called new merely from
the fact that it comes second in time; it is not merely "modern" [37]; it is, in the absolute sense of the term, the "last": *novissimum, sempiternum, novum et aeternum*. It is definitive, eternal,
destined to remain just as it was given by Christ: *"aeternum dicitur, quia in aliud testamentum non mutabitur sicut mutatum
est vetus in novum"* [38]*;* always new, *"quia numquam veteras-
cit"* [39]*;* renewing all things: *"novum dicitur, quia de immutabili-
bus et semper novis loquitur"* [40]*; "semper novum, quod semper
innovat mentes, nec unquam vetus, quod in perpetuum non mar-
cessit."* [41] It is the "Strength of God," *"quae transire aut
veterascere non potest"* (which can neither pass away nor grow
old).[42] "The Old Testament knows many real Nows, but not a
Now which does not wait for an indisputable Now. The New
Testament knows only one Now, which is not in any sense or
in any way disputable. . . . There is no question of repeating
the (new) covenant." [43] Not only will it not be added to, or
completed, but the understanding of it will not change: *intellectus
illius numquam mutatur.*[44]

37. The epithet, although rare, is nevertheless encountered:
 *Domus haec, de qua vetusta sonuit historia*
 *Et moderna protestatur Christum fari pagina* (Gautier, I, 174).
38. Amalarius, *Ep. 4* (*PL*, 105, 1334C). Beatus, *In Ap.* (Florez, 278–
279). Hervé, *In Is.* (*PL*, 181, 506B-C); *In Gal.* (1134B). Sicardus of
Cremona, *Mitrale*, l. 3, c. 6 (*PL*, 212, 130B).
39. Augustine, *In Ps.* 99, n. 1 (*CCL*, 40, 2178).
40. Isidore, *Etym.*, l. 6, c. 1 (*PL*, 82, 229). Ps.-Hugh, *In Hebr.*, q. 80
(*PL*, 175, 627A-B). Richard, *L. exceptionum*, l. 3, c. 10 (J. Châtillon,
121). See Innocent III, *In nat. Dom.*, sermo 2 (*PL*, 217, 455D).
41. Bernard, *In vig. nat. Dom.*, sermo 6, n. 6 (*PL*, 183, 112A).
42. Rupert of Deutz, *In Ap.*, l. 9, c. 14 (*PL*, 169, 1097C-D).
43. Karl Barth, *Church Dogmatics, The Doctrine of the Word of God*,
I, II (Edinburgh, 1936), sec. 14, p. 104.
44. Gregory, *In Ez.*, 1. 1, h. 6, n. 17 (*PL*, 76, 836–837). Likewise
for the *novissime* of Heb. 1; Hervé (*PL*, 181, 1521C-D).

Thus, there is a kind of opposition between the two Testaments: *"aliter tunc . . . aliter nunc."* [45] The condition of the still "primitive" Jewish people was really quite different from that of the Christian people "in the Truth of the Gospel." But, even so, there is union. Their relationship is ambiguous. The second derives from the first, but without repudiating it.[46] The second does not destroy the first: while fulfilling it, it gives it life, it renews it. The second transfigures the first. It absorbs it into itself. In a word, it changes the letter of the first into spirit. It is one and the same thing to understand the Bible *spiritualiter* and to understand it *evangelico sensu.*[47] *Sine ullo Veteris Testamenti velamine Spiritus Sancti jam veritas fulget* (No longer veiled by the Old Testament, see how the truth of the Holy Spirit shines forth).[48]

At the same time, the first Testament, in all those aspects of its letter which are not in conformity with the New, is surpassed, grown old, annulled—*antiquatum,*[49] as soon as the change is effected. If we were to attempt thereafter to preserve literal interpretation as a steady norm, that interpretation would become 'the letter which kills." [50] From this point on, the Old Testament has no existence for the believer except in its relationship to the New. In other words, it must thereafter be understood uniquely *secundum spiritum,* not as negating the interpretation which had once been given it *secundum litteram* but as opposed to the interpretation which might be given it today *secundum litterae vetustatem.*[51] The ancient Jews, those at least who were faithful, did understand Scripture, to the extent that God then willed that they understand it; but those Jews who, by refusing to recognize Jesus Christ, refused to

[45] Rhabanus Maurus, *In Num.,* l. 1, c. 13 (*PL,* 108, 631A).

[46] See Origen, *Selecta in Threnos: "Ecclesiam, quae veteris Synagogae filia est"* (*PG,* 13, 661–662B).

[47] Origen, *In Num.,* h. 11, n. 4 (59).

[48] Isidore (*PL,* 83, 313A).

[49] See Chrysostom, In 2 Cor., h. 7, n. 3: κατήργηται ὁ νόμος (*PG,* 61, 43).

[50] Isidore, *Etym.,* l. 6, c. 1, nn. 1–2 (*PL,* 82, 229A).

[51] Bruno of Segni, *In Ps.* (*PL,* 164, 696B-C); *In Deut.,* c. 34 (550D).

recognize the New Covenant lost their understanding of Scripture itself.[52] *Jam vetera sunt, quae per renovantem spiritum non intelliguntur* (all those things which are not understood through the spirit which renews have now become forever old).[53]

Note well that this transformation of the Old into the New does not come about from some sort of intellectual development. And it is not something which is spread over a period of time: it happens in a flash. In no sense is it a gradual progression; even though prepared for, it is a sudden change [54] when it finally occurs, a total transference,[55] a change of key which gives a different meaning to everything. The Church is the daughter of the Synagogue, but in the newness of the Spirit. Thanks to a new illumination, a sudden change appears in everything which made up what is now called the Old Testament: people, events, institutions, laws, temple, priesthood, etc.:

> Deep confusion overcame me, caused by the sudden introduction of the New Testament in place of the Old, when, instead of the books of the prophets and the law, which I knew to be divine and written by the Holy Spirit, I suddenly became aware that the preaching of the Gospel was spread over the whole world.[56]

Properly speaking, this is an alteration or mutation: [57] *non in eis nomen, sed intelligentia* (in all of this it is not the name but the understanding which has changed). "Passage," "transference," "mutation" are words which constantly recur in the texts: *"mutatio legis atque sacerdotii,"* [58] *"mutatio veteris testa-*

---

52. Hervé, *In Is.*, 1. 7 (*PL*, 181, 514C); *In Gal.* IV (1174D, 1177C).

53. Gregory, *In I Reg.*, l. 1, n. 9 (*PL*, 79, 68C). See *Catholicism*, New York, 1950, c. 6; *Histoire et Esprit*, Paris, 1950, *passim; Corpus Mysticum,* Paris, 1949, c. II.

54. Jerome, *In Gal.* (*PL*, 26, 428C). Alcuin, *In Ps. 127* (*PL*, 100, 630C). Bruno of Segni (*PL*, 164, 1009B-C). Godfrey of Admont, *h. dom.*, 55 (*PL*, 184, 359D).

55. Rhabanus Maurus, *In Paral.*, 1. 1 (*PL*, 109, 335D). *Glossa, In II Paral.,* IV, 21 (*PL*, 113, 675A). See *Leo, Sermo 59*, c. 5; *Sermo 68,* c. 3 (*PL*, 54, 340B, 374D).

56. Bede, *In Cant.*, 1. 5 (*PL*, 91, 1186A). Rhabanus Maurus (*PL*, 109, 22D, 26D).

57. Origen, *In Gen.*, h. 13, n. 3 (118).

58. Isidore, *L. de variis q.*, c. 12, n. 4 (37).

*menti in novum."* [59] Passage through the fire of the Spirit. Mutation effected by the right hand of the Most High. A still more expressive word, and no less frequent, is "conversion": [60] the conversion of letter to spirit.[61]

We must not confuse this fact, therefore, with the process which can be observed throughout the history of Israel, and which can also be observed, though with differences which need not be analyzed here, in the history of other peoples as well—the process of spiritualization, of increasing depth of insight, which can be traced back to its beginnings in more primitive times. "Allegorical interpretation," Beryl Smalley has written, "marks a stage in the history of any civilized people whose sacred literature is 'primitive'." [62] Actually, it is by this means that the inevitable conflict between the letter of what is taken as the norm and the demands of the new intellectual and moral situation is resolved. Thus, new problems receive a fitting solution and progress can be welcomed without causing any rupture of the sacred bond, without altering the fervent attachment to venerable prescriptions or teachings. It is thus that "new Scriptures, curious mixtures of fidelity and fancy, come forth" from meditation on the ancient Scriptures; expressions which originated in an early author emerge in new colors from a later one.[63] Yet this is not to say that everything in such a process is invariably arbitrary; the historian often finds himself admiring "the

[59.] Peter Lombard, *In Ps. 39 (PL, 191, 399A).* Jerome, *In Ps. 39 (An. mar.,* III, 1, 45). Isidore *(PL, 83, 392D); Sent.,* l. 1, c. 20, n. 2 (586B). Paul the Deacon, *De temp.,* h. 77 *(PL, 95, 1231B).* Bede, *Q. in Reg.,* l. 1, c. 1 *(PL, 93, 431A).* Claudius of Turin, *In Reg.,* l. 1 *(PL, 50, 1066A, 1053C).* Rhabanus Maurus, *In Reg.,* l. 1, c. 4 *(PL, 109, 26D).*

[60.] Bede, *In Sam.,* l. 3, c. 2 *(PL, 91, 614D).* Rhabanus Maurus, *In Ez.,* c. 43 *(PL, 110, 999–1000).* Othloh, *Dial. de trib. q.,* c. 46 *(PL, 146, 126C).* Sicardus of Cremona, *Mitrale,* l. 2, c. 1 *(PL, 212, 57B).*

[61.] Origen, *In Matt.,* X, 14: τὴν ἀπὸ τοῦ γράμματος ἐπὶ τὸ πνεῦμα μεάνοιαν (18). Remigius of Auxerre, *In Ps. 140 (PL,* 131, 393B). Baldwin of Canterbury, *De sacr. alt. (PL,* 204, 763C).

[62.] Beryl Smalley, *The Study of the Bible in the Middle Ages,* Notre Dame, 1964, 2. See "L. G.", "Allegorical Interpretation" in *The Jewish Encyclopedia,* I (1901), 403.

[63.] A. Robert, "Le genre littéraire du Cantique des Cantiques," *R. bibl.,* 52 (1945), p. 201.

truly living role of tradition which again and again occasions the resurgence of the great works so that they can increase and bear fruit in time." [64] This is notably true in the case of Israel. It acquired great breadth, and it brought forth rich fruit. "It was a people moved by a religious impulse impelling it always one stage further, rethinking on a more spiritual level what in the first place it had lived and thought in a way less worthy of God. The Old Testament is the history of continual forward movements; a novitiate, a growing spiritualization." [65] As a matter of fact, the process was continued within Judaism, although under different conditions, after the beginning of the Christian era. But what we are referring to here is another fact, later and more decisive. Since these facts are often confounded, it is necessary to put some emphasis on them.

The oldest feasts in Israel were agricultural ones. They were preserved, but transformed into feasts which commemorated the great events reported in the Book of Exodus: the flight from Egypt, the giving of the Law, the march through the desert, the conquest of the Promised Land. This historical reinterpretation was only a first step, however. At the time of the Prophets, there is an idealization of the nation's past, and a deepening of the providential significance which then becomes the springboard for greater expectations. From this point on, history serves as the key to the understanding of the present, and it is increasingly transformed into an allegory of the future. The benefits bestowed by God upon his people are the guarantees of benefits still more precious. The old tales take on new symbolism. As Père Daniélou says, "typology is rooted in the Old Testament"; for example, "the early history of the Patristic interpretation of the Exodus

---

64. J. Steinmann, *Le prophète Isaïe,* Paris (2d ed.), 1955, p. 312.

65. Albert Gelin, *Les idées maîtresses de l'Ancien Testament;* ET *The Key Concepts of the Old Testament,* New York, 1963, p. 8. Gelin, "Jérusalem dans le dessein de Dieu," *La Vie spirituelle,* 86 (1951), p. 366: "Jerusalem . . ., a word which denoted a reality which was ever more burdened. But do not all biblical words bear a double and triple burden? . . . Ultimately, we always find ourselves facing the same biblical stages: history, messianization, eschatologicization and spiritualization."

offers us a period in the Old Testament itself in which we see the Prophets proclaim a new Exodus of which the first was the type, as they also proclaimed a second cataclysm of which the Flood was the type." [66] For the author of the Book of Daniel, the fall of Babylon will have been prefigured by the destruction of the Tower of Babel. For Ezekiel, the description of the first paradise will be projected into the vision of the final Jerusalem.

Still more impressively, the sacred authors from generation to generation use, under the impulse of the Spirit, materials which had been assembled by earlier generations and thereby announce a purer and more interior religion. "Hearkening back to the experiences and traditions of the ancestors in the Holy Land, they had to submit them to careful review and readjustment in the light of novel conditions. Out of this painful striving and searching of the soul emerged the more definitive formulation of biblical Judaism." [67] This is particularly true of Jeremiah, Deuteronomy, Deutero-Isaiah. The "new song" which they sing constitutes "a new elaboration and a flowering" of truths which had already come to light in earlier times but had not yet borne fruit. This is true of the Song of Songs and of Psalm 40, which are reworkings of various themes from Hosea, Ezekiel, and Deutero-Isaiah for the purpose of making more profound the idea of the union of Yahweh and Israel through exploiting the analogy of the union of man and woman. It is also true of Ezekiel, as Renée Bloch has shown in a penetrating study: "The prophet-writer succeeded in constructing an original work, with materials received from his predecessors, so as to deliver a new message which answered to the needs of his times"; he rethought "the whole history of Israel and the significance of its great events in terms of the present situation."

We are in the presence of a reflective mind which, at a time of upheaval and confusion, anxiously questions the documents of the

[66]. Jean Daniélou, *Sacramentum futuri;* ET *From Shadows to Reality,* London, 1960, pp. 153–154. See A. G. Hebert, *The Authority of the Old Testament,* London, 1947, p. 146.

[67]. See S. W. Baron, *A Social and Religious History of the Jews,* vol. I, New York, 1952, p. 13.

past so as to find in them the light, the answers, the explanations, the assurances, the hopes which the present requires, a present which was particularly dismal. To this end, the prophet puts various texts side by side, particularly texts of Hosea, Jeremiah, Deuteronomy, in order to illuminate them, explain them, complete them by one another, and he somehow makes them react on one another . . . so as to evoke from them light which was in some respects new. . . . He takes up the oracles of the past, but he puts them in a setting which gives them a new meaning, a new significance—not *different* from that of the past, but an improvement on it—which is adapted to the needs of the present situation and in conformity with his own mission.[68]

This is precisely the genre of *midrash,* whose importance in Israel develops from the time of the exile. The genre enters into canonical and non-canonical literature alike,[69] and knowledge of it is indispensable for sound exegesis of the New Testament.

We must not think that a development of this kind totally escaped the notice of the early Christian commentators. They had acquired an excellent grasp of one of the essential methods of the prophets: *"Propheticae scientiae est pro gerendis gesta memorare."* [70] They had also known how to recognize the allegorization of prior history, whose "mystery" had been partially revealed even before the coming of Christ. Thus St. Augustine, for example, explaining Psalm 113:

Hear what is more wonderful still: the hidden and veiled mysteries of the ancient books are in some degree revealed by the ancient books themselves. For the prophet Micah speaks thus: As in the days when you came out of the land of Egypt I will show them marvelous things, etc. (Mic. 7, 15-19). You see, brethren, that

68. Renée Bloch, "Ezechiel XVI, exemple parfait du procédé midrashique dans la Bible," in *Cahiers sioniens,* X (1955), 193–223; 213, 216–217. See Georges Auzou, *La Parole de Dieu;* ET *The Word of God,* St. Louis, 1960, p. 96.

69. There are a number of examples in the Book of Wisdom, whose author "outlines a religious philosophy of history behind which lies a fresh interpretation of the texts" (*The Jerusalem Bible,* New York, 1966, p. 1005).

70. Hilary, *In Ps. 62,* 4 (218).

the hidden mysteries are here more clearly revealed. In this psalm, therefore, even though the wonderful spirit of prophecy looks to the future, it still seems to be recounting the things of the future as if they were things of the past.[71]

We might say, then, that the Prophets had already "softened" the hearts of the men of their era, and thereby enabled them to catch a glimpse of what was prefigured by the ancient history of Israel. According to St. Augustine again, this took place:

. . . so that we would not believe solely on the authority of the Apostle that these ancient facts are figures for us; the prophets themselves were not silent on the subject, so that we would be able, having been instructed and delighted by their explanation, to draw confidently from the treasury of God both new and old things, perfectly in harmony with each other.

Deuteronomy had, of course, attracted their attention to this aspect. Origen, observing that Deuteronomy sets forth "a clearer legislation," saw in this the symbol of the "evangelical precepts," the "second law which brings all to perfection," "the law of the Gospel which is written within the heart of the believer who hears and retains the Word of Christ." As was his habit, he looked still more deeply and also saw signified in it the second coming of Christ, which is to be "more brilliant and more glorious" than the first coming in the humility of the flesh.[72] Others, disregarding the latter application, will yet retain what Deuteronomy announced with more striking truth: The promulgation of the Gospel as the real and definitive "second Law." "*Secunda legislatio dicitur, quod significat evangelium.*" [73] "*Deuteronomium evangelicae veritatis.*" [74] Had not St. Paul himself, by means of a subtle exegesis, suggested that one of the passages of Deuteronomy contained "a prophetic announcement of evan-

[71.] *In Ps. 113,* n. 4 (*CCL,* 40, 1637–1638).
[72.] *De princ.,* l. 4, c. 3, n. 13 (343–344). *In Jos.,* h. 9, n. 4 (349–350). See *Glossa in Ex.* (*PL,* 113, 295B).
[73.] Bede, *Q. sup Deut.,* c. 2 (*PL,* 93, 409C). Claudius of Turin, *In Reg.,* 1. 1 (*PL,* 100, 1053C). See Augustine, *In Hept.,* l. 6, q. 30, on Josh. 24, 27 (*PL,* 34, 791–792).
[74.] Jerome *Ep.,* 78, n. 43: "*meditatorium evangelii*" (4, 92).

gelical justice," a kind of "anticipation of the economy proclaimed by Christ"? [75]

We can say, then, that the Fathers themselves recognized that there were "between a biblical theme and the patristic typological exegesis . . . a certain number of stages, constituted by the varying interpretations of the theme which are to be found in successive biblical authors." [76] Note, however, that the author of the lines just quoted adds that an identical theme is thus taken up again "by the Prophets, the Psalms, the Jewish Apocalypse, the New Testament, and finally by the Fathers of the Church—always by men who were turned towards the future." This is something to which neither the Fathers nor their spiritual heirs could ever subscribe. In their eyes, the "moment" of the New Testament was not—nor can it ever be to any Christian—an individual moment in a series analogous to the "moments" of the Psalms, the Prophets, or the Jewish Apocalypse. In their eyes, it was—to borrow a few words from Karl Barth—the "critical instant" which became the "eternal instant." It was the one and only καίρος. The substructure of Deuteronomy was not fully comparable to it; neither for them nor for St. Paul did Deuteronomy constitute a second Testament. [77] They knew perfectly well that if St. Paul had been able to "prolong" the meaning of the inspired writer without being false to it, the prolongation presupposed the unique intervention of the Christ-Fact. And the Fathers who, like Origen, may have exaggerated, in their opposition to the heretical Gnostics, the role of the revelations of the Logos prior to the incarnation, and simultaneously sensed more vividly the congenital imperfection of our knowledge up until the accession of the new Law, nonetheless proclaimed that the coming of the Logos in the flesh alone constitutes "the Coming of Truth." [78]

75. Stanislas Lyonnet, S.J., "Saint Paul et l'exégèse juive de son temps," in *Mélanges Robert* (1957), pp. 498–499.

76. Daniel Lys, "A la recherche d'une méthode pour l'exégèse de l'Ancien Testament," in *Etudes théol. et rel.*, 3 (1955), p. 5, n. 6.

77. Augustine, *In Hept.*, l. 5, q. 49 (*PL*, 34, 770).

78. Origen, *In Jo.*, 1. 28, XII: τῇ φανερώσει τῆς ἀληθείας (404); see I, VI (II); fr. *in Jo.* 9 (491).

*A fortiori,* they had no thought of seeing this coming as constituting a new "moment." Such a notion could only have been rejected by them as blasphemous. They did not presume to interpret the ancient texts differently from the way they had been interpreted in the past, nor did they project into the past the interpretation which had newly been received from the witnesses of Jesus. They were totally lost in wonder at the Newness, unique, unsurpassable, outside of any sequence whatever, transfiguring everything, which the "New Testament" constituted in their eyes; and if they were still turned towards the future, since every Christian naturally awaits the glorious return of Christ, they did not do so in the style of Israel's ancient seers, for they knew that the Christ had come—they certainly were not looking for another Christ, of whom the Christ of the Gospels would have been only another kind of prefiguration. Thus there is an essential difference "between the way in which the Temple of God grows during its preparatory phase and the way in which it must attain to the fullness of Christ in its ultimate phase. . . . In the new Covenant there was given once-for-all in Christ the fullness which one had been content in the old simply to await." [79] From now on, the entire expectation of believers could be "nothing other than the Now of Jesus Christ." [80] After having been prepared "from the beginning of time" by a full series of stages, salvation had at last come; the passage from shadows to reality had taken place:

> *Umbram fugat Veritas!*
> *Noctem Lux illuminat!* [81]

In a single stroke, the Lord Jesus had appeared, emerging from the dense forest of allegories, whose darkness had not been

[79]. Louis Bouyer, *La vie de la liturgie,* Paris, 1956, 183–184.
[80]. See Karl Barth, *Church Dogmatics, The Doctrine of the Word of God,* Edinburgh, 1936, I, I.
[81]. Adam of St. Victor, *Easter* (Gautier, 26). *Ibid.:*

> *Figuram res exterminat*
> *Et umbram lux illuminat* (32).

Peter Damian, *De petitionibus lucidarii* (*PL,* 145, 1177C-D); see *Op. 3* (58C). Ps.-Hugh (*PL,* 175, 914B).

in the least affected until then.[82] This was what none of the stages which had marked out the development of the religion of Israel had been able to accomplish. Without the Lord who was to show himself at last, all of those stages would have been pointless, *"inaniter currerent, nisi Christus in eis praedicaretur";* [83] contrasted with their term, every one of the stages merited to have said of it: *"Omne tempus ante Salvatoris adventum, quasi vacuum et inane permansit"* (All the ages which preceded the coming of the Saviour were as if empty and pointless).[84] This was the illumination which had been procured by none of the successive "re-readings" of the Sacred Books. There was no comparison to be made between any of those "re-readings" and the "re-reading" effectuated from then on in the Word and in his Spirit. We see, then, that the "evangelical innovation" was not just another degree higher in an ascent which was still to be pursued.[85] It is not to be questioned that it effected no change in the visible conditions of our present existence in the flesh. In that respect, it still had to be said that we walk as always among "shadows and figures," but from that point on we could at least walk "in the shadow of Christ." [86] The Lord Jesus was the unique and incomparable summit: *"mons montium, non unus de montibus."* [87] In him all of Scripture had, once for all, received its fulfillment. Moses and Aaron had at one time lived, but Christians, following the true Joshua, had entered into the land of evangelical promise.[88] They no longer sought to "actualize" ancient Scripture; they realized that it had been actualized in Jesus, once for all. Thus they were able to devote their atten-

---

[82.] Aelred of Riexaulx, *De oner.,* sermo 28 (*PL,* 195, 478A); Isidore, *L. de variis q.,* c. 29, n. 10 (86).

[83.] Werner, *Deflorationes SS. Patrum,* 1. 1 (*PL,* 157, 821D).

[84.] Helinandus, sermo 7 (*PL,* 212, 535D).

[85.] Rupert of Deutz, *In Ez.,* 1. 1, c. 6 (*PL,* 167, 1427C). Ps.-Bede, *In Gen.* (*PL,* 91, 225D).

[86.] Origen, fr. *in Cant.* (Procope; 181–182); *In Jos.,* h. 22, n. 5 (437); see *In Cant.,* 1. 3 (183). *Histoire et Esprit,* ch. 6.

[87.] Etherius and Beatus, *Ad Elip.,* 1. 2, c. 50 (*PL,* 96, 1006C).

[88.] *Libri Carolini,* I, c. 19 (*PL,* 98, 1048D; following Augustine). Peter Damian, *Op. 32, De quadrag.,* c. 9 (*PL,* 145, 559B-C). Leo, *Sermo 60,* c. 1 (*PL,* 54, 342–343).

tion to particularizing, in the joyful daring of their faith, the magnificent allegory which Scripture spread before them. They were fully aware that, through this endless activity, they neither prolonged nor completed in any way the total allegorization which had been definitely made of Scripture by Christ.

## 2. The Act of Christ

It is sometimes said that before we can properly understand biblical revelation we must first have some sense of history, some sense of evolution, of the continuity of God's work in time, an uninterrupted continuity of homogeneous historical development.[1] Nothing could be more accurate, as long as this very continuity and this evolution are not taken as "the character of being continually created . . . of sacred history, . . . the history in which it is God who acts";[2] as long as one knows how to see in them "a series of successive transpositions,"[3] transpositions "which are true metamorphoses."[4]

And yet nothing could be more incomplete. The history of revelation also offers the spectacle of unequalled discontinuity, and it is this which renders irreplaceable the traditional idea of allegory taken in its deepest essence. Allegory was far more than "the expression of a forward-looking prophetism," as has sometimes been said since the time of Edward Caird, and the "theory of evolution" could not possibly have sufficed to pass it on. The Ancients were fully aware of the fact that the history of Israel showed a progressive forward movement; the most "allegorical"

[1] J. Coppens, *NRT,* 71 (1949), 31.

[2] Louis Bouyer, *La Bible et l'Evangile;* ET *The Meaning of Sacred Scripture,* Notre Dame, 1958, p. 231; see pp. 228–229. In point of fact, the reality even of secular history does not consist solely in the denseness of a concrete and progressive time.

[3] Dom Charlier, *La lecture chrétienne de la Bible;* ET *The Christian Approach to the Bible,* Westminster, 1958, p. 185ff.

[4] Louis Bouyer, "Liturgie et exégèse spirituelle," in *La Maison-Dieu,* 7 (1946). *Le trône de la Sagesse;* ET *The Seat of Wisdom,* New York, 1960, p. 31.

of them were as well aware of this as the rest.[5] But when they spoke of allegory, they intended to refer to something else again.

It is perfectly true that in one sense the continuity always remains, and we can even call it "flawless": there is nothing which has not been prepared in advance. Jesus Christ did not appear *raptim*, without previous preparation, on a hostile or alien scene.[6] The Old Testament was a kind of sketch or model, a *prima adumbratio* [7]—a model of clay for vessels of gold. The New Testament is the fruit of the supernatural tree whose root, trunk, and leaves are the Old Testament, and "it is through the Law that we come to the Gospel." [8] The light which the Gospel causes to burst forth had already begun to shine in the Law: *"Quod lucet in veteri Testamento, hoc fulget in Novo."* [9] Yet in another sense there is a radical breach.[10] The New Covenant

[5.] What the moderns look for in the theory of evolution, so as to express history, the ancients would have looked for in the allegorical method, which would then have expressed "a prophetism of progress." More than one confusion is latent here. See Origen, *In Gen.: "Parvus erat Isaac in lege, sed processu temporis fit magnus in prophetia, . . ."*; repeated in Claudius of Turin, *In Gen.*, 1. 2 (*PL*, 50, 484C). Filastrius, *Haer.*, 138 (*CCL*, IX, 305–306).

[6.] Maximus of Turin, hom. 55 (*PL*, 57, 355B). Hildegarde, also, *Scivias*, l. 3, c. 11 (*PL*, 197, 716B). See *Catholicism*, chs. 5, 6, 8.

[7.] Augustine, *S. Mai* 158, n. 1 (Morin, 1930, 381). Bede, In Luc. (*PL*, 92, 584C-D).

[8.] Isidore, *De eccl. off.*, l. 1, c. 11, nn. 1–2 (*PL*, 83, 745–746).

[9.] Haimo of Auxerre, *In Ap.*, 1. 2 (*PL*, 117, 1008D).

[10.] This dual character is well noted in J. de Fraine, *Sciences ecclésiastiques*, 5 (1953), pp. 17–18: "There are numerous indications in the New Testament which bring out the continuity of the divine plan. . . . On the other hand, the inspired authors of the same New Testament insist on the discontinuity, the breach, on the insertion of a new and transcendent principle. No matter how well prepared for it might be made out to be, the coming of Jesus is still something completely new." The two points of view must be synthesized "in the sense of discovering a superior unity," rather than of "doing away with one of the terms." What follows immediately thereafter, however, is somewhat less impressive: "It is certainly a strange way of reconciling the two points of view . . ., when we put forward the absolute inadequacy of the Old Testament for the disciples of Christ, or even when we assert the impossibility of understanding it adequately without taking Christ into account."

is not like the Old Covenant.[11] The People of God are no longer to be an ethnic group. The divine Presence is no longer to be localized in a single place, the material tabernacle: henceforth, God will be in Jesus Christ, everywhere. When we attempt to explain a contrast like this, it is not enough to say that "the soul of Israel has matured." [12] The transposition which then took place constitutes "a new state and a transcendent consummation as complete as were the assumption into and the accomplishment by Christianity of the Old Testament prophecies." [13] There is no proportion between the "perpetual creation" which could previously be observed and the "new creation" which fulfills it.

Let us admit, however, that we are dealing with something unique, as far removed from likelihood as from analogy. Human history does not offer two "fullnesses of time." Nor does the history of revelation offer a long series of "staggered" testaments: after the Old Testament, there can be nothing but the New. Though there might have been a number of passages, there is only one—and it is the "last" in both senses of the word—which forever deserves the name of "Pascha." [14] It is only at that point that "Moses is dead," [15] so that another life, a higher life, might follow upon his. Until then, we had "shadow"; now we have "Truth." [16] Formerly, we had "the Law and the Prophets"; henceforth, "the Kingdom of God." [17] Thus, however astonishing, even disconcerting, be the findings which the historian must make, and which can lead him to an affirmation which is no longer dependent on history alone, we are still

[11.] Jer. 31, 31: "Behold, the days are coming, says the Lord, when I will make a new covenant with the house of Israel and the house of Judah, not like the covenant which I made with their fathers." See "La lumière du Christ," in *Affrontements mystiques,* Paris, 1950.

[12.] Although there certainly was some maturation; St. Irenaeus, *Adv. Haer.,* l. 4, c. 9, n. 3: *"per testamenta maturescere perfectum salutis"* (*PG,* 7, 998B).

[13.] Congar, *Le mystère du Temple;* ET *The Mystery of the Temple,* Westminster, 1962, p. 215.

[14.] See Augustine, *In Jo.,* tr. 55, n. 1 (*CCL,* 35, 463–4).

[15.] Origen, *In Jos.,* h. 1, n. 3: "Moses is dead, for the Law has ceased to be . . ." (290); h. 2, nn. 1–2 (296–298).

[16.] Jerome, *Ep.* 22, c. 23: *"Praecedit umbra, nunc veritas est"* (1, 134).

[17.] See Lk. 16, 16; Rom. 8, 3; Gal. 4, 4; Heb. 1, 1–2.

dealing with something which, in its uniqueness, will elude one who is a stranger to the viewpoint of faith. The change from the Old Testament to the New, or from the letter of Scripture to its spirit, can only be explained and accounted for, radically, by the omnipotent and unprecedented intervention of the One who is both *Alpha* and *Omega, Primus* and *Novissimus.*[18] It could only have occurred *operante Christo.*[19] "Ancient Word," [20] "born before the ages," and "come at the end of time," [21] Jesus Christ can, at the moment of the Incarnation, say: *"Ipse qui loquebar, adsum"* (I who then spoke to you, here I am now).[22] He can also truthfully say: "Before Abraham was,—before Abraham was—, I am." [23] *"Semen Abrahae, creator Abrahae"* (Seed of Abraham, creator of Abraham); *"Dominus prophetarum, impletor prophetarum"* (Lord of the Prophets, fulfilling the [oracles of the] Prophets).[24] He is the "Prototype" of all those who, having arrived on the biblical scene before him, can only be "types" [25] in relationship to him. He is the one who is both *"de quo et per quem omnis prophetia est."* [26]

Thus he is Master both of the first Testament and of the second. He made them for one another. He separates them, and he also unites them in himself. If, then, a passage can be effected from one to the other, it is because it is a passage to Christ: *transitus ad Christum;* [27] and at the same time a passage accom-

---

[18.] Rev. 1, 17. See 1 Cor. 15, 45. Bruno of Segni, *In Ap.,* 1. 1, c. 1 (*PL,* 163, 610C-D). Hildegarde, *Scivias,* III, c. 7 (*PL,* 197, 664B).

[19.] Ps.-Augustine, *Sermo 90,* n. 4 (*PL,* 39, 1919).

[20.] Rupert of Deutz, *In Ap.,* 1. 2 (*PL,* 169, 865A).

[21.] Haimo of Auxerre, *In Ap.,* 1. 1, (*PL,* 117, 960C); Mk. 1, 15.

[22.] Origen, *Selecta in Threnos,* IV, 20 (*PG,* 13, 657–658D).

[23.] Jn. 8, 53–58. Augustine, *In Ps. 139,* n. 3 (*CCL,* 40, 2013); *In Ps. 142,* n. 2 (2060).

[24.] Augustine, *In Jo.,* tr. 43, n. 16 (*CCL,* 36, 379).

[25.] And which can still be called, once this paradoxical relationship is accepted, both *"exemplar"* and *"exemplum":* Ps.-Hugh, *In Hebr.,* q. 76 (*PL,* 175, 626C). The Tabernacle which the Father has made ready from the very beginning: Origen, *In Matt.,* ser. 138 (285).

[26.] Hilary, *In Ps. 54,* n. 2 (147).

[27.] Augustine, *In Ps. 7,* n. 1 (*CCL,* 38). See Jerome, *Ep.* 121, c. 10 (*PL,* 22, 1031). Claudius of Turin, *In Reg.,* 1. 1 (*PL,* 50, 1066A). Hervé, *In Col.,* II (*PL,* 181, 1335D). See 2 Cor. 3, 16.

plished in Christ: *transitus in Christo.*[28] If all the "clouds" are dispelled at once, this can only be due to the unparalleled brilliance which is the brilliance of Christ: *"prae fulgore in conspectu ejus nubes transierunt."* [29] If truth follows upon shadow through a sudden illumination, this is because it is the Truth which shines in Christ: *"in solo Jesu Veritas Dei apparuit."* [30] If there is "mutation," it is something produced through Christ: *mutatio per Christum.*[31] "He did not render useless the former signs of things by arguing about them; he changed them by fulfilling them." [32] If there is "conversion," this can only be the doing of Christ: "By his coming in the flesh, the Lord turned all the shadows (the ceremonies of the Mosaic law) towards the light of spiritual life." [33] If there is transference, *translatio,* the reason is that Jesus Christ, penetrating into the Holy of Holies, sends us his Spirit.[34] If there is total renewal, the reason is that the Newness of Christ intervenes. In this regard, we may recall the well-known expression of St. Irenaeus: *"omnem novitatem attulit, semetipsum afferens";* [35] St. Ambrose says the same thing, and his formula is every bit as strong: *"Venit Dominus Jesus . . ., et illud quod erat vetus factum est novum"* (The Lord Jesus came . . ., and that which was old was made new).[36] If the effect of such a "shedding" is not only total but also definitive, if the "Christian meaning of the Bible" is "henceforth

28. Abelard, *Sermo 13* (*PL*, 178, 485C).

29. Bernard, *In dom. I post Epiph., sermo* 2, n. 1 (*PL*, 183, 158C). Richard (?), *In Nahum* (*PL*, 196, 745C).

30. Jerome, *In Eph.* (*PL*, 26, 507A).

31. Claudius of Turin (*PL*, 50, 1053C). See Origen, *In Gen.,* h. 13, n. 3 (118). Cassiodorus, *In Ps. 72* (*PL*, 70, 515D). Ps.-Bede, *In Jo.* (*PL*, 92, 694B).

32. Florus, *Exp. missae,* c. 4, n. 11 (Duc, 90).

33. Othloh, *Dial. de trib. quaest.,* c. 46 (*PL*, 146, 126C). Honorius (*PL*, 172, 842). Godfrey of Admont (*PL*, 174, 272D). Peter Lombard, *In Ps. 118* (*PL*, 191, 1067C).

34. Leo, *Sermo 68,* n. 3 (*PL*, 54, 374C).

35. *Adv. Haer.,* l. 4, c. 34, n. 1 (*PG*, 7, 1083C).

36. *De int. Job et David,* l. 1, c. 4, n. 12 (*PL*, 14, 802A). See *Glossa in Reg.,* l. 4, 13–14 (following Rhabanus Maurus) (*PL*, 113, 619D). Richard, *L. except.,* P. II, l. 8, c. 10 (Châtillon, 349).

and forever affirmed," [37] the simple reason is that God has, through successive stages, "led his people to the feet of Someone." [38] Christ was the sole end of all biblical history and of all biblical reality.

> Lex est umbra futurorum,
> Christus, finis promissorum,
> Qui consummat omnia![39]
> Lex antiqua novam firmat, veterem nova complet;
> In veteri spes est, in novitate fides;
> Sed vetus atque novum conjungit gratia Christi.[40]

In short, the spirit of the letter is Christ: *Spiritus ipsius litterae, Christus.*[41] The Gift of which Prophecy and the whole Law spoke prophetically is Christ.[42] The New Testament is Christ: *Novum Testamentum, qui est Christus.*[43] The Gospel is Christ: *Evangelium, Christus est.*[44] The Breath of our nostrils is Christ the Lord: *Spiritus ante faciem nostram, Christus Dominus.*[45]

Thus Jesus Christ effects the unity of Scripture because he is its end and its fullness. Everything in Scripture is related to him. And he is its unique Object. We could even say that he is the totality of its exegesis. According to St. Augustine, this is what is meant by the notation, *"in finem,"* which we frequently find in the titles of the Psalms: *"Cum audis psalmum dicere: in finem, corda convertantur ad Christum"* (thus, when you hear the Psalm say, *to the end,* let hearts be turned to Christ).[46] Scripture leads us to him, and once we have arrived at this goal,

[37] Georges Auzou, *The Word of God.*
[38] Charles Hauret, "Comment lire la Bible?" in *La Table Ronde,* November 1956, 141.
[39] Adam of St. Victor, Sequence, "Zyma vetus expurgetur," v. 19–21 (Gautier, 47). Hervé, *In Rom.: Christum, consummationem legis"* (*PL,* 181, 740D).
[40] Paulinus of Nola, *Ep. 32, ad Severum,* n. 5 (*PL,* 61, 333A).
[41] John Scotus, *In Jo.,* fr. 2 (*PL,* 122, 331B).
[42] Origen, *Selecta in Threnos* (*PG,* 13, 659–660C).
[43] Bede, *Q. in Reg.,* l. 1, c. 1 (*PL,* 93, 431A).
[44] Amalarius, *De eccl. off.,* l. 2, c. 20 (*PL,* 105, 1096B).
[45] Lam. 4, 20. Bernard, *In Cantica,* sermo 75, n. 2 (*PL,* 183, 1145B).
[46] Augustine, *In Ps. 139,* n. 3 (*CCL,* 40, 2013).

we have nothing further to seek: *"ad quem dum pervenimus, nihil ultra perquiremus."* [47] The cornerstone, he joins two Testaments together, just as he joins two peoples together.[48] He is the Head of the body of Scripture, just as he is the Head of the body of his Church. He is the Head of all sacred understanding, just as he is the Head of all the elect.[49] He is the complete contents of Scripture, just as he contains it all in himself:

The entire body of divine Scripture, the Old as well as the New, contains the Son of God. . . . In him is contained all Law, both the old and the New.[50]

The whole of divine Scripture is a single book, and this unique book is Christ, for the divine Scripture speaks of Christ, and the whole divine Scripture is fulfilled in Christ. [51]

The Word of God, the only Son of God, our Lord, Jesus Christ . . ., appears as a magnificent firmament of Truth in the eyes of anyone who is capable of interpreting Scripture so as to perceive its mystery, namely, the Lord himself who instituted it.[52]

But this unity in Christ has another aspect as well, by which the unity is still more forcefully revealed. Just as he is the exegesis of Scripture, Jesus Christ is also its exegete. He is really its Logos, both in the active sense and in the passive sense.[53] *"Christus, qui solus intelligentiam Scripturarum aperit."* [54] It is he and he alone who explains it to us, and in explaining it to us

---

[47.] Cassiodorus, *Expositio in psalterium*, praef., c. 3 *(PL, 70, 14–15)*. Manegold, *In Ps. 63 (PL, 93, 810B)*; but Manegold's opinion is that this reference in the title of the Psalms means that they have no meaning other than in relation to Christ. See Cyril of Alexandria *(PG, 68, 700C-D)*.

[48.] Ps.-Chrysostom, *H. in Luc.*, 11, 1 *(PG, 50, 798)*.

[49.] Hervé, *In Rom.*, 11 *(PL, 181, 1336D)*. Jerome, *Ep.* 121, c. 10 *(PL, 22, 1031)*.

[50.] Gaudentius, *Tr.* 2, *in Ex.* (26).

[51.] Hugh, *De arca Noe mor.*, l. 2, c. 8 *(PL, 176, 642C)*.

[52.] Godfrey of Admont, *H. dom.* 60 *(PL, 174, 401B-C)*.

[53.] See Martin Heidegger: "logos is both λεγειν, to utter, and λεγόμενον, that which is uttered." *Essais et conférences*, A. Préau trans. (1958). p. 251.

[54.] Hervé, *In Is.*, 1. 8 *(PL, 181, 557D)*.

106

he is himself explained: *"Liber ipse aperit seipsum."* [55] And who, after all, could be a better interpreter of him than he himself? [56] He and he alone shows us that the whole of Scripture, from one end to the other, has no meaning other than the Gospel, that is, himself: *non aliud quam Evangelium, id est, seipsum.*[57] During his earthly life, he had said to the Jews who were questioning him: "You search the Scriptures . . . and it is they that bear witness to me." [58] Yet that could only be an anticipation. But one evening on the road to Emmaus, we see him giving such instruction more openly to the two men who walk at his side: "And beginning with Moses and all the prophets, he interpreted to them in all the Scriptures the things concerning himself." [59] And this time, on the contrary, there is a second time, which assumes the fulfillment of the mystery. *"Magis ac magis aperire Salvator sacramentum suae incipit passionis, quod cum Evangelio concordare non dubium est"* (The Saviour begins to set more and more before them the mystery of his passion, and there can be no doubt that it agrees with the Gospel).[60] In this way he makes understandable an explanation whose substance has already been established; he invites us to see something which has just been cleared up forever.

The point is that the exegesis of Christ, in all its essential and decisive aspects, is not principally a matter of words: it is something in act. It is Act itself. *"Omnis enim dubietas tollitur*

55. See Bernard, *In die s. Paschae, s. de 7 signaculis,* 12 (*PL,* 183, 280C).

56. Jerome, *In Jonam,* prol. (Paul Antin ed., *SC,* 43, 1956, 55).

57. Paschasius Radbertus, *In Matt.,* praef. (*PL,* 120, 39B-C).

58. Jn. 5, 39. Godfrey of Admont, *H. dom.* 60 (*PL,* 174, 401B).

59. Lk. 25, 25ff. Julian of Toledo, *De comprobatione aet. sextae* (*PL,* 96, 562–563). Hervé, *In Is.* (*PL,* 181, 515C). *In Nahum* (*PL,* 96, 745C-D). Humbert, *Adv. Graec. cal.,* c. 38 (*PL,* 143, 954D). See J. Dupont, "Les pèlerins d'Emmaüs," in *Misc. biblica B. Ubach,* Montserrat, 1953, on vv. 27 and 44: "This fashion of defining the paschal message in its object and in its method corresponds exactly to the types of paschal preaching which Luke has preserved for us in the Acts. . . . The apologetic use of Scripture goes back to the origins of even the apostolic preaching. . . . It is perfectly appropriate to assume that the apostles were simply repeating the teachings of Jesus."

60. St. Ambrose, *In Ps. 40,* v. 15 (239).

*et veritas declaratur, ubi non verbis sed rebus ipsis Veritas probatur"* (For all doubt is dispelled and all truth declared, where Truth is established not by words but by realities).[61] Before he explained to his disciples on Easter evening how the ancient Scripture bore witness to the New Testament and so was changed into it, Jesus had effected this change. In other words, prophecies and figures were explained by their fulfillment, —and they could not have been explained otherwise. The mysteries of Scripture are *opere revelata.*[62] According to St. Jerome's translation of Origen, this is the double signification of the Greek word used by St. Luke at the beginning of his Gospel, a word which can only be translated by connecting the two words "fulfilled" and "manifested." [63] "The night," sang the Psalmist, "is bright as the day": this is what happens at the Saviour's coming.[64] Then "the east Portal, whence comes the true Light" [65] is opened. Then "the Old Testament was opened, and the spiritual understanding concealed therein was revealed to the faithful." [66] *Christus, inluminator antiquitatum.*[67]

Jesus, thus, is Exegete of Scripture in himself, in all his mystery. In principle, he is this Exegete from the first instant of his incarnation. This is what Origen was explaining in the fourth book of the *Peri Archon,* a book which is too often taken simply as a treatise on hermeneutics in the narrow sense of the word, as if it were the *books* of the Bible which were at issue rather than the very *realities* of the dual Testament:

The splendor of Christ's advent has, therefore, by illuminating the law of Moses with the brightness of the truth, withdrawn the veil

61. Peter of Corn., *Disp. adv. Sim. jud.* (R. W. Hunt, in *Studies in Medieval History,* 1948, 154).

62. Ambrose Autpert, *In Ap.* 1. 7 (573C).

63. *In Luc.,* h. 1, Jerome trans.

64. Cassiodorus, *In Ps. 138,* n. 12 (*CCL.,* 98, 1247).

65. Jerome, *Ep. 121,* preface (*PL,* 22, 1007).

66. Berengarius, *In Ap.* v. 4 (*PL,* 17, 874C). St. Justin, *Apology,* c. 32, n. 2: Jesus is "the interpreter of prophecies which had not been understood" (Pautigny ed., 63).

67. Tertullian, *Adv. Marc.,* l. 4, c. 40 (Kroymann ed., 560). Origen, *In Ex.,* h. 12, n. 4 (266).

108

which had covered the letter and has disclosed, for everyone who believes in him, all those "good things" which lay concealed within.[68]

It is possible, however, to speak in less general terms. Jesus is Exegete of Scripture pre-eminently in the act in which he fulfills his mission, at the solemn hour for which he came: in the act of sacrifice, at the hour of his death on the Cross. It is then that he says in substance: Behold, I make all things new, *Ecce nova facio omnia.*[69] It is then that he *kills* the shadows and images, as to their letter, and reveals their spirit, from which those who believe in him will live.[70] This is divine alchemy, which is effected solely by the *virtus Dominicae passionis* (the power of the Lord's passion.)[71] *"Dum in Cruce Salvator suspenditur, sanctae Scripturae intelligentia mundo expanditur."* [72] As he uttered the *"consummatum est"* on the Cross which is symbolized by the last letter of the Hebrew alphabet, Jesus bestows its consummation upon the whole of Scripture,[73] "thereby revealing the whole mystery of man's redemption, which had until then been hidden in the twenty-two books of the Old Testament." [74] The Cross of Jesus is the key, unique and universal.[75] By the sacrament of the Cross, he unites the two Testaments into a single body of doctrine, blending the ancient precepts with the grace of the Gospel.[76] The Lion of Judah, he wins through

[68]. *De princ.,* l. 4, c. 1, n. 6 (302); ET *Origen on First Principles* (G. W. Butterworth trans.), London, 1936, p. 265.

[69]. Rev. 21, 5. See Rom. 5, 17; 1 Cor. 15, 47–49; Eph. 4, 28. See Bruno of Segni, *In Ps.* (*PL,* 163, 696C). See Congar, *Le mystère du Temple;* ET *The Mystery of the Temple,* Westminster, 1958, pp. 148–150, 168.

[70]. Claudius of Turin, *In Reg.,* 1. 4 (*PL,* 50, 1179C).

[71]. Aelred of Rievaulx, *S. ined.* (Talbot ed., 42).

[72]. Irimbert, *In Jud.,* 1. 1 (Pez, 4, 196).

[73]. *Vitis myst.,* c. 14, n. 16 (*PL,* 184, 663D). See Chromatius, *In Matt.,* tr. 6, c. 1, n. 2 (*CCL,* 9, 409).

[74]. Helinandus, *Sermo 10* (*PL,* 212, 567B).

[75]. Augustine, *In Ps. 45,* n. 1 (*CCL,* 38); *Sermo 300,* n. 3 (*PL,* 39, 1378). Stephen Langton, *Postillae super Bibliothecam, glossa in Ruth* (Lacombe, *AHDLMA,* 5, 112). On the cross as key to the Old Testament according to Augustine, see Maurice Pontet, *L'exégèse de Saint Augustin prédicateur,* 373, 374.

[76]. Peter Damian, *Sermo 18* (*PL,* 144, 606C).

his death the victory which opens the Book which was sealed with seven seals.[77] He enters into the Temple which contained the holy Ark.[78] He rips open the veil which covered the mysteries of grace.[79] With a single stroke, he demonstrates the deepest meaning of what was written.[80] And, at the same time, opens for all those who do not resist the eyes which are needed to see him: *"in morte quippe sua nostrae oculos mentis aperuit."* [81]

Thus does the light of truth burst doubly forth from the Cross.[82] All tradition repeats it: *"spiritualem intellectum aperit"* [83]; *"Scripturae sacrae eloquia spiritualiter intelligi facit"* [84]; *"umbram et figuram in veritatem convertit"* [85]; *"litterae finem imponit et spirituali novaeque intelligentiae principatum tribuit"* [86] (It opens spiritual understanding: it makes the words of sacred Scripture spiritually understandable; it converts shadow and figure into truth; it places a limit on the letter and grants the primacy to the spiritual and new understanding). The blow of the centurion's lance accomplished in truth what the ring of Moses, struck against the rock, had accomplished in figure: from

[77.] Caesarius of Arles, *In Ap.* (*Opera omnia,* Morin, II, 222). Gregory, *In Ez.,* l. 2, h. 4, n. 19 (*PL,* 76, 984A). Berengarius, *In Ap.,* v. 1 (*PL,* 17, 789A); v. 3 (808D). Gerhoh of Reichersberg, *In Ps. 77* (19, 482D). Absalon, *Sermo 25* (*PL,* 211, 149–150).

[78.] Ambrose Autpert, *In Ap.,* 1. 7 (573C).

[79.] Origen, *In Luc.,* fr. 26 (244–245). Augustine, *In Ps. 143,* n. 2 (*CCL,* 40); *Sermo 300, n. 4* (*PL,* 39, 1378). *De spir. et litt.,* c. 15 (*PL,* 44, 218). Ambrose Autpert, *In Ap.,* 1. 4: *"Sua passione velum scidit"* (484H). Paschasius Radbertus, *In Matt.,* 1. 12 (*PL,* 120, 963–964). Dungal, *Adv. Claud.* (*PL,* 105, 493B). Ps.-Hugh, *In II Cor.* (*PL,* 175, 546B). See Abelard, *Dominica ad Laudes: "Velamen exuunt figurae mysticae"* (*PL,* 178, 1779B). Leo, *Sermo 53,* c. 2 (*PL,* 54, 318A). Absalon, *Sermo 25* (*PL,* 211, 150A). On the manifold symbolism of the rent veil, see André Pelletier in *RSR,* 46 (1958), pp. 161–180.

[80.] Claudius of Turin, *30 Q. sup. libros Reg.,* q. IV (*PL,* 104, 772C). Haimo of Auxerre, *In Hebr.,* c. 10 (*PL,* 117, 888C).

[81.] Gregory, *Moralia,* l. 29, c. 14, n. 26 (*PL,* 76, 491A).

[82.] Beatus, *In Ap.* (Florez, 157). See Origen, *In Exod.,* h. 11, n. 2 (253–254).

[83.] See Gregory, *In Ezechielem,* l. 2, h. 9, n. 2 (*PL,* 76, 1042C).

[84.] Ambrose Autpert, *In Ap.,* 1. 2 (541H). See 1. 3 (477D-E).

[85.] Haimo of Auxerre, *In Hebr.* (*PL,* 117, 934A).

[86.] Bruno of Segni, *S. in octava Dom.* (*MBVP,* 6, 700C).

the side pierced by the lance the fountains of the New Testament gushed forth: "If Jesus had not been struck, if water and blood had not come from his side, we would all still be thirsting for the Word of God." [87] On Calvary, then, the Book of the Design of God is opened wide and is henceforth readable by all:

The thought of God is a huge book. . . . In the Apocalypse and in Isaiah, the book is sealed. But Ezekiel draws nourishment from it by opening it wide. . . . Ezra reads from it in a clear and open way, when he gazes upon it lifted up on the wood of the cross, where the soldier opened with his lance Christ's side, where, in blood and water, all the lamps of the Christian faith were lighted, so that there would be nothing more still hidden, but all would be revealed.[88]

Behold the page once turned which clarifies everything, like the missal's great illuminated leaf. . . . Here, brilliant and painted in red, is the great Page which separates the two Testaments! All doors open at once, all conflicts are dispelled, all contradictions are resolved.[89]

> Terris illabitur lux illa supera,
> Qua mortis pellitur caligo misera;
> Res nova geritur; panduntur vetera:
> Jam nil relinquitur clausum sub littera.[90]

Just as the "universal recapitulation" was effected by the Sacrifice of Jesus,[91] so also, and at the same time, were the opening and the definitive condensation of the ancient Scripture. But since the sacrifice of Jesus is fulfilled in the resurrection, from which death is inseparable, it is the resurrection which is responsible for both.[92] He who opens the Book is inevitably "the Lamb who was sacrificed and the Lion who returns from the dead," —and this is the reason, according to Ambrose

---

87. Origen, In Ex., h. 11, n. 2 (254).
88. Peter of Celle, In annunt., sermo 1 (PL, 202, 705–706).
89. Paul Claudel, L'epée et le miroir, 74.
90. Gautier of Châtillon (late twelfth century) (Wilmart, RB, 49, 164).
91. Eph. 1, 10. See Georges Auzou, The Word of God, p. 231.
92. Bernard, De div., sermo 57, n. 2 (PL, 183, 681C-D). Hervé (PL, 181, 278C). See Origen, In Matt, t. XII, n. 20 (114). Apringius. In Ap., c. 5 (Vega, 32).

Autpert, why the lion is, in the Book of Revelation, the first of the four living creatures.[93] When he came forth from the sepulchre, Christ pushed aside the stone which had covered it over, the stone of the letter which had until then been a hindrance to the springing forth of spiritual understanding, the stone which he had already removed prophetically from the tomb of Lazarus.[94] The new Jacob, he lifted the cover from the well, so that the whole world could henceforth quench its thirst and be refreshed.[95]

The Act of Christ in fulfilling the Scriptures and simultaneously bestowing the fullness of their meaning upon them is also compared by Christian tradition to the act of eucharistic consecration. For in truth Scripture is bread, but bread which becomes for the Christian the life-giving food which it must be only after it has been consecrated by Jesus:

> Then the Lord Jesus took into his hands the bread of the Scriptures, when, incarnate according to the Scriptures, he underwent his passion and rose again; then, I say, having taken the bread into his hands, he gave thanks, when, thus fulfilling the Scriptures, he offered himself to the Father as a sacrifice of grace and truth.[96]

93. *In Ap.*, 1. 3 (466–467).

94. Bruno of Segni, *In Jo.*, P. II, c. II, (*PL*, 165, 544B); following Augustine and Bede. See Origen, *In Gen.*, h. 13, n. 1, about the well of Haran, citing 2 Cor. 2, and undoubtedly alluding to Mk. 16, 3 (114).

95. Gregory, *Dial.*, 1. 4, c. 4, n. 43 (*PL*, 77, 401A). Remigius of Auxerre, *In Gen.*, XXIX, 2 (*PL*, 131, 106C); *In Gen.*, XXIV (99A). Apringius, *In Ap.*, v. 7 (35).

96. Rupert of Deutz, *In Jo.*, 1. 6 (*PL*, 169, 443B-D). To say, with A. Vaccari, *Scritti di erudizione e di filologia*, II (1958), 158, that "the Alexandrians, with their allegorical interpretation of the Old Testament, recognized hardly any difference at all between the Old and the New Covenant," is probably to take too little account of the fact, so consistently brought out by them, of the transfiguration of the ancient Scripture which was effected by Christ.

## 3. Harmony of the Two Testaments

The Church, born from the side of Christ on Calvary, drawing life from faith in his resurrection, and animated by his Spirit received at Pentecost, henceforward takes the place of Israel. The Church is Abraham's posterity,[1] and alone possesses his inheritance, for "no one can receive the inheritance of Abraham except those whose thinking will be completely conformed to the faith of Abraham with full awareness of all its mysteries."[2] In her living reality, she now possesses and forever preserves "the truth of that which had been prefigured."[3] She is the "just Remnant," of which Isaiah spoke; the "people of the new covenant," promised by Jeremiah; the Israel "risen from the dead," as in the vision of Ezekiel; the "people of the saints of the Almighty," prophesied in the Book of Daniel.[4] While the city whose faith is no more has become "Sodom and Egypt," the new Jerusalem inscribes the names of the twelve tribes on her twelve mystic portals.[5] Her leaders, the twelve Apostles, are the twelve true sons of Jacob. They gather together from everywhere the "redeemed," whom ancient Israel had had the mission of foreshadowing as well as preparing. The Book—not the "codices" with their material letters, but the Prophecy of Christ, the spiritual Book which Christ himself is—is now in their hands. It rightfully belongs to this new people, because this is the people of Christ: *"Pars mea haec, qui in Christum credo."*[6] The great passage has been realized. All the "sacraments" have been fulfilled.[7] The Church takes over from the Synagogue, which, now blind and sterile, is no longer anything but her

---

[1]. Gal. 3, 29. Augustine, *In Ps. 113,* sermo 1, n. 2 (*CCL,* 40, 1636).
[2]. Justin, *Dial.,* c. 44 (Archambault, 1, 197).
[3]. Hesychius, *In Lev.,* 1, 2 (*PG,* 93, 872B).
[4]. See C. H. Dodd, *The Bible Today,* New York, 1947, p. 63. Today it is the Christian who possesses the noble blood of Israel: Origen, *In Gen.,* h. 16, n. 4 (141).
[5]. Rev. 11, 8; 21, 12.
[6]. Augustine, *In Ps. 58,* sermo 1, n. 22 (*CCL,* 39, 744).
[7]. Quodvultdeus, *De prom.,* P. II, c. 18, n. 33 (*PL,* 51, 787B).

113

librarian: *"Codicem portat Judaeus, unde credat Christianus"*
(The Jew bears the book from which the Christian draws his
faith).[8] "Your books," St. Justin early remarked to Tryphon, the
Jew, "or, rather, ours: for it is we who follow them; while you,
on the other hand, even as you read them, do not understand
their meaning . . . It is we who are the true race of Israel, the
spiritual one." [9]

Now it is in the Spirit that the Church, "the authentic Israel,"
"Israel according to the spirit," [10] receives her inheritance and
truly understands it. The "true" meaning of the Scriptures, their
complete and definitive meaning, can really be nothing other than
the meaning "which the Spirit gives to the Church." [11] Although
the Jews still have the letter, the Christians, having the spirit,
have the whole.[12] They have the true Deuteronomy, the one
which consists *"in volumine cordis," "in mystico intellectu," "in
puriore intelligentia mentis."* [13] Henceforth, the Ark of the
Covenant is theirs: *"Nam lata est gloria Domini, quia capta est
arca Dei"* (The glory has departed from Israel, for the Ark of
God has been captured).[14] In a subtle balance, ordered by an
extremely sure instinct, the Church affirms from the time of her
birth and will maintain during the whole course of her history
"the precise and indissoluble interdependence of the Old and
New Testaments." [15] Despite temptations which immediately
assailed her and were to be ceaselessly renewed, she will inde-

8. Bernard, *In Cantica,* sermo 73, n. 2 (*PL,* 183, 1134D). Augustine,
*In Ps. 56,* n. 9 (*CCL,* 39, 700); *Civ. Dei,* l. 4, c. 34 (*PL,* 41, 140).

9. *Dial.,* c. 29, n. 2 (Archambault, 1, 128); c. 11, n. 5 (55). Origen,
*In Jer.,* h. 14, n. 12 (116–117).

10. Rom. 2, 20; 8, 5. Origen, *In Rom.,* l. 2, c. 11 (*PG,* 14, 895–896).
Augustine, *Doct. chr.,* 1. 3, c. 34, n. 49 (Combès-Farges, 408–410). Leo,
*Sermo 30,* c. 7 (*PL,* 54, 234B). Ps.-Maximus, *C. Judaeos qui sunt sec.
litteram Judaei, non sec. spiritum* (C. H. Turner, *JTS,* 20, 293).
Rhabanus Maurus, *In Jud.* (*PL,* 108, 1153B). Bernard, *In vig. nat. Dom.,*
sermo 2, n. 1 (*PL,* 183, 90B). Hervé, *In Rom.* (*PL,* 181, 629B).

11. Origen, *In Lev.,* h. 5, n. 5 (343).

12. Jerome, *In Ez.,* 1. 14 (*PL,* 25, 480D).

13. John of Salisbury, *Polycraticus,* l. 4, c. 6 (*PL,* 199, 522C-D).

14. 1 Sam. 4, 22; Gregory, *In I Reg.,* l. 3, c. 2, n. 21 (*PL,* 79, 172–173).

15. See Augustine, *De musica,* 1. 6, c. 17, n. 59 (Thonnard, 476).
Aponius, *In Cant.,* 1. 6: The teacher who does not transmit both Testaments, whether as a Jew or as a Manichean, is *"homicida animarum"*
(114–115).

fatigably resist those who would reject the Old Book and those too who might wish to make it live again according to the letter. For "the strength of the Gospel is found in the Law," and this Law cannot grow old "for one who explains it according to the meaning of the Gospel." Thus "each Testament is for us a new Testament, by newness of understanding rather than in terms of age," [16] and anyone who would accept the one to the exclusion of the other thereby becomes *"a Testamento Dei alienus."* [17]

All of Israel mysteriously relives in the Church—its history, its personalities, its battles, its trials, its destiny, its expectation. In the Church the heavens of Scripture, like the heavens we see, participate in the universal harmony,[18] in the harmony which still denotes the Covenant established between God and man through the redemptive incarnation.[19] For the two Testaments are "brothers." [20] They are the two wings which bear the Covenant aloft.[21] There is constantly to be discovered between them a connection,[22] an agreement, a "concordance," [23] a "con-

[16.] Origen, *In Num.*, h. 9, n. 4 (59). Rhabanus Maurus, *In Num.*, l. 2, c. 19 (*PL*, 108, 685–686). Bruno of Segni, *In Ex.*, c. 25 (*PL*, 164, 305D). Peter of Celle (*PL*, 202, 1059A-B).

[17.] Bede, *In Marc.*, l. 1, c. 1 (*PL*, 92, 134D).

[18.] Othloh, *Dial. de trib. q.*, c. 43 (*PL*, 146, 119D); c. 44 (121C-D). See John Scotus, *Div nat.*, l. 1, c. 72 (*PL*, 122, 517C); l. 3, c. 6 (637–638).

[19.] Augustine, *De Trinitate*, l. 4, c. 2, n. 4 (*PL*, 42, 889). Involved here are both the accord established between God and man and the "one-two" relationship which is at the basis of music; it is remarkable that these are the same words which serve to express the relationships of the two Testaments as well. Paschasius Radbertus, *In Matt.* (*PL*, 120, 624A).

[20.] Origen, *Selecta in Jos.*: ἀδελφὰ τῆς παλαισᾶ τὰ νέα (*PG*, 12, 820B).

[21.] Haimo of Auxerre, *In Ap.*, l. 2 (*PL*, 117, 1010C).

[22.] Hilary, *In Ps. 76*, n. 9 (302).

[23.] Gregory of Elvira, tr. 11 (117). Ambrose Autpert, *In trans. Dom.*, n. 14 (*PL*, 89, 1314C). Alcuin (*PL*, 101, 1226D). Haimo (*PL*, 117, 1008A). Claudius of Turin, *In Reg.*, l. 3 (*PL*, 50, 1138B-C). Gerhoh, *In Ps. 41* (*PL*, 193, 1514C), and *XL* (*PL*, 194, 995D). Adam Scotus (*PL*, 198, 759A). Baldwin of Canterbury, *Liber de sacr. alt.* (*PL*, 204, 731). See Augustine, *In Ps. 67*, n. 19 (*CCL*, 39, 882); *In Ps. 150*, n. 2 (40, 2193). Amedeus of Lausanne will show Christ *"tam dulci concordia veritatis organa modulantem"* (*PL*, 188, 1307B; 1305B: *"veritas consona"*).

115

sonance," [24] a "fittingness," [25] a "congruence," a "consensus," [26] a "concert." [27] This is a *"concordiae consensus"* [28] whose overall affirmation will never again cease, nor will its drive towards verifying, deciphering, or at least illustrating, signifying down to the smallest details, through a second degree of symbolism. To the *sed tunc* and the *nunc autem* of contrast will succeed the *jam tunc* and the *et nunc* of inclusion. In an earlier time, the contrast had to be stressed. Was this not foretold by the Old Testament itself? "Behold, the days are coming, says the Lord, when I will make a new Covenant with the house of Israel and the house of Judah, *not like* the Covenant which I made with their fathers." [29] We are familiar with the commentary of St. Paul, and the commentary of the Letter to the Hebrews: on the one hand, a blazing fire, and darkness and gloom, and a tempest, which made Moses and Sinai tremble with fear; on the other, Mount Zion and the city of the living God, the heavenly Jerusalem and innumerable angels, the "festal gathering" to which are welcomed in peace all those who were purified by the blood of Jesus.[30] St. Augustine comments as follows on this commentary: *"illic etiam fumus, hic vero ignis serenus"* (there was also smoke there, while here there is a tranquil fire); this is something which makes us appreciate the *"distantiam evidentissimam"* [31] between the Old Testament and the New. But at the

[24.] Tertullian, *Adv. Marc.*, l. 4, c. 39 (556). Origen, *In Lev.*, h. 6, n. 3 (363); *In Rom. I*, 10 (*PG*, 14, 856C). Augustine, *Contra Faustum*, l. 12, c. 41 (*PL*, 42, 275); *In Ps. 49*, n. 4 (*CCL*, 38, 577). Othloh, *Dial. de trib. quaest.*, c. 44 (*PL*, 133, 118D), (121C-D).

[25.] Origen, *In Matt.*, t. XIV, n. 4 (280). Isidore, *L. de var.* 2 (20).

[26.] Origen, *loc. cit.*, and *In Lev.*, h. 3, n. 2 (302). Augustine, *In Ps. 67*, n. 19 (*CCL*, 39, 882). Maximus of Turin, h. 11 (*PL*, 57, 245B-C). Adam Scotus, *Sermo 7*, n. 8 (*PL*, 198, 138A).

[27.] Paschasius Radbertus, *In Matt.* (*PL*, 120, 624A). See Macrobius, *In somm. Scrip.*, 1. 1, c. 5: *"coeli harmoniam, id est concinentiam"* (Eyssenhardt ed., 494).

[28.] Richard, *Benj. major*, l. 4, c. 19 (*PL*, 196, 160D).

[29.] Jer. 31, 31–34.

[30.] Heb. 12, 18–29. See 2 Cor. 3.

[31.] *Sermo 155*, nn. 5–6 (*PL*, 38, 843–844). Glossa, *in Hebr.*, XII, 18 (*PL*, 114, 668A). Ps.-Bede, *In Jo.* (*PL*, 92, 662A). See J. Lécuyer, *Le sacerdoce dans le mystère du Christ*, Paris, 1957, pp. 43–44, 59.

very moment that the gift of the New Testament creates the contrast, it suppresses it. The distance is at once filled in. We find that the Old Testament itself has been unified, and the two Testaments together speak with a single voice.[32] *"Invenitur Christus in eis, quoniam et Christus ipse consensus est"* (We find Christ in them, for it is Christ who is their consensus).[33] Once the Gospel has been proclaimed, Prophets and Apostles make up a single choir, and the believer contemplates them in their wondrous conjunction.[34] *Scriptura enim sancta haeret sibi tota, et uno spiritu copulata est* (For the whole of Scripture is coherent, united as it is by a single spirit).[35]

How many texts, analogous to these, could be quoted! Sometimes it is contrast which is emphasized, and sometimes harmony, and yet they never contradict each other. The majority express the passage of the first moment to the second. We see this in a hymn of Adam of St. Victor for Pentecost:

> *Lex praecessit in figura,*
> *Lex paenalis, lex obscura,*
> *Lumen Evangelicum.*
>
> *Spiritalis intellectus,*
> *Litterali fronde tectus,*
> *Prodeat in publicum!*[36]

And of how many other doctors, besides St. Hilary, could this Sequence of Poitiers not also be sung:

> *Aenigmata prophetarum*
> *Et figuras Scripturarum*
> *Verbis evangelistarum*
> *Concordavit omnia!*[37]

---

[32]. Augustine, *In Ps. 49,* n. 4 (*CCL,* 38, 577). Fortunatian of Aquileia, *In ev.,* fr. 1 (*CCL,* 9, 367).

[33]. Origen, *In Matt.,* t. XIV, n. 4 (281).

[34]. Rupert of Deutz, *In Ap.,* 1. 9, c. 14 (*PL,* 169, 1096B). *In reg. s. Ben.,* 1. 2, c. 9 (*PL,* 170, 506B).

[35]. Jerome, *In Marc.* (*An mar.,* III, 2, 328). Gregory of Elvira, tr. 11 (118). Isidore, *L. de var. q.,* c. 1 (5).

[36]. Strophe 2 (Gautier, 66–67).

[37]. *M. W.,* 1, 525.

It is the principle which deserves our interest here, rather than the details, whose inventiveness is suggestive of a turn of mind which is quite alien to us. The principle is undoubtedly the basis of a system of apologetics, a system whose living actuality was to be preserved by the persistence of Judaism within Christendom as well as by the perpetual revivals of Gnosticism and Manicheism. Origen was constantly thinking of these two contrasting enemies of the Christian synthesis. And it was of them that St. Gregory the Great was thinking—at the very least, they were in the background of his thinking—when he wrote: *"Sic Novum Testamentum Ecclesia catholica recipit, ut Vetus non abjiciat; sic Vetus veneratur, ut Novum semper in ipsis sacrificiis carnalibus per spiritum intelligat* (The Catholic Church receives the New Testament in such a way as not to reject the Old, which she venerates in such a way as always to understand, in spirit, the New).[38] And the medieval exegetes were often thinking of them also, as of an always present danger—and the danger was often there in actual fact.[39] In this way they repulse the "calumnies" directed against Scripture,[40] and simultaneously the Christian faith. But there is much more besides.

Throughout the whole of Christian exegesis, and even as early as certain utterances of St. Paul, there is something more to be observed than mere defensive argumentation. There is a note of triumphant joy. This *"admirabilis divinae operationis concordia,"* [41] this *"consona utriusque Testamenti veritas"* [42] is admired, relished, celebrated for its own sake. It is found to be "delight-

---

[38.] *Sup. Cant.,* c. 7 (*PL,* 79, 538C).

[39.] This was a constant concern. On neo-Manicheanism, see Fliche-Martin, *Histoire de l'Eglise,* VII, 459–460; IX, 91–99, 330–344. Héfélé-Leclercq, *Histoire des conciles,* V, II, 1112. H. A. Borst, *Die Katharer* (1933). Rodulphus Glaber, *Historiae,* l. 2, c. 11; Bernard, *In Cant.,* sermones 65–66 (*PL,* 183, 1089, 1094); Egbert of Schönau, *Sermones c. Catharos* (*PL,* 195, 69ff.); Geoffrey of Auxerre (Leclercq, *Studia anselmiana,* 31, 196). Raoul of Argences, *In ep. et ev.,* p. 2, h. 19 (*PL,* 155, 2010–2013).

[40.] Augustine, *In Ps. 145,* n. 14 (*CCL,* 40, 2115); see *in Ps. 58,* sermo 1, n. 22 (*CCL,* 39, 744).

[41.] Claudius of Turin.

[42.] Raoul of St. Germer, *In Lev.,* l. 17, c. 13 (212F).

ful." The light derived from it is a feast for the understanding. The imagination becomes active in behalf of an initial insight which will always be stronger and more extensive than any of its inventions. The Christian, meditating on Scripture, enjoys it as he enjoys a piece of music.[43] The harmonious concert of the Testaments, more than the music of the spheres, more than the *"carmen universitatis,"* has its climax in establishing in him a state of contemplative peace, similar to the slumber of ecstasy.[44] No matter how many centuries pass, the wonder is ever new. It is always the "new song" which rings out.[45] The "glorious face of Moses" is always the object of the same fascination.[46] *"Vide quantum consonat Evangelium cum lege!* [47] *Vides ubique sibi concordare mysteria!"* [48] That was Origen speaking. Nine centuries later, this is St. Bernard: *"Vides quam pulchre et concorditer . . . sibi invicem concinant!"* [49] *"Videte, fratres, quanta est unitas Scripturarum!"* [50] And Geoffrey Babion: *"Ecce quantum conveniunt Vetus et Novum Testamentum!"* [51]

This kind of agreement is something unique and could not be perfectly brought out by any one model, although the vocabulary used to define it is borrowed from music and music provides a number of clarifications. It is not the agreement of a simple parallelism, nor of a simple hierarchy; it is the agreement of a simple unity. But this kind of unity is not a confusion either. It is a consonance, a harmony, a "harmonious sweetness" which is achieved by the convergence of things which are initially un-

---

43. Augustine, *De musica*, l. 6, c. 11, n. 29 (Thonnard, 424).

44. Augustine, *In Ps. 67*, n. 19 (*PL*, 36, 824). A modern author has spoken rather lightly of "false mysticism" on this subject.

45. See Bruno of Segni, *In Ps.* (*PL*, 164, 696B-C).

46. Sicardus of Cremona, *Mitrale*, l. 6, c. 5 (*PL*, 213, 261A).

47. Origen, *In Ex.*, h. 5, n. 3 (187). Same tone in Chrysostom, *In Gal.*, IV, 30: ὁρᾷς διὰ πάντων τὸν τύπον τηρούμενον (*PG*, 61, 664).

48 Origen, *In Gen.*, h. 10, n. 5 (100). *In Ez.*, h. 1 (*PL*, 25, 697C).

49. *Sup. missus est*, h. 2, n. 11 (*PL*, 183, 66C).

50. Bernard, *In festo Omnium sanctorum*, sermo 2, n. 4 (*PL*, 183, 467A).

51. *S. in Pent.* (*PL*, 171, 593D). Maurice of Sully (*PL*, 171, 714B). See Leo, sermo 51, c. 4 (*PL*, 54, 311B).

like and recognized as such; [52] a wonderful peace, which follows upon what seems to be a war; [53] a symphony, *"vocum disparium inter se dulcis concentus."* [54] Between the two parts of the Book, there is a strict coaptation; an organic disposition and flawless correspondence. *"Vetus Lex Novae congruit; id ipsum Moyses, quod Apostolus."* [55] The fabric of the New Law is, as it were, woven with the thread of the Old: *"Nova Lex de Veteri Lege texta est."* [56] The bond can also be compared to the marriage bond,[57] or to the bond between brothers: *"Novum Testamentum jungitur Veteri fraterno faedere."* [58]

A series of formulas define this bond for us. All of the formulas amount basically to the same thing, but the abundance and variety of the analogies are meaningful. The Latins were the ones who emphasized them the most. St. Augustine, influenced by Tychonius, seems to have been their principal artisan. In the *De catechizandis rudibus*, he says: *"In Veteri Testamento est occultatio Novi, in Novo Testamento est manifestatio Veteris";* [59] in one sermon: *"Vetus Testamentum est promissio figurata, Novum Testamentum est promissio spiritualiter intellecta";* [60] and in another sermon: *"Vetus Testamentum in*

---

[52.] Regino of Prüm, *De harmonica inst.*, c. 10 (*PL*, 132, 491D), following Boethius. Othloh, *Dial. de trib. q.*, c. 43 (*PL*, 146, 119–120). See John Scotus, *De div. nat.*, l. 1, c. 72: *"Est enim ipse [Deus] similium similitudo, et dissimilitudo dissimilium, oppositorum oppositio et contrariorum contrarietas. Haec enim omnia pulchra ineffabilique harmonia in unam concordiam colligit atque componit . . ."* (*PL*, 122, 517B-C).

[53.] Origen, *In Matt.*, t. II, commenting on *"Beati pacifici"*; in *The Philocalia of Origen*, (J. Armitage Robinson ed.), Cambridge, 1893, pp. 49–50.

[54.] See Augustine, *In Ps. 150*, nn. 7–8, on the diversity among the saints, John Scotus, *De div. nat.*, 1. 5, c. 36 (*PL*, 122, 965–966).

[55.] Jerome, *ep. 64*, n. 20 (5, 137). Isidore, *L. de var. q.* (180, 188).

[56.] Hildegarde (*PL*, 197, 1010A).

[57.] Isidore (*PL*, 83, 313A). Haymo of Halberstadt, *In Is.* (*PL*, 116, 756D).

[58.] Peter of Celle, *De tab. Moysi* (Leclercq, *La spiritualité de Pierre de Celle*, 1629). See G. Jouassard, *Mélanges Salaville* (1958), pp. 109–110.

[59.] Combès-Farges, *op. cit.*, pp. 548–550.

[60.] *Sermo 4*, c. 8, n. 9 (*PL*, 38, 37). See *In Ps. 74*, n. 12 (*CCL*, 39, 1033); *In Ps. 143*, n. 2 (*CCL*, 40, 2073).

*Novo revelatum, in Vetere Novum velatum vides."* [61] Not long
afterwards, Primasius, who also depends on Tychonius, likewise
explains why we must always refuse to accept one of the two
Testaments without the other: "The Old Testament is the forerunner and the veil of the New, and the New is the fulfillment
and the revelation of the Old." [62] Then, St. Gregory, taking an
image from the first vision of Ezekiel which was to become
particularly famous: "The wheel within a wheel is the New
Testament within the Old, because the object denoted by the Old
Testament is the same as that demonstrated by the New." [63]
The Venerable Bede asserts what all the Doctors who preceded
him had already said: *"Vetus Testamentum in Novo dilucidatum,
Novum in veteri adumbratum."* [64] Beatus of Liebana, commenting on the Book of Revelation, again takes up the symbol used
by St. Gregory and draws this condensed formula from it: *"Prophetia Testamenti Novi, Testamentum Vetus est; et expositio
Testamenti Veteris, Testamentum Novum."* [65] We again find the
same symbol in St. Ambrose Autpert, who explains it in similar
fashion:

What is the wheel within a wheel if not the New Testament revealed
in the Old? . . . But if the Old and New Testaments are said to be
a single book, this is because the New can no longer be distinguished
from the Old, nor can the Old be distinguished from the New. For
the Old Testament is the forerunner and veil of the New, while
the New is the fulfillment and revelation of the Old.[66]

This combines St. Gregory and Primasius. Equivalent formulas can be found in Rhabanus Maurus,[67] in Haimo of Auxerre,[68]

[61.] *In Ps. 105,* n. 36 (*CCL,* 40, 1576).
[62.] *Sup. Ap.,* 1. 2: *"Nec novum sine vetere, nec vetus sine novo. Nam
. . ."* (*PL,* 68, 821A).
[63.] *In Ez.,* 1. 1, h. 6, n. 15 (*PL,* 76, 835B). See Aponius, *In Cant.,*
l. 6 (115).
[64.] *De tab.,* 1. 2, c. 6 (*PL,* 91, 439D).
[65.] *In Ap.* (Florez, 278); see 274, 276. Gregory, *In Ez.* (*PL,* 76,
836A-B).
[66.] *In Ap.,* 1. 3 (467H, 469H).
[67.] *In Ez.,* 1. 2 (*PL,* 110, 527–528); this is also one of Gregory's
formulas, *In Ez.,* 1. 1, h. 6, n. 12 (*PL,* 76, 834A).
[68.] *In Ap.* XII (*PL,* 117, 1013C); this is the formula of Primasius,
*In Ap.* IV (1008D).

in Claudius of Turin, who concluded: *"Omnia resonant novitatem."* [69] The same can be said for Bruno of Segni,[70] Richard of St. Victor,[71] Wolberon,[72] and many others. Letbert of St. Ruf will write: *"Vetus est prophetia Novi, et Novum Veteris expositio"* (The Old is the prophecy of the New, and the New is the exposition of the Old),[73] which is more or less the same as the formula of Beatus. And Hervé du Bourg-Dieu: *"Si spiritualiter intelligatur Vetus, nihil discrepat a Novo"* (If the Old is spiritually understood, it differs in no way from the New).[74] There is probably no one who found a better turn of phrase than Berengarius, in his explanation of the Book of Revelation. He does not only say, for example: *"Novum Testamentum apertio est Veteris Testamenti"* (The New Testament is the opening of the Old),[75] but he also twice uses this perfect formula, which, as close as it is to St. Gregory's as repeated by Beatus, still has something more germinal about it: *"Spiritualis intelligentia in Veteri Testamento, nihil est aliud quam Novum Testamentum"* (Spiritual understanding in the Old Testament is nothing other than the New Testament).[76] It is true that St. Augustine had also said of the Law: *"Spiritualiter intellecta, Evangelium est."* [77] And, earlier, Origen: "The entire divine Scripture is Gospel." [78]

If this is how things are, then the *corpus* of the Jewish Scriptures unreservedly enters into the collection of Christian Scriptures. Just as there is only one *Verbum*, only one Word, there is for the faith only one Scripture, only one Book, *"unus liber."* [79]

[69]. *In Gen.*, 1. 1 (*PL*, 50, 958C).

[70]. *In Ps. 49* (*PL*, 164, 875C).

[71]. *In Ap.*, l. 2, c. 3 (*PL*, 196, 755B).

[72]. *In Cant.*, always with reference to the two wheels of Ezekiel (*PL*, 195, 1059B-C).

[73]. *In Ps. 41* (*PL*, 21, 809A).

[74]. *In Gal.* (*PL*, 181, 1134A).

[75]. V. 3 (*PL*, 17, 838D); speaking of the Cross, he also says: *"quae redemptio,"* or *"quae victoria,"* *"apertio fuit veteris Testamenti"* (808A-D).

[76]. V. 3 (*PL*, 17, 807D). V. 7 (956C); see 923C. Hervé, *In Gal.* (*PL*, 181, 1134A).

[77]. *Sermo 25,* n. 2 (*PL*, 38, 168).

[78]. *In Jo.*, l. 1, c. 15 (19).

[79]. Wolberon, *loc. cit.* Hervé, *In Is.*, 1.4 (*PL*, 181, 277C). Jerome, *In Eccl.*, XII, 12 (*PL*, 23, 115B).

*"Universa Scriptura, liber unus suavissimus."* [80] The two Testaments *"sunt unum,"* [81] and the artisan as well as the principle of their unity is, once again, Christ: *"unanimes in unitate Christi inveniuntur—Christus ipse eorum consensus est."* [82] The first collection's unity with the second consecrates the unity of all the parts which make up the first collection, however disparate they may sometimes humanly be: *"Divina eloquia, etsi temporibus distincta, sunt tamen sensibus unita"* (The divine utterances, although distinct as to time, are nonetheless united in meaning).[83] It can then be said of all the inspired books, taken together, what is said of the various prophetic books, for example: just as many churches form but a single Church, and just as the different heavens form but a single Heaven, so all these works form but a single work, "in a wonderful and divine unity." [84] These affirmations are only the more remarkable in that the sacred Books —*"numerosa Scripturarum volumina"* [85]—had not yet been gathered into a definitive canon, which was to bestow upon the Bible a kind of visible and material unity. One spoke, as of two quite different collections, of the divine or "heavenly" Scriptures and of human scriptures.[86] One devoted himself to the study *"omnium divinarum Scripturarum";* one said: *"divinarum Scripturarum series,"* or *"omnis Scripturarum sacrarum ordo."* [87] Well beyond the middle of the twelfth century, John of Salisbury would still, to satisfy a correspondent, look into the question of the number of books which made up the two Testaments.[88]

[80.] Origen, *In Jo.,* V (Robinson, *The Philocalia of Origen,* pp. 42–48).
[81.] Ambrose Autpert, *In Ap.* (469H). Haimo of Auxerre (*PL,* 117, 1014C). Rupert of Deutz (*PL,* 167, 1119D).
[82.]Paschasius Radbertus, *In Matt.,* 1. 8, c. 18 (*PL,* 120, 623–624). Scripture must be approached as a single body: Origen, *In Jo.,* 1. 10, c. 18 (189).
[83.] Gregory, *In Ez.,* l. 1, h. 6, n. 14 (*PL,* 76, 835A).
[84.] Peter Lombard, *In Ps. 150* (*PL,* 191, 1295C-D).
[85.] Willibald, *Vita S. Bonifatii,* c. 11, n. 8 (*MGH, Scr.,* II, 336).
[86.] See Jerome, *Ep. 22,* c. 30, end of the "dream": *"tanto dehinc studio divina legisse, quanto mortaliae ante legeram"* (I, 146).
[87.] Jonas, *Vita Columbani,* l. 1, c. 3 (1905 ed., 156–157). Aldhelm (*MGH, A. ant.,* XV, 492). A bishop of Merida in the seventh century, teaches his successor *"omnem bibliothecam Scripturarum divinarum,"* *Vitae P. Emer.,* IV, 4 (Marrou, 442).
[88.] *Ep. 143* (*PL,* 199, 124D).

There was no reference yet to "the Bible," but to "the Library," "the heavenly library." [89] And yet it was affirmed: *"Tota Bibliotheca unus liber est, in capite velatus, in fine manifestus"* (The whole Library is a single book, veiled at the beginning, manifest at the end).[90]

Without and within, before and after, shadow and body, figure and truth, letter and spirit, prophecy and realization; ultimately, two Testaments: the unity of these pairings is the same unity, and the understanding of the one is the understanding of each of the others.[91] This is a unique Mystery, but its resonances are endless, and its varied expression is everywhere to be found in the Fathers and in those who read them. It is at the center of their exegesis. It dominates all their teaching on biblical meanings. It is what inspires St. Hilary to look upon these formulas as equivalent: *"Spiritalis intelligentia—spiritalis praeformatio —praefigurationis significatio—Ecclesiae praeformatio";* [92] or a St. Augustine, words such as: *"prophetatio," "praenuntiatio,"* [93] *"allegorica praefiguratio,"* [94] and so forth. It is what makes a St. Gaudentius of Brescia see, in the very facts which are set down in Exodus, the historical understanding proper to the Jews *"usque ad Christi praesentiam"* and also the spiritual understanding which must alone prevail today.[95] It is what makes a St. Gregory of Elvira say, when explaining the Bible: "For our own part, we shall demonstrate that the power and the spiritual reason of all the actions (recounted in the Bible) are ordered

[89.] Aldhelm, *Ep. 5;* Cuthbert (*MGH, A. ant.,* XV, 492). Abelard, *Ep. 8* (*PL,* 178, 310A). *Vita S. Gertrudis virg.* (seventh century) (*MGH, Rer. merov.,* II, 458). And even in 1209 Albricius will call P. Riga *"bibliothecae versificator"* (*MGH, Scr.,* 23, 889). A. Mundo, "Bibliotheca," *Bible et lecture de carême d'après S. Benoît, RB,* 60, 65–92 (discussed by G. Penco, *Rivista liturg.,* 38, 1951, 210–217).

[90.] Etherius and Beatus, *Ad Elip.,* l. 1, c. 99 (*PL,* 96, 956A-B).

[91.] Sicardus of Cremona, *Mitrale,* l. 1, c. 6 (*PL,* 213, 30C). Haimo of Auxerre, *In Ap.,* 1. 2 (*PL,* 117, 1013C-D).

[92.] *Tr. myst.,* l. 1, c. 39–40; l. 2, c. 5 (28, 31, 33). Claudius of Turin: *"praesignabat," "praefiguraverat"* (*PL,* 104, 758B, 772D, 773A).

[93.] *Civ. Dei,* l. 10, c. 32, n. 2 (*PL,* 41, 314).

[94.] *Civ. Dei,* l. 17, c. 5, n. 2 (*PL,* 41, 526). *In Jo.,* tr. 9, n. 10 (*PL,* 35, 1463–1464).

[95.] *Tr. 7* (56).

to the prefiguring of the New Testament," [96] and so forth. St. Isidore of Seville will speak in the same vein of a *"praefigurationis mysterium"* and of *"promissivae figurae,"* [97] just as St. Augustine had spoken of *"sacramenta prophetica"* [98] and Quodvultdeus of *"figuratae promissiones."* [99] And Baldwin of Canterbury of a *"mystica significatio secuturae veritatis"* (mystical signification of the truth which must follow).[100] Scripture itself, Berengarius says, incites us to this spiritual understanding of everything which it recounts to us; with the Gospel of St. John, it says to us: "Come and see," which is to say "Come, not by the steps of the body, but by those of the spirit, and understand spiritually that the facts which you have read about are realized historically in time." [101]

Over and over again, tradition will repeat: "The former things are historically ordered in such a way that they appear completely new spiritually." [102] It will not repeat this in words and in writings alone, but in images also. We know how the great art of the Middle Ages represented these correlations through sculpture and through stained-glass window. Suger himself told how he had commissioned, for the basilica of Saint-Denis, a series of windows, for each of which he had composed a caption in verse; for example:

*Sicut serpentes serpens necat aeneus omnes,*
*Sic exaltatus hostes necat in cruce Christus.*

Or:

*Qui Deus est magnus, librum Leo solvit et Agnus.*

The altar, the chalices, and other objects of worship were similarly decorated with what Suger calls *"allegoriae jocundae,"* always with one or two explanatory verses, following the old

96. *Tr. 13* (141). *Tr. 7* (76).
97. *PL*, 83, 207B, 321B.
98. *In Ps. 103*, sermo 3, n. 1 (*CCL*, 40, 1499).
99. *De prom.*, p. 2, c. 40, n. 93 (*PL*, 51, 818A).
100. *PL*, 204, 712C.
101. *In Ap.*, v. 3 (*PL*, 17, 813C).
102. Rhabanus Maurus, *Ep.* 12 (*MGH, Ep.* 5, 399); *In Deut.*, praef. (*PL*, 108, 839A).

form of versified *tituli* which originated in the inscriptions of Damasus:

Hoc quod Abram pro prole litat, Christi caro signat. Botrum vecte ferunt qui Christum cum cruce quaerunt.[103]

In one of the drawings in his *Hortus deliciarum,* a work which contains "as in a golden vial, the fine flower of medieval culture" [104] and which sums up in an original way the symbolism of his age, Herrad of Landsberg showed "two winged heads, joined by a stole crossed over the breast and brought around again behind the back," with this inscription: *"Vetus et Novum Testamentum in simul junctum."* [105] The same inspiration guided the Mosan goldsmith, Nicolas de Verdun, in 1181, when he was making the famous enamelled ambo of the Augustinian abbey of Klosterneuburg in Austria, "the most complete typological sequence left to us by the twelfth century"; as in still older works, the small panels which make it up are arranged in groupings of three rather than two—each mystery of the New Testament is framed by two scenes from the Old Testament prefiguring it, the first being taken from the age of the law of nature, and the second from the age of the law of Moses; thus, the Baptism of Christ appears as prefigured both by the passage through the

103. *L. de rebus in admin. sua gest.,* c. 32 (*PL,* 186, 1233, 1237).

104. Robert Will, *Revue d'histoire et de philosophie religieuse,* 17, (1937), 565. On Herrad see Manitius, 3, 1010–1014.

105. Pl. 23 (p. 16–17). At the Uffizi Museum in Florence there is a tapestry showing scenes of the Patriarchs, with this legend:

*Vera refert pictura pia haec,*
*Sed mystica, lector,*
*Ecclesiam et Christum*
*Sancta figura tegit.*

In this second Middle Ages, the relationships of the two Testaments to each other occasioned niceties and combinations according to an artificial schematization. Thus a painting attributed to one of the students of Fra Angelico (Florence, San Marco) shows the twelve Prophets opposite the twelve apostles, with each apostle uttering an article of the Creed which corresponds to a prophecy. (In the same painting, the seven-branched candelabra is a figure of the seven sacraments.)

Red Sea and by the molten sea which stood upon twelve oxen in Solomon's Temple; his Ascension is framed between that of Enoch and that of Elijah,[106] and so forth. This ordering will also be adopted by the *Speculum humanae salvationis* (1324), a work which was to be so much in vogue for more than two centuries. Much earlier still, at St. Gall, Eckhardt IV (ca. 980–1060) composed his *Versus ad picturas,* in which he described (with fidelity, it was thought) a series of scenes drawn from each Testament, such as he had seen them painted on the walls of the Cathedral of Mainz and possibly his own church as well.[107] And even earlier than that, when Benet Biscop, the founder of Wearmouth and Yarrow who made six trips to Rome, returned to England from his fourth trip in 684,[108] he brought with him, in addition to another collection of books, a collection of large symbolic pictures, *"summa ratione compositas,"* Bede tells us, which were designed to impress upon the people this wonderful "harmony" of the Testaments.

Without going all the way back to the art of the very first centuries, let us take a few more early examples. A sixth-century poet, whose identity is uncertain but who may have been the friend of Sidonius Apollinaris, Rusticus Helpidius Domnulus, who died as the Bishop of Lyons (501–502), composed some tristichs which are correlated, the relationship being sometimes of contrast (Tower of Babel—Pentecost), and sometimes of direct prefiguring (sacrifice of Isaac—crucifixion of Christ). The adverb *hic,* which frequently recurs in these verses, as well as their extreme brevity (which sometimes makes them barely

[106.] Louis Réau, *L'art du moyen age, op. cit.,* p. 28. The symbolism is still rather external. The same disposition can be seen on the tapestries at La Chaise-Dieu (fifteenth century).
[107.] M. Seidlmayer, *Lexikon für Theologie und Kirche,* 3 (1931), 609. E. de Bruyne, I, 282. See Raby, *A History of Secular Poetry in the Middle Ages* (1934), I, 222, on the frescoes at St. Albanus in Mainz, following Ermoldus: on the left, the *gesta Dei* of the Old Testament; on the right, the *vitalia gesta* of Christ.
[108.] Bede, *H. abb. Wisem.,* cc. 4, 6 (*PL,* 94, 720B-C). B. Capelle, *L'Angleterre chrétienne avant les Normands* (1909), 140–143, 198.

intelligible), really suggest that they were intended to be inscribed at the bottom of frescoes: caption and painting were to
explain each other.[109] The genre was imitated in the quatrains
which make up the "Dittochaeon" (*"duplex cibus," "refectio
duplex"*) of Prudentius, also undoubtedly intended to illustrate
paintings which represented interconnected scenes from each
Testament.[110] At Rome, in the apses of Santa Costanza, we can
still see a mosaic of Moses receiving the tablets of the Law, while
another mosaic, close by, shows Peter receiving the Gospel from
the hands of Christ: a "correlation of the two Covenants," [111]
which can be interpreted in many ways. Let us close this section
by extracts from two poems in which St. Paulinus of Nola com-
placently describes the paintings which decorated his beloved
basilica of St. Felix. In the first poem, he asks his friend Nicetas
to lift his head up to look at them:

> *Nunc volo picturas fucatis agmine longo*
> *Porticibus videas, paulumque supinas fatiges*
> *Colla, reclinato dum perlegis omnia vultu.*
> *Qui videt haec vacuis agnoscens vera figuris,*
> *Non vacua fidem sibi pascet imagine mentem.*
> *Omnia namque tenet serie pictura fideli,*
> *Quae senior scripsit per quinque volumina Moses,*
> *Quae gessit Domini signatus nomine Jesus,*
> *Quo duce Jordanis, suspenso gurgite, fixi*
> *Fluctibus, a facie divinae restitit arcae.*[112]

[109.] *In historiam V. et N. T. carmina* (*PL*, 62, 534–536). See Samuel
Cavallin, *Le poète Domnulus, étude prosopographique* (*S. Er.*, VII,
1955, 49–66). An *Elegia* of Sedulius, entitled *Collatio Veteris et Novi
Testamenti*, is made of fifty-five parallel distichs.
[110.] Prudentius, 4 (M. Lavarenne), 201–216. Lavarenne, *Prudentius,
Psychomachie* (1933), 16. Eleventh-century gloss on the *Psychomachia*
(*S. Er.*, IX, 66). But although there is an equal number for each Testament, they are not placed in a parallel order through a symbolic correspondence.
[111.] Marcel Laurent, *L'art chrétien des origines à Justinien* (1956),
p. 176.
[112.] *De S. Fel. nat. carmen 9*, p. 27, vv. 511–520 (*PL*, 61, 660A-B).
A mosaic at San Apollinare in Ravenna (sixth century) shows the same
kind of disposition.

The second poem subtly interweaves the relationships of the two successive Testaments with those of the old church of Nola and the new:

> In veteri nobis nova res adnascitur actu
> Et solita insolito crescunt solemnia ritu.[113]

After calling upon us to admire the porches and the interior of the basilica which was transformed by his efforts, Paulinus comes to the paintings with which he has decorated it:

> Miremurque sacras veterum monumenta figuras:
> Et tribus in spatiis duo Testamenta legamus.[114]
> Hanc quoque cernentes rationem lumine recto
> Quod nova in antiquis tectis, antiqua novis lex
> Pingitur: est etenim pariter decus utile nobis
> In veteri novitas, atque in novitate vetustas.[115]

---

113. *De S. Fel. nat. carmen 10*, p. 28, vv. 1-2 (*PL*, 61, 663A). Vv, 214-222:

> Hinc operum tempus confunditur et nitet extra
> Parietibus novitas, latet intus operta vetustae:
> Fronte juventutis tegitur fucata senectus:
> In pueram faciem veterana refloruit aetas.
> Suntque simul vetera et nova; nec nova nec vetera aeque.
>
> Non eadem simul atque eadem quae forma futuri
> Praesentisque boni est; namque et nunc utile nobis,
> Deterso veteris vitae squalore, novari
> Mente pia, Christumque sequi, regnisque parari (668A).

114. Do not these "two in three" indicate a disposition which is analogous to the one we just saw on the ambo at Klosterneuburg? See vv. 22-23:

> At geminas quae sunt dextra laevaque patentes,
> Binis historiis ornat pictura fidelis,

followed by the connection of Job with Tobit, and of Judith with Esther (663C).

115. Vv. 170-175 (*PL*, 61, 666-667). Paulinus will be extensively quoted by Dungal, *Adv. Claud. Tur.* (*PL.* 105, 468-470).

129

## 4. Symbols of Harmony

There are many symbols drawn from Scripture itself in which this mystery of the two Testaments is expressed. To begin with, there are, of course, those which are exploited as such in various passages of the New Testament: in particular, there is the Pauline symbol of the veil which covered the face of Moses, the veil of the letter which formerly concealed the secret of the spirit, which is facially expressed.[1] But there are many others also. Some of them signify merely the first aspect of the mystery, or its first phase: that of the blotting out of the Old Testament as far as the letter is concerned. Thus, Zechariah, the father of John the Baptist, entered the temple "at the hour of incense," the hour when night is coming on, because, just as the sun was then setting behind the temple, so was evening falling on the Jewish religion; the day of the Law was growing dim, so as to give way to the dawn of the Gospel.[2] Or the clouds, which in the prophecy of Nahum are the dust on the feet of the Lord, represent the temporary darkness which flees at the approach of Truth.[3] The silver and the bronze are the two Testaments, for *"argentum sonat et lucet, aes sonat et non lucet"* (silver rings and also gives light, but brass merely rings and gives no light).[4] For some, a liturgical detail will have an analogous lesson to teach: if, at a pontifical Mass, two candles are lighted for the reading of the Gospel, this is done to signify that the Law and the Prophets bear witness to it; when they are extinguished after the Gospel has been read, the reason is that, once the Gospel has been proclaimed, the Law and the Prophets no longer have an object and therefore vanish.[5]

[1.] 2 Cor. 3, 12–18. Rupert of Deutz, *In Ex.*, l. 2, c. 4 (*PL*, 167, 611–612). Peter of Celle, *Sermo 87* (*PL*, 202, 903C).

[2.] Peter Chrysologus, *Sermo 86* (*PL*, 52, 443B).

[3.] Richard (?), *In Nahum*, n. 75 (*PL*, 196, 745B-D): *"umbra fugit dum redit claritas; typus transit, dum adest Veritas."*

[4.] Alan of Lille, *Distinct.* (*PL*, 210, 710A).

[5.] Sicardus of Cremona, *Mitrale*, I, 3, c. 4 (*PL*, 213, 107B-C).

But the majority of the symbols emphasize, rather, the second phase, in which the two Testaments are now but one by reason of the conversion and exaltation of the Old in the New. They show how "the flight of the darkness" is the same as "the illumination of the night."

The Gospel offers a good number of such symbols. The loaves multiplied by the Lord are broken by the Apostles to be distributed to the crowd, because the role of the Apostles is precisely to explain the Gospel, to break it, so to speak, in order to separate letter and Spirit; to open it, in order to extract from it the substance which must nourish the understanding of the faithful.[6] The two denarii of the Good Samaritan each bear the image of the eternal King, since Christ is the end of the Law.[7] The saying of Jesus about the two women grinding at the mill, one of whom would be taken and one left on the Day of the Lord, was at first applied to the Church and to the Synagogue, different interpretations, one sterile and the other fruitful, being drawn from the same Scripture.[8] But there was no stopping at that: in order to grind, is it not necessary to have two stones? These two millstones are the two Testaments, but the first is of no use unless the second is there to rub against it, and from the mill thus set up the pure flour finally comes forth. One of the homilies of Maximus of Turin [9] develops the comparison with a wealth of ingenious detail, none of which will be forgotten later on.[10] More important, and also better founded in the very intention of Scripture, are the two great symbols of the Transfiguration and the miracle at Cana. Both are explained by Origen.

6. Augustine, *Sermo 130*, n. 1 (*PL*, 38, 725). John Scotus, *In Jo.*, fr. 3 (*PL*, 122, 346A-B). Hildebert (*PL*, 171, 1278C-D.)

7. Bede, *In Luc.* (*PL*, 92, 470A). Werner, *Deflorationes SS. Patrum*, 1. 2 (*PL*, 157, 1120C-D). Victor of Pettau, *In Ap.* (Haussleiter, 24).

8. Maximus of Turin, h. 111 (*PL*, 57, 514C).

9. H. 3 (*PL*, 57, 227–230). Earlier still, Ambrose, *De paenit.*, 1. 1, c. 15, n. 82 (*PL*, 16, 491).

10. Peter Damian (*PL*, 145, 1031A, 1082C-D). Paschasius Radbertus, *In Matt.*, 1. 11 (*PL*, 120, 830D). Bruno of Segni, *In Deut.* (*PL*, 164, 529C-D). Baldwin of Canterbury, *L. de sacram. alt.* (*PL*, 204, 761–762). Or else the mill is the Cross of Christ, and the woman who is grinding is the Church; Irimbert, *In Jud.*, 1.1 (Pez, 4, 310–311).

Christ, on the mountain, is shown with Moses and Elijah in attendance, for it is always the Old Testament which bears witness to the New; the garments of Moses and Elijah are white like the garments of Jesus, for it is the glory of the New Testament which is reflected on the Old; yet when the three privileged spectators again raise their eyes, they see no one but Jesus, for the New Testament has just absorbed the Old; [11] and thus there is now no need for more than one tent, for "the Law and the Prophets are recapitulated in the Gospel." [12] St. Jerome borrowed this beautiful symbol from Origen; [13] we find it again in St. Augustine [14] and in the later course of the Latin tradition, notably in Ambrose Autpert, who spends a good deal of time on the three Apostles but still manages to say what is essential: *"Veteris ac Novi Testamenti facta concordia";* [15] in Paschasius Radbertus, who sees in the bright cloud the Holy Spirit covering with his shadow "those who, in the Gospel, were one with Christ"; [16] and better still perhaps in Hervé du Bourg-Dieu, in a homily which was for a long time attributed to St. Anselm:

And when they lifted up their eyes, they saw no one but Jesus only —that is to say, the New Testament.

Indeed, once the cloud had passed away, and Moses and Elijah had disappeared with it, only Christ remained in sight: in other words, after the shadow of the Law and the Prophets had withdrawn, the true light, derived from the radiation of the grace of the Gospel, began to shine. For when the shadow of Law and

[11.] Jerome, *In Marc.* (*An. mar.,* III).

[12.] *In Lev.,* h. 6, n. 2 (302). See *Histoire et Esprit,* 276–277; *Aspects du Bouddhisme;* ET *Aspects of Buddhism,* New York, 1953, ch. III. This is not "a substitution of Scripture for the person of Jesus," as Marguerite Harl says in her *Origène et la fonction révélatrice du Verbe incarné* (1958), p. 253. R. P. Jacques Guillet rightly emphasizes the importance of this symbol; *RSR,* 34, 292.

[13.] Jerome, *In Matt.,* l. 3, c. 17 (*PL,* 26, 122C); *In Marc.* (Morin, 350–353). See Tertullian, *Adv. Marc.,* l. 4, c. 22 (492–495). Ambrose, *In Luc.,* l. 7, n. 21 (Tissot, *SC,* 52, 16).

[14.] *Sermo 78,* nn. 2–3; *Sermo 79* (*PL,* 38, 490–491, 493); *Sermo 252,* n. 10 (1177).

[15.] *H. in transf. Dom.,* n. 14 (*PL,* 89, 1314C). Jerome, *In Marc., loc. cit.*

[16.] *In Matt.,* l. 8, c. 17 (*PL,* 120, 583–584).

prophecy, which covered the minds of men with its veil, withdraw, both are found again in the Gospel. Whereas they had been three, they become one. At the beginning, three were seen; at the end, only one is seen. The reason is that Law, prophecy, and Gospel, as long as they are observed according to the superficiality of the letter, are seen as three; but if they are thought of in their inner meaning, then they appear as one. For law and prophecy, spiritually understood, are nothing other than the doctrine of the Gospels.[17]

As for the miracle at Cana, its symbolism is as rich as it is simple. Jesus changes the water of the letter into the wine of the spirit.[18] Inheriting the Old Law, he transforms it into the grace of the Gospel.[19] *"Aquas Legales in vina Evangelica vertit virtute sua"* (His power makes of the waters of the Law the wine of the Gospel).[20] By the same activity of his omnipotence, he changes at the same time the hearts of those whom he calls to newness of life in newness of understanding,[21] and even then transforms their mortal condition by pouring upon them the

[17.] *In Matt.* XVII, h. 4, (*PL,* 163, 616A). See Wilmart, *AHDLMA,* 1927, pp. 5–29. As a result of having systematically disregarded the light of tradition, the author of a scholarly thesis finds only this meaning in this passage of the Gospel: "Jesus is related to the world of the beyond; he converses with Moses and Elijah"; then, summing up his interpretation of the scene, an interpretation which seems to him to be "absolutely evident," he takes no account whatever of Moses and Elijah.

[18.] Thus Bede, *Prov.,* A (*PL,* 40, 1091D). Ps.-Bede, *In Jo.* (*PL,* 92, 657–662). Othloh (*PL,* 146, 302B), Ps.-Maximus of Turin, h. 2 (*PL,* 57, 917D). Following Gregory, *In Ez.,* l. 1, h. 6, h. 7 (*PL,* 76, 831B-C). Earlier, Origen, *In Jo.,* l. 13, c. 62 (24–25); *In Jo.,* fr. 74 (541). Gaudentius, tr. 8 (64–66). Augustine, *In Jo.,* tr. 9 (*PL,* 36, 10–100). Thus it is not simply a question of "an ingenious Gregorian comparison" (Batiffol, *Saint Grégoire le Grand* [1928], p. 95).

[19.] Thus Odilo of Cluny, *Sermo 2* (*PL,* 142, 997C). Othloh, *De curs. spir.,* c. 10 (*PL,* 146, 212C). Godfrey of Admont (*PL,* 174, 1196C-D). Rupert of Deutz, *In Jo.* (*PL,* 169, 284–290). Collect. of Hildebert, *In Ep.,* sermo 1 and 3 (*PL,* 171, 409, 415); poems (1278B). Aelred of Rievaulx, sermo ined. 3 (Talbot, 39–46). Joachim of Flora, *Sup. 4 ev.* (Buon., 20, 128, 146).

[20.] Prose (tenth-eleventh century), *M. W.,* I, 145. *"Hic ante illius adventum—littera legalis quasi aqua potatur; . . . Nunc in vinum vertitur, —Christo conviva":* Einsiedeln (eleventh century), Blume-Bannister, 1911, 57.

[21.] Othloh, *Liber de cursu spirituali* (*PL,* 146, 213A).

germ of the glorious resurrection.[22] Of all the symbols in the Gospel, this is the one which is the most exploited, both in the literature of exegesis and in the liturgy. It makes it possible for us to take full account of the historical preparation for the coming of Jesus and also, though somewhat less impressively, of the preparation of each soul to receive him, without any risk of overemphasizing them. If we direct our attention to the replacement of the ordinary wine, which is just running out, by a better wine, we see especially the progress registered by the New Covenant over the Old, which it fulfills; *Et Nova Lex Veterem superat gustata saporem* (When it is tasted, the New Law prevails over the old flavor).[23]

If we are interested rather in the miraculous change of water into wine, we can measure still better the total newness of the work accomplished by Christ,[24] and, in line with the most rigorous criticism, we recognize the necessity of the "transference" which alone permits the allegorical interpretation of the ancient Scriptures:

The Word of God, made flesh, fulfilled the Old Testament, opened up the ancient Scriptures, changed them into wine, making them pass over in the allegorical and moral meaning.[25]

St. John's account lent itself to many another ingenious remark. Wonder is expressed, for example, at how much better are the waters of the Gospel than the wine of prophecy, since they provide delicious wine for the end of the banquet.[26] There are long-spun-out subtleties about the stone jars, their number, their contents, and about the role of the *architriclinus* and the role of the servants, all of this in accordance with classical allegorical

[22]. Ps.-Ambrose, *Sermo 8*, n. 6 (*PL*, 17, 620A).

[23]. Marbod, *Carmen 25, De Epiphania* (*PL*, 171, 1663A). Following Origen, *In Cant.*, 1. 1 (94). Hildebert (1278B).

[24]. Geoffrey Babion, *Sermo in Epiph.* (*PL*, 171, 415C). Rupert of Deutz, *In Jo.*, 1. 11 (*PL*, 169, 286C-D).

[25]. Herbert de Losinga, *Sermo in Epiph.* (G.-S., 260). Ps.-Hildebert, *s.* 13 (*PL*, 171, 409B).

[26]. Gregory of Elvira, *In Cant.* (*BLE*, 1906, 241; see 245).

procedure.[27] The mystery of Cana is related to the mystery of Bethlehem and with the mystery of the Jordan, as the liturgy suggests,[28] or with the Song of Songs, as the wedding context suggests.[29] It is even seen as prefigured in the first page of Genesis, in the transformation of primordial fire and of light first diffused in the brilliance of the sun,[30] and so forth. But, in the final analysis, as has been recognized by good exegetes in our own time, all this effort simply translates, without either falsifying it or exhausting it, the original idea which inspired St. John when he reported the miracle.[31] Jesus changing water into wine during a wedding banquet: [32] is this not the incarnate Word, come to invite mankind to the divine espousals, and, through the effects of death and resurrection, changing letter into spirit, weakness into strength, man into God? [33] "The literal meaning of [the passage of] Scripture is changed, like the water into wine, when, through spiritual understanding, it is poured on the wedding guests," [34] says Rupert. This is the idea which is summed up in a sermon of Yves of Chartres (?):

[27.] *Allegoriae* (*PL*, 112, 1078). Gerhoh of Reichersberg, *In Ps. 18* (*PL*, 193, 911A). Isaac of Stella, *Sermo 10* (*PL*, 194, 1725D). Garnier of Rochefort, *Sermo 8* (*PL*, 205, 621C-D). Bonaventure, *In Hexaem.*, col. 19, n. 8 (Quaracchi, 5, 421).

[28.] Thus Aelred of Rievaulx, *In Epiph., de trib. gen. nupt.* (sermo ined. 3; Talbot, 39–57).

[29.] Bede, *In Cant.*, l. 2, c. 1 (*PL*, 91, 1085C). Rupert of Deutz, *In Jo.*, 1. 2 (*PL*, 169, 285C-D).

[30.] Hugh, *In Gen.*, c. 6 (*PL*, 175, 35B).

[31.] M. E. Boismard, *Du Baptême à Cana*, Paris, 1956, pp. 139–140: "The wine symbolizes Scripture: when the Law and the Prophets come to eat, Christ brings a new teaching. . . . There are excellent reasons which urge acceptance of the interpretation proposed by Origen." The same explanation is to be found in C. H. Dodd and in R. H. Lightfoot.

[32.] Gregory of Elvira, *In Cant.* (*BLE*, 1906, 241–242). Rupert of Deutz (*PL*, 167, 447C); *"Verus Isaac, scilicet Dominus Jesus Christus, matrem omnium nostrum, sanctam Scripturam, secundum quam Deo renascimur, in conjugium suum, id est evangelicae praedicationis usum assumpsit"* (449A).

[33.] Adam Scotus, *Sermo 47*, c. 18 (*PL*, 198, 439–440). Garnier of Rochefort, *Sermo 9* (*PL*, 205, 633A). See Gerhoh, *Ad Petrum phil.* (*Op. in.*, I, 358). Bede, *In Job* (*PL*, 91, 932B). Hugh, *De savam.*, l. 1, P. I, c. 15 (*PL*, 176, 199A).

[34.] *In Jo.*, 1. 2 (*PL*, 169, 288A).

Mystically, the water changed into wine at the wedding signifies the following: When God united himself to human nature, and they became two in one flesh—Christ and the Church—the Law, which until then had been carnally observed, began to be understood, in the dispensation of Christ's humanity, in its spiritual meaning. And we too passed over, thanks to this union of Christ and the Church, from the future [?] and insipid life of the old man to the state of adopted sons of God.[35]

The symbols taken from the Old Testament are more numerous. The two cherubim of the Ark of the Covenant, the "cherubim of glory" of which we read in the Letter to the Hebrews,[36] are a magnificent symbol. It was natural to put them side-by-side with the two seraphim in the vision of Isaiah 6, 2. The symbolism, which was to become classic, had, however, been preceded by another. St. Jerome has a few things to tell us on this subject. According to him, Origen had had the unfortunate idea, the "impious" idea of seeing in the two seraphim the Son and the Spirit, overshadowing the invisible Father.[37] Jerome could also have said that Origen interpreted in the same way the two cherubim of the Tabernacle, and also the "two living creatures" of the Canticle of Habakkuk.[38] Let us make only the observation that Origen's exegesis had none of the "impious" and "blasphematory" character ascribed to it by Jerome and the author of the treatise *In Isaiam*, 6, 1–7, in the fury of belated polemic; and, moreover, that the assimilation of Word and Spirit (Wisdom) to cherubim and to seraphim, which stemmed from Judeo-Christian circles, was already to be found in St. Irenaeus.[39] "I changed," Jerome goes on, "this detestable

[35]. *Sermo 10* (*PL*, 162, 575B-C). Ps-Hildebert (Geoffrey Babion), *Sermo 15* (*PL*, 171, 415C).

[36]. Heb. 9, 5. Ex. 25, 17–20 and 37, 6–9.

[37]. *In Is.*, l. 3, c. 6 (*PL*, 24, 94C). See *Ep.*, 18, n. 4 (I, 75–78). *In Isaiam*, VI, 1–7 (*An. mar.*, 3, p. III, 119–121). See, on how this small treatise is related to Jerome, F. Cavallera, *Saint Jérôme*, II, 81–86.

[38]. Origen, *In Is.*, h. 1, n. 2; h. 4, n. 1 (244–245; 257–259). See *In Rom.*, l. 3, c. 8 (*PG*, 13, 948A-C). *De princ.*, l. 1, c. 3, n. 4 (52–53).

[39]. *Proof of the Apostolic Preaching* (J. P. Smith trans. and ann.), Westminster, 1952, c. 10, 53–54, 35, 146, n. See Jean Daniélou, *Théologie du judéo-christianisme*; ET *The Theology of Jewish Christianity*, Chicago, 1964, pp. 134–140. M. Th. d'Alverny, "Les anges et les jours," *Cahiers archéologiques*, 9 (1957), p. 292.

explanation into that of the two Testaments." [40] As a matter of fact, even before Jerome, "some of the Latins," as he himself points out elsewhere, had suggested this new way of understanding the symbol.[41] Gaudentius of Brescia had just repeated it. It was ultimately to prevail. St. Gregory adopts it, and brings with him the whole Latin tradition, with respect to the two cherubim of pure gold with folded wings which face one another, inside the Dwelling-place of Yahweh, at the two ends of the mercy seat, with their gaze directed towards it. After all, does not "cherubim" mean "fullness of knowledge"? Do not the two Testaments in some way border the Mediator, the one prophesying what the other shows as fulfilled? The pure gold of the two cherubim is the pure truth of the two Testaments; their extended wings are the protection against error and sin which we find in Scripture when we question it properly; they touch the two opposite sides of the tabernacle because one of the two Testaments was given to the Jews and the other found welcome among the Gentiles. Just as the two cherubim or the two seraphim are inseparable, so are the two Testaments *"semper simul pergunt, simul et docent et praedicant"* (they always walk together, teach and preach together), and if we open to them the citadels of our hearts, they together prepare for the coming of the Lord.[42] But the most meaningful feature of all is that they look at one another, *"quia utraque Testamenta in nullo a se discrepant"* (because the two Testaments differ from each other in nothing),[43]—*"quia Testamenta pari de Domino attestatione*

40. *Ep.* 84, n. 3 (4, 127–128). See *Ep. 18,* nn. 9, 14 (1, 64, 68–69).
41. *In Is.,* l. 3, c. 6, 2–3 (*PL,* 24, 95A). Gaudentius, tr. 9 (87).
42. Gregory, *In Ez.,* l. 1, h. 5, n. 15 (*PL,* 76, 835–836). Bede, *De tab.,* l. 1, c. 5 (*PL,* 91, 404–406); *De templo Sal.,* c. 13 (766–767). Rhabanus Maurus, *In Num.,* l. 1, c. 13 (*PL,* 108, 834B); *In Paral.,* l. 3, c. 3 (*PL,* 109, 429–432). Angelome of Luxeuil, *In Reg.,* 1. 3 (*PL,* 115, 428–429). *Miscell.,* 1. 7, tit. 22 (*PL,* 176, 877C-D). Godfrey of Admont, *In Script.,* h. 13 (*PL,* 174, 1115–1116). Adam Scotus, *Trip. tab.,* p. 3, c. 8, n. 153 (*PL,* 198, 759A-B). Richard, *L. except.,* p. 2. l. 3, c. 13 (Châtillon, 259). See Cassian, *Conference 14,* c. 10 (*SC,* 54, 196).
43. Gregory, *loc. cit.* Beatus, *In Ap.* (277). Isidore, *L. de variis q.,* c. 1 (1).

*consentiunt,"* [44]—*"quia idem sentiunt, consona dicunt."* [45] This mutual gaze "signifies the friendship and the harmony of the two Testaments" [46] in Christ: *"quoniam tota sacra Scriptura, tam Novi quam Veteris Testamenti, ad solum respicit Christum"* (for the whole of sacred Scripture, the New no less than the Old, is turned towards the one Christ).[47] Rupert of Deutz, commenting on the fourth gospel, sees in this particularly the intimate union of the two Johns, the Apostle and the Baptist: *"maximae tubae duorum Testamentorum: hic Joannes praecipuus evangelistarum, et ille alius Joannes maximus prophetarum"* (the two greatest trumpets of the two Testaments, the one John being the principal evangelist and the other John the greatest of the prophets).[48] Going back to the seraphim in Isaiah (which he calls cherubim, as a matter of fact), Stephen Langton will note that they "shouted to each other" the divine praise just like the two Testaments which proclaim the same truth and "contain each other." [49]

From the same book (Exodus), the waters of Marah, which Moses made sweet by throwing into them the tree which Yahweh had shown him,[50] were well fitted to signify the ancient Scripture: carnally understood, it is bitter, with a bitterness which is fatal today, and the soul cannot quench its thirst with it; in the spiritual meaning communicated to it by the tree of the Cross, it is the very sweetness of the Gospel: *"Legis amaritudo vincatur amaritudine Crucis"* (Let the bitterness of the

[44.] *Libri carolini,* 1. 1 (*PL,* 169, 1052A). Claudius of Turin, *loc. cit.* (1127B).
[45.] Rupert of Deutz, *In Jo.,* 1. 1 (*PL,* 170, 225C). *In Ex.,* l. 4, c. 6 (*PL,* 167, 702–703). *De div. off.,* l. 3, c. 15 (*PL,* 170, 74B-D). Gerhoh, *Exp. sup. canonem* (*Op. in.,* I, 13).
[46.] Bruno of Segni, h. 137 (*PL,* 165, 845A-B); h. 141 (859B-C); *In Is.* (*Sp. casin.,* III, 21). See the mosaic of Theodulf at Germigny-sur-Loire (apse, circa 810), the symbolism of which is both simple and manifold.
[47.] Godfrey of Admont, *h. dom. 15* (*PL,* 174, 108B). Richard, *Benjamin major.,* 1. 4, c. 19 (*PL,* 196, 160–161).
[48.] *In Jo.* (*PL,* 169, 225B-C).
[49.] Smalley, in *Speculum,* 6 (1931), p. 75. Hervé, *In Is.,* 1. 1 (*PL,* 181, 91C-D).
[50.] Ex. 15, 23–25.

138

Law be overcome by the bitterness of the Cross).[51] From the time of Tertullian [52] and Origen,[53] this extremely simple yet extremely striking image was repeated again and again.[54] The water of Marah become sweet is compared with the sterile and fatal waters changed by Elisha into life-giving waters.[55] Still more, it corresponds to the water of Cana changed into wine.

The Psalms offer innumerable symbols of the same great fact. As "deep calls to deep," each Testament calls to the other and the more profoundly they are understood the more they deserve the name of "deep," and the more loudly do they call.[56] *"O quam hic abyssus Veteris Testamenti abyssum invocat Novi! O quam antiquiora recentioribus concinunt!"* (Oh how the deep of the Old Testament calls to the deep of the New! Oh what harmony the ancient things make with the recent!)[57]

> *Dumque rei testis exstat, abyssus abyssum*
> *Invocat. Utraque Lex nomen abyssus habet.*[58]

[51.] Bruno of Segni, *In Ex.* (*PL,* 164, 267B). Abelard, *Inv. s. Crucis, ad Laudes:* "*Lignum amaras—Indulcat aquas—Eis immissum*" (*PL,* 178, 1797). Adam of St. Victor (?) (Gautier, 227).

[52.] *De bapt.,* c. 9, n. 2 (*SC,* 35, 78).

[53.] *In Ex.,* h. 7, n. 1 (206); n. 2 (207). *In Jer.,* h. 8 (*PL,* 25, 64–644).

[54.] Hilary, *Tr. myst.,* l. 1, cc. 33–35 (Brisson, *SC,* 19, 128–132). Ambrose, *De nupt.,* c. 3, n. 14 (*SC,* 25, 112). Ps.-Ambrose, *Sermo 19,* n. 5 (*PL,* 17, 641D). Augustine, *Q. in Hept.* (*PL,* 34, 615–616). Jerome (*PL,* 25, 468C, 817B). Quodvultdeus, *De prom.,* p. 1, c. 38, n. 55 (*PL,* 51, 765B). Maximus of Turin, h. 39 (*PL,* 57, 312–314). Gregory of Elvira. *Tr.* 15 (164). Isidore (83, 297A). Berengarius, *In Ap.,* v. 3 (*PL,* 17, 827C-D). Ps.-Hildefonsus (*PL,* 96, 173). Rhabanus Maurus, *In Ex.,* l. 2, cc. 5–6 (*PL,* 108, 76–77); *In Num,* l. 4, c. 8 (*PL,* 108, 813D). Odo of Cluny, *Occupatio,* l. 6, v. 167 (Swoboda, 124). Rupert of Deutz, *In Ex.* (*PL,* 167, 655B). See Peter of Celle, *Sermo 58* (*PL,* 202, 814B-C). Adam of St. Victor (Gautier, 253).

[55.] 2 Kgs. 3. Jerome, *In Os.,* prol. (*PL,* 25, 817B).

[56.] Jerome, *Ep. 120,* c. 1 (6, 122). Braulio, *Ep. 44* (Madoz, 203). Rhabanus Maurus, *De univ.,* l. 11, c. 6 (*PL,* 111, 314–315). John Scotus, *H. in prol. Jo.* (*PL,* 122, 291D). Haymo of Halberstadt, *In Ps. 41* (*PL,* 116, 341A). Bruno of Segni, *In Ps. 35* (*PL,* 164, 818C); *In Ps. 41* (845–846). Letbert of St. Ruf, *In Ps. 41* (*PL,* 21, 809A). Gerhoh, *In Ps. 41* (*PL,* 193, 1514B-C). Peter Lombard, *In Ps. 41* (*PL,* 191, 419D). *Répertoire cistercien* (Wilmart, *Mémorial Lagrange,* 315).

[57.] Ratherius of Verona, *Sermo 10,* n. 3 (*PL,* 136, 746, 746C). Gilbert of Holland, *In Cant.,* sermo 18, n. 4 (*PL,* 184, 94A).

[58.] Anonymous poem, v. 1198 (Leyser, 1721, 749; Glunz, 1937, 185).

As "day to day pours forth speech," thus each of the Testaments is addressed to the other, and both in this exchange equally become light;[59] in Christ they are both day, and since it is the same Christ who shines on each, they make but one light[60]: David heard two things, yet "God spoke only once," for, even if, from man's viewpoint, there were two "tenses" in revelation—"*pro captu temporis, aut nova, aut vetera*"—the more deeply we look into these two things, old and new, the more we see them coming together in a single reality.[61] Just as the skies, like a skin, are stretched across the firmament, so too the sky of Scripture, in order for the mysteries enclosed therein to be visible to the eyes of all.[62] And just as the breath of the Lord sends forth living waters, opening the closed garden and unlocking the sealed fountain, so too the Spirit which breathes at the coming of the incarnate Word opens up the garden of Scripture and causes to spring from its fountains torrents of spiritual understanding; but until this occurred, "*sacramenta Ecclesiae nondum manifestata fuerunt, spirituales intelligentiae Scripturarum nondum emanaverunt.*"[63] And again, just as the archer pulls on the cord of his bow and the rigidity of the wood or of the horn is relaxed by the tension on the cord, so too the Lord, the divine archer, pulls on the cord of the New Testament and, by that fact alone, "*a duritia litterae Vetus Testamentum inclinat, et ad intellectum spiritualem flectit.*"[64]

---

[59.] Maximus of Turin, *Sermo 65* (*PL,* 194, 664A-B). Honorius, *In Ps.* (*PL,* 194, 581B).

[60.] Jerome, *In Ps. 94* (*An. mar.,* 3, p. 2, 134–135).

[61.] Victor of Pettau, *In Ap.* (Haussleiter, 24). Ambrose, *In Ps. 61,* n. 33 (*PL,* 14, 1180). Caesarius of Arles, *Exp. in Ap.* (Morin, II, 212). Apringius, *In Ap.,* c. 4 (Vega, 25). Isidore, *L. de Variis* q., c. 1 (V.-A. 7).

[62.] Honorius, *In Ps. 103,* 2 (*PL,* 194, 622A). *In Ps. 103,* sermo 1, nn. 7–8 (*CCL,* 40, 1479). *Répertoire cistercien* (Wilmart, 317).

[63.] Absalon, *Sermo 35* (*PL,* 211, 205A). See Gregory, *Moralia,* l. 17, c. 26, n. 38 (*PL,* 76, 28A-C). Bruno of Segni, *In Ps. 73* (*PL,* 164, 982A).

[64.] Gregory, *Moralia,* l. 19, c. 30, n. 55 (*PL,* 76, 134A-B). Earlier, Augustine, *In Ps. 7,* n. 14 (*CCL,* 38, 45). Rhabanus Maurus, *In Reg.,* l. 4, c. 13 (*PL,* 109, 244A-B). Haymo of Halberstadt, *In Ps. 7* (*PL,* 116, 219A). Remigius, *In Hab.* (*PL,* 117, 192B). Manegold, *In Ps. 7* (*PL,* 93, 521B). Letbert of St. Ruf, *In Ps. 7* (*PL,* 21, 673C). Gerhoh,

*Utraque lex, arcus: cornu vetus et nova chorda;*
*Chorda rigens cornu flectit, veterisque rigorem*
*Legis. Ab historia nova flectit ad allegoriam.*[65]

Or else the two Testaments are the two ends of the bow, and the cord which, by being pulled upon, brings them together, is the sign of their harmony.[66]

Among other symbols, we see again the two-edged sword in the mouth of the Horseman of the Apocalypse; [67] and the two breasts of the spouse in the Song of Songs; [68] and the ladder of Jacob with angels ascending and descending; [69] and the animals which chew their cud and those with cloven hooves; [70] and the wheels within wheels of the chariot of Ezekiel, on which St. Gregory commented so successfully: [71]

*Et Vetus et Nova Lex intelligitur rota duplex:*
*Exterior velat, velata secunda revelat.*[72]

Then there is Jacob's well, "the well of the One who lives and the One who sees," which is the well of the knowledge of the

---

*In Ps. 7 (PL*, 193, 735B, 736D). Peter Lombard, *In Ps. 7 (PL*, 191, 117C). *Glossa, In 4 Reg. 13–14* (following Rhabanus; 113, 619D; see 855A). Serlon of Savigny (Wilmart, *Revue Mabillon*, XI, 37). Innocent III, *Sermo 13 (PL*, 217, 516B-D).

65. Ps.-Hildebert, *Locorum Scripturae moralis applicatio*, 37 (*PL*, 171, 1269C).

66. Prudentius of Troyes, *Tr. sup. aedif. Prudentii* (Pitra, 3, 424).

67. Victor of Pettau, *In Ap.* (24). Jerome, *In Ps. 148 (An. Mar.*, III, 2, 314). Augustine, *In Ps. 149*, n. 12 (*CCL*, 40, 2185–2186). Caesarius of Arles, *In Ap.* (*Opera*, II, 212).

68. Honorius, *Spec. Eccl.* (*PL*, 157, 893D). Justus of Urgel, *In Cant.* (*PL*, 67, 977C).

69. Abelard, *Sermo 28 (PL*, 178, 553A-B).

70. Bruno of Segni, *Tr. de sacram. Eccl.* (*PL*, 165, 1095A).

71. *In Ez.*, l. 1, h. 7 (*PL*, 76, 844–848). Rhabanus, *In Ez.*, 1. 2 (*PL*, 110, 526D; see 528–529). Paschasius Radbertus, *In Matt.*, 1. 11, c. 24 (*PL*, 120, 830–831). Odo of Cluny, *Occupatio*, l. 6, vv. 671–672 (138). Rupert of Deutz (*PL*, 167, 1433C). Honorius *In Cant.*, 1. 1 (*PL*, 172, 359C). Hervé (*PL*, 181, 83A). Aelred of Rievaulx, *Sermo 3, in app. Dom.* (*PL*, 193, 230B-C). Philip of Harvengt, *De somnio Nabuchodonosor* (*PL*, 203, 590C). Paschasius Radbertus, *loc. cit.*, compares the symbol of the mill.

72. Twelfth century? (Neuss, 1912, 236).

Scriptures, to which the road of the Passion of Christ leads; [73]
and the *"duo cleri"* of the Psalm, between whom there is rest
for him who reads the Bible in Christian fashion—although they
are interpreted in various ways, the same doctrinal meaning is
always arrived at; [74] and the scene of Jacob before his blind
father: *"Recognovit Isaac stolam Scripturae veteris, et ideo cog-
novit esse mutatum"* (Isaac recognized the tunic of the ancient
Scripture, and this is why he knew that it had been changed); [75]
and the two tablets of stone which had been engraved by the
finger of God, that is, by his Spirit; and the two mountains of
Zechariah; and the two Living creatures of Habakkuk; [76] and
again the two portals of the sanctuary of Ezekiel which close
over on one another, *"ut in historia spiritus habeas intelligentiam,
et in tropologia historiae veritatem"* (so that you might have in
history the understanding of the spirit, and in tropology the truth
of history).[77] The two wooden beams of which the cross is
made are visibly expressive of the *"geminata figura"* [78] of the
two Testaments, etc. Let us point out some other symbols not
taken from the Bible. Here are two numerical symbols: The
number fifteen signifies the harmony of the two Testaments, because it is the sum of seven, the characteristic number of the
Old Testament, and eight, the number which is proper to the
New; [79] more simply, the indivisible numbers signify their indivisible unity.[80] And here is a liturgical symbol: the two alpha-
bets which the bishop writes on the ground when he consecrates
a church not only indicate that Christians receive both Testaments, but also represent the dual knowledge of Scripture, or

[73.] Origen, *In Gen.,* h. 7, n. 5 (75–76). Claudius of Turin, *In Gen.,*
l. 2, on Gen. 20, 62 (*PL,* 50, 977–978). Remigius, *In Gen.* (*PL,* 131,
99A, 106C, 163A).
[74.] Letbert of St. Ruf, *In Ps. 67,* n. 14 (*PL,* 21, 914–915). Alan of
Lille, *Dist.* (*PL,* 210, 743D).
[75.] Ambrose, *De Jacob et vita,* b., l. 2, c. 2, n. 9 (*PL,* 14, 618B).
[76.] Isidore, *L. de var. q.,* c. 1 (5–6).
[77.] Rupert of Deutz, *In Ez.,* l. 2, c. 28 (*PL,* 167, 1489B-C).
[78.] Aponius, *In Cant.,* 1. 5 (102).
[79.] Augustine, *In Ps. 150,* n. 1 (*CCL,* 40, 2191). Gerhoh, *In Ps. 150*
(*PL,* 194, 995D).
[80.] Aponius, *In Cant.,* 1. 9 (174).

knowledge of the two Testaments according to the letter and according to the Spirit.[81] Cassiodorus proposes a symbol from nature: as the two eyes enhance each other's beauty and converge in a single glance, so also *"sacrorum Testamentorum pulcherrima duo volumina," "ad unum respiciunt, unum sapiunt"* (the two splendid volumes of the sacred Testaments look at a single object, and have the same unique savor).[82] St. Gregory did not look down on a cosmic symbol:

No matter what side of the North Star is showing it points to the Pleiades, which signify the New Testament, because, through everything expressed by the Old Testament, the works of the New Testament are foretold.[83]

Let us end this incomplete listing by a return to the Song of Songs: the two Testaments are the two lips of the Spouse, revealing the same secret, giving the same kiss.[84]

These symbols evidently are not all of the same calibre. Some of them are quite artificial. Many are products of the "allegorical" process at what seems to us its most childish. But whatever be their character and whatever be the name by which we designate them, we shall not confuse them with what they are intended to signify, with what is the principle of scriptural allegory itself. They are merely illustrative of it, by way of "similitudes," even if the similitudes are intended as "authentic." [85] Nor shall we confuse this scriptural allegory, integrally understood, with what is today called "typology," [86] a modern term

[81.] Bruno of Segni, *De sacr. Eccl.* (*PL,* 165, 1094D). Sicardus of Cremona, *Mitrale,* l. 1, c. 6 (*PL,* 213, 30C). See Honorius, regarding the bell-rope, *Gemma animae,* l. 1, c. 143 (*PL,* 173, 589A); *Sacramentarium,* c. 30 (763B-C). See John of Avranches, *L. de off. eccl.* (R. Delamare, 12).

[82.] *De anima,* c. 9 (*PL,* 70, 1295B).

[83.] *Moralia,* l. 29, c. 31, n. 73 (*PL,* 76, 518B-D); Garnier, l. 1, c. 10 (*PL,* 193, 48C).

[84.] Gilbert of Stanford, *In Cant.* (Leclercq, *Studia anselmiana,* 20, 227).

[85.] Rupert, *De div. off.,* l. 9, c. 6 (*PL,* 170, 250C).

[86.] See J. D. Michaelis, *Entwurf der typischen Theologie* (1763); G. Rau, *Untersuchung über die Typologie* (1784); Chr. Blasche, *Neue Aufklärung der mosaischen Typologie* (1799). Cited by Patrizi, *Inst. de*

which has had a great deal of use. Scriptural allegory provides a justification for typology, provides a foundation for it and contains it within itself. But if only the typology were to be seen, we would not have gotten to the heart of the traditional teaching on Scripture. In addition to the fact that typology, as it is usually defined,[87] does not have a foundation of its own, typology by itself says nothing about the dialectical opposition of the two Testaments nor about the conditions for their union. It does not explain the unique passage from prophecy to Gospel. Therefore, it is not sufficient to show with the proper forcefulness the work accomplished by Jesus Christ. It does not provide a fundamental explanation either of the New Testament's roots in the Old or, more importantly, of its emergence and sovereign freedom. Having assumed the task of establishing "correlationships among historical realities at different moments in sacred history," it lacks the ability to show that the New Testament is something other than a second Old Testament which, at its term, would still leave us completely within the thread of history.[88] It does not express the connection between spiritual understanding and the personal conversion and life of the Christian,[89] or the relationship between "New Testament" and "New Man,"[90] between newness of understanding and newness of

---

interpr. Bibliorum (2d ed., 1876), p. 174; see p. 165. In 1875, the author of the dissertation, De sensu spiritali, remarked, following Perrone: "Tota haec disciplina, typologiae nomen a recentioribus scriptoribus inditum habet" (Cornelius a Lapide, Opera, 20, 2).

[87.] Thus K. J. Woollcombe, Essays on Typology (1956), 39: "Typology, considered as a method of exegesis, may be defined as the establishment of historical connexions between certain events, persons or things in the Old Testament and similar events, persons or things in the New Testament."

[88.] See Alberto Vaccari, Scritti di Erudizione e di Filologia, II (1958), 352: "realtà storiche figure di realtà storiche, quello precisamente forma l'essenza delle tipologia"; "la tipologia si mantiene sempre sul terreno della storia e della realtà materiale."

[89.] See Origen, In Rom. (PG, 14, 1206C); repeated by Sedulius Scotus, In Rom., c. 11 (PL, 103, 110B). In Lev., h. 1, n. 1 (281). Ambrose, In Luc., l. 9, n. 18: "Duobus enim testamentis vulnera nostra curantur" (SC, 52, 146).

[90.] Bernard, In vig. nat. Dom., sermo 6, n. 6 (PL, 183, 112A).

spirit.[91] Neither does it retain a role for antithesis or "contrasting parallelism" which received so much emphasis in early Christian generations and was always maintained by the Church's tradition.[92] It stops the spiritual impulse at the half-way mark. Even in its best features, it still remains apart from the great Pauline inspiration which gives life to the entire doctrine.

"The old has passed away, and everything has become new! The letter yields, the Spirit prevails; the shadows fade away, the Truth enters upon the scene." [93] Here then is the era of the Spirit, which is the era of the call of the Gentiles and of the mystical espousals.[94] This is the unique καιρός, the *"dies nostrae novitatis."* [95] It is the era of the great "recapitulation" as well as of the great expectation. For us, even the Old Testament becomes a new song.[96] In the old tales and in the old laws, a new banquet has been prepared for us.[97] Having been filled with a new spirit, poured into us by the incarnate Word, we must adore God in a new way.[98] We must listen to the Spirit of truth, the life-giving Spirit, which snatches us away from the dead letter.[99] Henceforth we must live *"in novitate spiritus, non in vetustate litterae"* (in

[91.] Sedulius Scotus, *In Rom.* (*PL*, 103, 66B). Rupert of Deutz (*PL*, 168, 528B). Bernard, *In Epiph.*, sermo 2, n. 2 (*PL*, 182, 148B); *De diversis*, sermo 50, n. 2 (672D). See M. A. Dimier, *Pour la fiche Spiritus libertatis, RMAL*, 3, 56–60.

[92.] Paul employs "typological antithesis": Lucien Cerfaux, *Le Christ dans la théologie de S. Paul;* ET *Christ in the Theology of Saint Paul*, New York, 1959, pp. 190–192. See *Histoire et Esprit*, pp. 384–395. There is an example of this parallelism in the canticles of Anne, the mother of Samuel, and Mary, the mother of Jesus: see Bouyer, *The Seat of Wisdom*, p. 31.

[93.] Gregory Nazianzus, *Disc. 38* (December 25, 379), c. 2 (*PG*, 26, 313A). See Origen, *In Lev.*, h. 10, n. 3 (445). G. Durand, *Rationale*, l. 6, c. 1 (Lyons, 1551, f. 154r).

[94.] Origen, *In Gen.*, h. 6, n. 3 (68–69).

[95.] *Sermo Galterii in Pascha* (Delhaye, *RTAM*, 21, 207).

[96.] Rupert of Deutz, *In Ap.*, l. 9, c. 14 (*PL*, 169, 1092C).

[97.] Peter of Celle, *Sermo 34* (*PL*, 202, 739D); see *Sermo 20* (699–700).

[98.] See Irenaeus, *Adv. haer.*, l. 3, c. 10, n. 2, with reference to the *Benedictus* (*PG*, 7, 874A).

[99.] Didymus, *De Spiritu Sancto*, c. 39 (*PG*, 39, 1063C).

the new life of the Spirit, not under the old written code).[100]
We must receive all things "with the freedom of the Spirit," [101]
which is the freedom of the Gospel.[102] *"Non mediocris est Deus,
nec angustus"* (God is not indifferent, nor contracted)! [103] *Intelligentia spiritualis,* St. Augustine clearly defines, is *libertas
Christiana;* it is what makes the spiritual man, the new man, the
free man; [104] so let us reject, when we read Scripture, carnal
slavery, and retain the understanding which liberates us.[105] St.
Bernard says: *"Egredimini de sensu carnali ad intellectum mentis, de servitude carnali ad libertatem spiritualis intelligentiae"*
(Abandon the carnal meaning for spiritual understanding, carnal slavery for the freedom of spiritual comprehension).[106] Let
us pay attention, says his disciple, Isaac of Stella, "to the freedom of the spirit in the sacred words." [107] In remarks such as
these, there is neither confusion nor extrapolation. These are
simply faithful commentaries, we can even say literal commentaries, on texts in St. Paul, notably in Second Corinthians:
*"Cum autem conversus fuerit ad Dominum, auferetur velamen.
Dominus autem Spiritus est. Ubi autem Spiritus Domini, ibi
liberatas . . ."* (But when a man turns to the Lord the veil is
removed. Now the Lord is the Spirit, and where the Spirit of the
Lord is, there is freedom . . .).[108] Christian exegesis is an exegesis in faith, but it certainly does not entail the naïvetés which
have sometimes been imputed to it. If we take it in its totality

100. Rom. 7, 6. Irenaeus, *Demonstratio,* c. 90 (Froidevaux, *SC,* 62,
157.)

101. Odo, *Epit. Mor.,* 1. 30 (*PL,* 133, 450A).

102. Haimo of Auxerre, *In Zach.* (*PL,* 117, 233D).

103. Novatian, *De Trinitate,* c. 6 (*PL,* 3, 896A).

104. *Doctrina christiana,* l. 3, cc. 5–8, nn. 9–12 (Combès-Farges, pp.
351–357).

105. *Contra Adimantum Manichaei Discipulum,* c. 15, n. 3 (*PL,* 42,
155). Hervé, *In Gal.* (*PL,* 176, 1173C). See Bede (*PL,* 92, 270D, 594D).
Rupert, *In Ex.,* l. 1, c. 2 (*PL,* 167, 569A).

106. *In Epiph.,* sermo 2, n. 2 (*PL,* 183, 148B). See *Libri Carolini,* l. 1,
c. 19 (*PL,* 98, 1048A-B).

107. *Sermo 42* (*PL,* 194, 1830C).

108. 2 Cor. 3, 16–17; see Ex. 34, 34. Rhabanus Maurus, *In Ez.,* l. 6,
c. 10 (*PL,* 110, 640A).

rather than in its details, in its substance rather than in its refinements, it is an act of faith in the great historical Act which has never had and never will have an equal, for the Incarnation is unique. This exegesis is aware of being developed by virtue of a creative, or more precisely a transfiguring, principle, but it does not posit this principle. It merely draws from this principle the infinite consequences, by using the tools which each age offers it. It can be defined by saying, with Raoul of Argences, *"Legant ergo et intelligant ministri Novi Testamenti sacras Scripturas non ex sensu quem faciunt, sed ex sensu ex quo fiunt."* [109] This is a profound observation, which can be understood in two ways, both of them true. (Let the ministers of the New Testament read and understand the sacred Scriptures not by following a meaning which they make for themselves but by following the meaning by which they become what they are [or: by which the Scriptures become what they are].) Christian exegesis believes in Jesus Christ, who bestows this meaning on the Scriptures. It believes in Jesus Christ, who has transformed all things and renewed all things. In him the ancient Scripture is "converted"; like those who are now its ministers, it is "a new creature," *ac toto surgit gens aurea mundo.*[110]

## 5. The Meaning of the Spirit

Such is the profound meaning of the Christian distinction between the letter and the spirit. It was fixed from the very beginning, as to several definitive features, by the Apostle Paul, whose only desire in doing so was to be the witness of Christ, the exegete of his Exegesis. And the distinction is unanimously supported. It is not marked by a double line of traditions, such as marks less basic divisions or explanations. Needless to say, its meaning is grasped with varying degrees of comprehension,

[109]. *PL*, 155, 2035.
[110]. Quodvultdeus adds this quotation from Virgil, *Eclogues,* IV, 9, to those from St. Paul. *De prom.*, p. 3, c. 33, n. 34 (*PL*, 51, 831B).

and it is analyzed with various degrees of perspicacity: not all commentators on Scripture are Origens or Augustines! Quite naturally also, it is possible to differentiate what might be called two families of mentalities, each of which will prefer exploiting one of the two formulas which divide the triple from the quadruple sense. The first are more attentive to the interior principle of spiritual understanding, which is the Holy Spirit,[1] while the second give more consideration to its essential Object, which is Christ.[2] The first are pre-eminently men of the spirit, whose primary goal in Scripture is *spiritualis vitae intelligentiam*,[3] while the second are pre-eminently men of doctrine, whose primary interest is *spiritualia de Christo arcana*.[4] But what is explicit in one group is implicit in the other, and vice versa. The first do not propose to exhaust the spiritual life by cutting it off from its source, and the second do not propose to blaspheme the source by denying or neglecting its spiritual fruitfulness. All are equally aware that Christ is never recognized except through the Spirit, and also that this Spirit is always the Spirit of Christ. *Lex in Christo spiritualiter debet intelligi*.[5] All Scripture is evangelical, when contemplated, as it must be, "in the sincerity of faith," "in the Spirit of the Lord." [6]

Whether one's purpose be to denounce their eccentricity and archaic character or, more seldom, to justify them, particular attention is almost always paid to the methods of ancient exegesis. The mechanism is taken apart, and the sources are inventoried, without asking in any precise fashion why these methods have been employed; or else the variety of its contents is described, without making any effort to discover the principle

---

[1.] Ps.-Remigius, *In Ps.* (*PL*, 131, 757D). Rupert of Deutz, *In Nahum*, 1. 2 (*PL*, 168, 555B). Bernard, *In Cant.*, sermo 51, n. 2 (*PL*, 183, 1025B-C).

[2.] Jerome, *In Gal.* (*PL*, 26, 390).

[3.] Othloh, *Dial. de trib.*, c. 33 (*PL*, 146, 102A).

[4.] Ambrose Autpert, *In Ap.*, 1. 4 (484G).

[5.] Alcuin, *In Ps.* (*PL*, 100, 597A). Hilary, *Instr. Ps.*, n. 21 (17).

[6.] See Gilbert Foliot, *Fifth hom. ined.*, quoted by Charles Dumont, *Collectanea OCR*, 1957, 218.

which confers on these thousand details their real significance, the principle which is the basis and the measure of their objectivity and insures their mutual connection. For the historian, analyses of this sort do have some passing interest. They seem ultimately pointless to us, however, and they can even be seriously misleading, when they are not accompanied by another effort at understanding. The indispensable effort to which we refer must seek not to explain, by an analytical breakdown, but on the contrary to understand in all its originality the great synthetic idea which is always present in the background of this exegesis, crops out frequently in the various texts, is asserted on numerous occasions, and not infrequently is magnificently expressed.

Once they are explained, these things can appear utterly simple, even too simple. And then one is tempted, after having perhaps suspected that the ancient exegesis was made up of nothing but the bizarre, to see no more in its "principle" than the banal. The reason, of course, is that we have been living on this principle for twenty centuries. If, on the contrary, one is not content to take a less inaccurate view of it and one succeeds in "realizing" the wealth of meaning in the ancient exegesis, it is then possible that, instead of sharing the sense of wonder which gave rise to so many speculations on Scripture, one will judge their boldness to be excessive. One of the reasons for a judgment like this may be that our faith, the faith which these speculations had helped to "construct," is suffering a bit of depression. But let us return to our modest objective. Let us return to the story we undertook to tell, a simple story of a few words and a few classifications.

*Spiritualiter intelligere debemus. Post historiae veritatem, spiritualiter accipienda sunt omnia* (We must understand spiritually. After the truth of history, everything must be received spiritually).[7] After centuries of unanimity, a unanimity for which there is no end of evidence from the very first Christian

7. Jerome, *In Is. prol.* (*PL*, 24, 20B).

149

generation right down to the most recent ecclesiastical documents,[8] we are entitled to be surprised when we see a number
of contemporary authors who not only criticize certain particular aspects of a complex theory, certain methods, certain
applications, certain outgrowths, but even go so far as to reject
the very expression "spiritual meaning," to condemn it as "ambiguous"—and what expression, in what language, does not lend
itself to ambiguity?—and even to speak of it as if it were some
novelty, as if its terminology stemmed from some personal choice
or other, and even from suspect thought. And yet it was not
very long ago that there were any number of theologians who
noted that this was a common term, *"maxime omnium com-
munis ac trita";* and there were any number of theologians who
asserted that the reality of the "spiritual meaning," which had
been denied by some anti-Catholic writers, was a matter of
faith.[9]

We are also entitled to remain a little skeptical about the conviction expressed by a few exegetes that the progress made in
their particular discipline has shattered the traditional distinction in its very principle. This conviction can be explained by
the fact that such exegetes assume that the distinction is entirely
attributable to ignorance in the field of science; consequently,
they think that it cannot be excused in the ancient exegetes
except as a kind of "temporary substitute." This sort of *a priori*
thinking does not make for ready understanding.

We can recognize thoroughly the role of science, and yet predict the failure of the well-meaning efforts of some exegetes to
absorb, without destroying, the spiritual meaning by making it
a part of a so-called *"plenior"* literal meaning. "Properly understood," the *sensus plenior* would, they think, embrace everything

[8.] Leo XIII as well, in the encyclical *Providentissimus Deus:* "The
Church received this mode of interpretation from the Apostles, and she
has approved it by her example, as the liturgy clearly brings out." And
by Pius XII in many instances in the encyclical *Divino afflante spiritu.*

[9.] Thus *De sensu spirituali,* in Cornelius a Lapide, *Opera,* 21 (1875),
I and XII. See J. Ev., Gartnerus, *De arcano, S. Scripturarum sensu,* ass.
7, n. 21 (*S.d.,* seventeenth century). See Théodore de Régnon, *Études
de théologie positive sur la sainte Trinité,* III, 1, Paris, 1892, p. 146.

demanded of the spiritual meaning by the ancient tradition; it could constitute a "scientific demonstration of the harmonies of the two Testaments." This is a very generous point of view, analogous to that of certain psychologists—"depth psychologists," —who think they are able, by a method which is still "scientific" but somewhat enlarged, thanks to their "integral psychology," rediscover the total reality of the mind, which classical psychological science, based on considerations of space, had either denied or proscribed.[10] And it is a point of view which possesses a measure of truth. In its authentic bearing, the spiritual meaning really is a *sensus plenior*. It makes us see how the very prophecies which were first realized in the history of Israel *"tamen spiritualiter in Christo et Apostolis verius pleniusque complentur"* (are nevertheless fulfilled with greater truth and plenitude when they are spiritually fulfilled in Christ and the Apostles).[11] It gives to the Christian who reads Scripture *"ea quae sunt plenitudinis sentienda";*[12] introduces him "to the evangelical fullness," to the "fullness of Christ,"[13] to the "fullness of the Word" which St. Gregory distinguishes from the simple "fullness of the Book," as the object of a living understanding rather than of a dead science.[14] It is the *sensus plenus* recommended by Benedict XV in the encyclical *Spiritus Paraclitus*.[15] But we must be wary of confusing levels and methods. For, even if the examination of the texts makes this "fullness" accessible, it still is not acquired without the Gospel—and we are not talking about the Gospels consulted like historical documents, but about the Gospel as received in faith; the *sensus plenus* presupposes a transposition which is impossible or unseemly without "newness of spirit." The only *sensus plenior*

[10] For example, Charles Baudouin, *Psychanalyse du symbole religieux* (1957), pp. 12–13.

[11] Jerome, *In Jer.*, l. 6, c. 32 (*PL,* 24, 900A).

[12] See Origen, *In Jer.*, h. 21, n. 2 (*PG,* 13, 536C).

[13] Lanfranc, quoting Jerome, *In Col.,* II, 26 (*PL,* 24, 20B). Origen, *In Jo.*, l. 6, 3, 15 (Preuschen, 109).

[14] *In I Reg.,* l. 4, c. 4, n. 49 (*PL,* 79, 267–268).

[15] *"Ad plenum ex sacris libris sensum eruendum"* (*Enchiridion biblicum,* 498).

which is completely coherent in idea does not really seem, then, to be the one which a number of authors have recently sought to advance.[16] It "is situated on the level of faith." [17] It is an "essential appeal of the faith." [18] It is the meaning which the Church recognizes and which is recognized in the Church.[19] Thus spiritual understanding, which is the recognition of spiritual meaning, cannot be something purely technical or purely intellectual. No matter what suppleness of mind is brought to determining this meaning, no matter what changes are rightly envisaged in the ways leading naturally to it, the Spirit of Christ cannot be omitted. It is a gift of this Spirit. In order to receive it, it is not enough, therefore, to "press hard," to "seek"; it is

[16.] Following the example particularly of Father Pesch (1906) as to the approach itself, and of Father Fernandez (1925) for the nomenclature. See G. Courtade, "Les Ecritures ont-elles un sens 'plénier'?", in *RSR*, 37 (1950), pp. 481–499. The author refuses, we think properly, to recognize the existence of a *"plenior"* meaning which is not the spiritual meaning.

[17.] J. Coppens, *ETL*, 1958, p. 17. See R. Aubert, *La théologie catholique au milieu du XXe siècle*, p. 26; J. Renie, *Manuel d' Écriture sainte*, I, p. 189. And see the judicious remarks of Karl Rahner, S.J., *Theological Investigations*, I, Baltimore, 1961, pp. 87–89.

[18.] P. Grelot, in *Introduction à la Bible*, I, 1957, 180; ET *Introduction to the Bible*, New York, 1967. Lagrange, *R.bibl.*, 9, p. 141.

[19.] Marian theology is an example. Louis Bouyer says that "true marian theology is at once a requirement and an outcome of the entire word of God. The few passages in which Mary is mentioned by name are, as it were, the core of several great scriptural themes, which, so far from occurring as a kind of by-product of revelation, are bound up intimately with its principal teachings. These, in turn, *once they find in the Virgin of the Gospels the beginning of their development,* themselves unfold round her as their centre. The great marian tradition is simply this development. We shall see in it how the *Church,* reading the marian texts of the New Testament, came to recognize what in the Old had its bearing upon Mary as well as upon herself." *The Seat of Wisdom,* p. 1 (emphasis added). And: "What the Old Testament does is to lay down the lines of thought that must be followed in order to understand the significance of the New. At the same time, it only sketches them in provisional form, and it is not till the coming of Christ that they come together in perfect unity. Christ, then, did more than bring out with greater clarity and force what was already given in the Old dispensation. What in fact took place was that the themes previously treated underwent a transposition which was made possible only by the new factors brought in by the Gospel." (*ibid.*, p. 30).

152

also necessary to "pray," to "implore." [20] *Quisquis enim Mysteria Scripturarum sine Dei Spiritu reserare posse se aestimat plane veluti sine luminibus alienos parietes erroneus palpat* (For anyone who thinks he is able to do without the Spirit of God and yet uncover the Mysteries of the Scriptures is exactly like a man who, without a light, loses his way and has only unfamiliar walls to touch).[21]

Spiritual understanding has always been understood this way within the Church. It does not disturb the scientific efforts of the exegete, nor can it be replaced by such efforts. The "true science" of the Scriptures, in the ancient sense of the expression, does not depend *wholly* on "science" in the modern precise sense, even though it may derive much benefit from it. It is not separable from "the sight through which Christ is recognized." [22] Just as it is closely related to faith, it is also related to humility,[23] to purity of heart,[24] to perfection of life.[25] This is yet another teaching of the mystery of the Transfiguration: *"Soli illi qui mente terrena desideria transcendunt, majestatem sanctae Scripturae, quae in Domino est adimpleta, perspiciunt"* (Only those whose minds rise above earthly desires perceive the majesty of

20. L. Lallemant, *Doctrine spirituelle:* The gift of understanding "is especially necessary for rightly comprehending the sense of Holy Scripture" (ET *The Spiritual Teaching of Father Louis Lallemant,* New York, 1928, p. 136). Origen, *In Matt.,* sermo 40 (78); *In Ex.,* n. 4, n. 5 (176); *In I Cor.,* II (JTS, 9, 240); *The Philocalia of Origen* (Robinson, 67); *In Rom. (PG,* 14, 919B).

21. Guibert of Nogent, *Trop. in Os.,* 12, 4 *(PL,* 156, 402C). Jerome, *In Mich.,* l. 1, c. 10, n. 15 and *In Gal.,* v. 19; quoted by Benedict XV in the encyclical *Spiritus Paraclitus.*

22. Paschasius Radbertus, *In Lam.,* 1. 2 *(PL,* 120, 1105A).

23. Caesarius of Arles, *In Ap.,* h. 19 *(PL,* 35, 2452). Gregory, *Moralia,* l. 20, cc. 8–9, nn. 18–20 *(PL,* 76, 147–149). Peter Comestor, *Sermo 3 (PL,* 198, 1731A). See Origen, *In* Jer., fr. 1 (195). Augustine, *Confessions,* l. 3, c. 5, n. 9.

24. Lallemant, *The Spiritual Teaching of Father Louis Lallemant,* p. 136: "Holy Scripture is difficult to understand, because therein God speaks his own thoughts, which are infinitely removed from ours; but he tempers them in such wise that by purity of heart we are able to understand them." Cassian, *Coll.* 14, c. 9 *(SC,* 54, 195).

25. Jerome, *In Is. (PL,* 24, 266B).

holy Scripture, whose fulfillment is in the Lord).[26] Such a science of Scripture does indeed lead to "eternal life." [27] In its fullness it is identified with the Kingdom of Heaven. One of the great patrons of exegetical science, who cannot be suspected of despising or neglecting human effort, proclaims: *Regnum caelorum, notitia Scripturarum* (The Kingdom of Heaven is knowledge of the Scriptures).[28]

Between these two kinds of "science," there are surely many links—which several recent works have helped to define better [29] —but still there is no homogeneity. The gap which exists between them seems to us to be rather like the gap between scholastic theology and mystical theology within the faith. Mysticism can no more turn down its nose at theology than spiritual understanding can disdain the historical meaning which exegesis has established; and yet it is something other than theology, and is in no sense a natural extension of it. And like mysticism, spiritual understanding depends on an illumination which can only be given from above.[30] It is received rather than mastered or found.[31] Human effort has a role to play in it, as in every work of salvation, and each century brings to it the resources at its command, resources which each individual is invited to assimilate, indeed to bring to perfection as best he can. But this kind of effort can never furnish anything other than a better historical knowledge. To put it another way, in the perspective of our problem, human progress in exegesis consists in making us reread the texts of the "New Testament" in the ever

26. Bede, *In Marc.* 8 (*PL*, 92, 218B).
27. Haimo of Auxerre, *In II Cor.,* III (*PL*, 117, 618A-B).
28. *In Matt.* (*PL*, 26, 90A). Bede (*PL*, 92, 62D).
29. For example, L. Bouyer, *La Bible et l'Évangile;* ET *The Meaning of Sacred Scripture,* Notre Dame, 1958, ch. 22 and Appendix A. Célestin Charlier, *La lecture chrétienne de la Bible;* ET *The Christian Approach to the Bible,* Westminster, 1958. Jean Levie, *La Bible, parole humaine et message de Dieu;* ET *The Bible, Word of God in Words of Men,* New York, 1962. There are also a number of suggestions in *Histoire et Esprit.*
30. Cassian, *Coll.* 14, c. 10 (*SC,* 54, 195).
31. Rupert, *In Ez.,* l. 1, c. 18 (*PL,* 167, 1449D). Augustine, *Doctr. chr.,* l. 3, c. 37, n. 56 (Combès-Farges, 422).

more revealing light of the Old. The fruit is precious. The method is a very necessary one. And it is in this regard that we may have principally to surpass or to correct the ancient exegesis which is studied in this work. But then it is still necessary to "recapture" the Old Testament by an inverse movement and to reread it in the light of the New as given to us by the faith, and thus to lead it *"ad sensum Evangelii."* [32] This is an approach which not only leads to superior human learning, guaranteed by greater doctrinal security,[33] but also to better spiritual "edification," both for the Church as a whole and for each one of us. Thus we are no longer studying an historical document but are receiving, as addressed to ourselves, *hic et nunc,* the Word of God. This, in any event, is the dual movement which is characteristic of patristic and medieval exegesis. But it is not by perfecting or by correcting the former that we shall ever be able to do away with the latter. *Si vis intelligere, non potes nisi per Evangelium.*[34] *Sancta Scriptura, quae spiritualibus loquitur regni Dei Mysteria, saecularibus hominibus est quasi parabola* (If you want to understand, you can only do so through the Gospel. Holy Scripture, which speaks to the spiritual man of the mysteries of the Kingdom of God, is like a parable to worldly men).[35]

This is what John of Salisbury, among many others, explains when he compares some professors of his period, who were too proud of their learning and too little concerned with the spiritual life, to the eunuch of the Queen of Ethiopia:

In the chariot of the Queen of the Ethiopians, the eunuchs are reciting the Scriptures. They are reading with their eyes closed, and either do not deign to see or are unable to see him who is

32. Rhabanus Maurus, *In Mach.,* 1. 2 (PL, 109, 1243A).

33. See Romano Guardini, *Freedom, Grace, and Destiny,* New York, 1961, p. 242, n. 117: "Once the Old Testament is depreciated, the attack is switched to the New Testament, which is then treated from the standpoints of philosophy and psychology and becomes meaningless."

34. Origen, *In Ex.,* h. 7, n. 7 (213). See Leclercq, *L'amour des lettres et le désir de Dieu;* ET *The Love of Learning and the Desire for God,* New York, 1961, pp. 103, 133–134).

35. Godfrey of Admont, *h. dom. 23* (PL, 174, 154D).

"like a lamb that is led to the slaughter" (Is. 53). Surely, even though they are sitting over the wheels of Scripture and are being carried by the force of the winged animals, their tongues, when they begin to discourse of exalted subjects, lick the ground, and they do not understand the Scriptures, because the Master of learning does not open their hearts.[36]

Thus in the final analysis "it is not human wisdom which Scripture needs for the understanding of what is written, but the revelation of the Spirit, in order that we, discovering the true meaning of the things contained therein, might draw abundant profit from them." [37] It is clear that we must, with material and tools renewed, imitate as best we can the ancients who studied the Bible *"proprio sudore et ingenii subtilis sibi innati exercitio"* (in the sweat of their brow and by the exercise of the subtle spirit which was innate in them).[38] It is an illusion "to imagine that we can attain the spiritual meaning of the Old Testament by means of symbolic transpositions, by a kind of cross-word puzzle." But neither can we attain to the whole of the spiritual meaning by a purely human science, "by defined methods, those of religious history," adapted to the "grounding of proofs." [39] In our effort to escape illuminism, let us not fall into scientism. Finally, we must keep "the eyes of the inner man" [40] open, eyes which are sensitive to another light than are the eyes of the scholar. We must acquire, as Richard of St. Victor said, "the eye of the dove." [41] St. Jerome said that "we cannot succeed in understanding Scripture without the help of the Holy Spirit who inspired it." [42] *Spiritualis sensus, quem Spiritus dat Ecclesiae*

36. *Polycraticus*, l. 8, c. 17 (*PL*, 199, 784A-B). See *Ep. 284* (in 1168): Of how many professors might one say today, as was said of old to the Ethiopian eunuch, *"Putas intelligis quae legis?"* (319D).

37. Chrysostom, *In Gen.*, h. 21, n. 1 (*PG*, 53, 175).

38. Jocelyn of Furness, *Vita Walteni, ASS*, vol. I (quoted by Amédée Hallier, *Aelred de Rievaulx*, 1959).

39. See J. Guillet, "Deux aspects du sens spirituel de l'Ecriture," in *Analecta gregoriana*, 68 (1954), 303.

40. Othloh, *L. de cursu sp.*, c. 3 (*PL*, 146, 146C). Augustine, *In Ps. 111*, n. 1: *"in gratiam spiritualis intellectus extenditur"* (*CCL*, 40, 1625).

41. Richard, *In Cant.*, c. 15 (*PL*, 96, 450B-D).

42. Jerome, *Ep. 120*, q. 10 (6, 149; the Letter to the Romans is at issue); see *Ep. 53*, c. 5 (3, 14). Gregory, *In Ez.*, l. 1, h. 7, n. 17 (*PL*, 76, 848D).

(The Spiritual meaning, which the Spirit gives to the Church).[43]
*Unctione Spiritus revelante, ad intelligentiam Scripturarum animus dilatatur* (As a result of the revealing unction of the Spirit, our mind is expanded for the understanding of the Scriptures).[44]

To sum up, learning and spirituality are not in the least incompatible. Normally, they must give each other a hand, and it is obviously desirable that they be combined in the same individual. But it is not ordained by God that the most learned will inevitably be the most believing, nor the most spiritual; nor that the century which sees the greatest progress realized in scientific exegesis will, by that fact alone, be the century with the best understanding of Holy Scripture. We need, then, both men of learning, who will make us read Scripture historically, and men of the spirit—who must be "men of the Church"—to deepen our spiritual grasp of it. If the former deliver us from our ignorance, it is still only the latter who possess the gift of discernment which protects us from interpretations which are dangerous for the faith.[45] St. Augustine compares them to the hills towards whose summits the psalmist lifts up his eyes:

*Levavi oculos meos in montes. Intelligimus montes, claros quoque et magnos Ecclesiae spirituales viros. . . . Per ipsos nobis Scriptura omnis dispensata est. Prophetae sunt, evangelistae sunt, doctores boni sunt: illuc levavi oculos meos in montes, unde veniet auxilium mihi.*[46]

The informed theologian thus knows beforehand that the veil is only removed for him who consults the sacred text *"studiose ac pie."* [47] While accepting the progress achieved by science and guarding himself from eternalizing all those forms in which faith in the divinity of Scripture was expressed in the past, he forthrightly acknowledges the existence of a dual meaning, literal and

---

43. Origen, *In Lev.*, h. 5, n. 5 (343).
44. Henry of Clairvaux, *De perc. civ. Dei*, tr. 16 (*PL*, 204, 384D).
45. See Augustine, *In Ps. 103*, sermo 3, n. 5 (*CCL*, 40, 1503).
46. *In Ps. 39*, n. 6 (*CCL*, 38, 429). "I lift up my eyes to the hills.— By the hills, we understand the great and distinguished spiritual persons in the Church. . . . By them, all Scripture has been dispensed to us. They are the prophets, the evangelists, the second teachers: to these do I lift up my eyes, to these hills, whence my help shall come."
47. Augustine, *De ut. cred.*, c. 3, n. 9 (Pegon, 228).

spiritual, as an inalienable *datum* of tradition. It is part of the Christian patrimony.[48] On the condition, of course, that this duality is accepted as tradition has handed it down to us. We shall therefore be wary of describing as "spiritual" any meaning which was considered "edifying, pious, religious" as opposed to one thought "banal and vulgar." [49] This would be to accept the spiritual meaning itself in a banal sense. It is, let us repeat with the Fathers, the *New Testament* itself, with all its fecundity, being revealed to us "as the fulfillment and transfiguration of the Old." The passage from one meaning to the other, just as from one Testament to the other, thus somehow expresses "the very movement of our faith." If we are now able to reread the whole of Scripture "hearing Jesus speak in it," the reason is that "Jesus likened himself to it, after having taken from it in some way his body of flesh, and revealed all its mysterious meaning when he handed this body over on the Cross and poured out his Spirit upon the world." [50]

---

[48.] Scheeben, *Dogmatik*, n. 237. C. Passaglia, S.J., *De immac. conc.* (1854), p. 985: *"Nemo est catholicorum qui universim non probet duplicem Scripturarum sensus, immediatum et mediatum, litteralem et spiritualem, historicum et mysticum."*

[49.] *RSPT*, 1948, pp. 90–91. Père Spicq properly protests against such a usage, "since, in hermeneutics, the 'spiritual meaning' has a very precise acceptation, denoting the reality suggested by the literal meaning."

[50.] René Marlé, S.J., "Bultmann et l'Ancien Testament," *NRT*, 78, (1956), p. 483.

# 3. THE CHRISTIAN NEWNESS

## 1. The Fact of Christ

In the Christian exegesis of the Bible, the relationship of "allegory" to "history" is primarily, as we know, a relationship of "after" to "before." But, though it might be this in essence, it is not this alone. It not only makes us pass, as St. Augustine says, *"ex illis quae facta sunt usque ad ista quae fiunt"* (from past facts to present facts),[1] but also, and by the same movement, makes us pass from things *"quae sub umbra legis historialiter accidisse leguntur"* (which one reads as having occurred historically under the shadow of the Law) to those which *"spiritualiter eveniunt in populo Dei tempore gratiae"* (occur spiritually in the people of God in the age of grace).[2] Thus, it is also in the qualitative order. The "history" of the Old Testament prefigures the "grace" of the Gospel.[3] With respect to this subject, we really could speak of an "infinite qualitative difference": something which Richard of St. Victor expresses, alluding to the table of the tabernacle which was fashioned of wood and of gold, by comparing history to wood and allegory, or mystical meaning, to gold.[4] *Et tunc enim Regnum Dei intra nos est* (And then indeed is the Kingdom of God within us)[5]—the Kingdom

---

[1]. *De fide rerum*, c. 5, n. 10 (Pegon, 332).

[2]. *Gesta Inn. III* (Muratori, 2, 539, quoted by du Cange).

[3]. Peter Lombard, *In Ps. 77*: "*Mystice haec omnia, et sub historia Veteris Testamenti gratia evangelica declaretur*" (*PL*, 191, 732A).

[4]. *Nonnullae allegoriae* (*PL*, 196, 199C-D).

[5]. Rupert of Deutz, *In Ap.*, 1. 3 (*PL*, 169, 904B); *In Ez.*, 1. 2, c. 6: "*Limen exterius, littera; limen vero interius in Scriptura sacra, allegoria est; quia enim per litteram ad allegoriam tendimus, quasi a limine quod est exterius ad hoc quod est interius venimus*" (*PL*, 168, 1468A).

of God which is none other than Christ. It is absolutely necessary for us to understand this difference, *"ut ex toto appareat
profunditas sacramenti"* (so that the depth of the mystery might
be wholly apparent).[6] If we failed to recognize it, we would be
making of the allegorical meaning, which is a *spiritual* meaning,
a new literal meaning; and this would, for all practical purposes,
constitute a denial of the Christian mystery. And we would
thereby deprive ourselves of the "inner restoration" which should
be the fruit of spiritual understanding.[7] We would not be reading Moses, as we ought, *"ad intelligendam Christi gratiam."* [8]
We would not be promoting "the Synagogue" to the position of
the Church, but would again be changing Church into Synagogue.[9] By affirming only the succession and not the difference
of ages, we would be suppressing the difference, integral to the
legitimate inheritance, between "Christian people" and "Jewish
people." [10] The prophecies called "historical" (as distinguished
from messianic or eschatological prophecies) "have hardly any
success at all among contemporary exegetes"; [11] in the majority
of cases, they did not have much more success among the exegetes of the Middle Ages, but the reasons for this were not primarily critical, as they are today, but spiritual. Even so, the
temptation to degrade the object of "prophecy" or of "allegory"
to the level of extrinsic history and to keep it there is a perpetual temptation. Whether through timidity of thought, or
through flabbiness of spirit, or through a tendency towards day-

6. See Paschasius Radbertus, *In Matt.,* l. 1, c. 1 (*PL*, 120, 59A).

7. Hervé, *In Is.: "de spirituali intelligentia pinguedinem internae re-
fectionis"* (*PL*, 181, 505C).

8. Rhabanus Maurus, *In Deut.,* l. 3, c. 25 (*PL*, 108, 961C). *Libri
Carolini,* I, c. 20: *"Litteram Veteris Testamenti evangelicae gratiae
plenam esse mysteriis"* (*PL*, 98, 1052B).

9. Paschasius Radbertus, *In Matt.,* l. 1, c. 1: *"Quia nimirum Synagogam
Christus provexit in Ecclesiam, et non Ecclesiam rursus mutavit in
Synagogam"* (*PL*, 120, 54C).

10. Rhabanus Maurus, *In Ez.,* 1. 13. *"Quae omnia, non tantum juxta
historiam ad plebem priorem et legis tempora, sed etiam multo magis
secundum allegoriam ad tempus Novi Testamenti et ad populum Christianum transferri possunt"* (*PL*, 109, 847B-C).

11. Henri Crouzel, *BLE,* 1957, p. 81, n. 10.

dreaming, or sometimes through fear of seeming to "Platonize," more than one exegesis would be contaminated by it. Examples of this are to be found in every period. But on the whole the Middle Ages did not succumb to the temptation. Following the example of St. Gregory, it understood that seeking the *incarnata Dei Sapientia* (incarnate Wisdom of God) in the ancient Scripture was essentially *"sensum ad interiora reducere et . . . juxta spiritum . . . perscrutari"* (to direct the meaning towards interior things and then examine it according to the spirit).[12] It knew how "to elevate to the splendor of mystery" [13] the mystery *"ad instar solis radiis rutilans"* (which shines as do the rays of the sun).[14] Through the mystery of Christ, or, more exactly, in this very mystery, it knew how to penetrate directly to "the depths of God."

*Altum intus!* Thus Christian allegory is fulfilled.

If we were only to take account of a few words, without giving any consideration to things, Christian allegory might occasionally seem to resemble philosophical allegory, such as the ancients frequently practised it, as we have seen, in their myths and in their poems: *Latet sub fabulo mysterium altus.*[15] And yet a great deal of misunderstanding was required, a great deal of polemic spirit, and also a great deal of contempt in dealing with texts, for two things so mutually opposed to become confused during the course of the last few centuries, merely because of a few common words and a few analogous practices. Some even went so far as to suggest that a pagan exegesis and a pagan form of thought had been applied to the Bible, even though allegory was, on the contrary, the proper note of Christian thought and the form in which its unique originality was expressed. To be sure, there is no historical basis for Christian allegory, either in

---

[12] *Moralia*, l. 12, c. 4, n. 5 (*PL*, 75, 988B-D). Rhabanus Maurus, *In Ez.*, 1. 8 (*PL*, 110, 696D).

[13] Origen, *In Num.*, h. 5, n. 1 (25). Jerome, *In Gal.* (*PL*, 26, 391A). Gregory, *Moralia*, l. 21, c. 1, n. 3 (*PL*, 76, 189B). Rhabanus Maurus, *In Ex.*, l. 4, c. 1 (*PL*, 108, 376B).

[14] Bruno of Segni, *In Ex.*, c. 34 (*PL*, 164, 376B).

[15] Coluccio Salutati, *De laboribus Herc.* (v. 1400), quoted by Marcel Simon, *Hercule et le christianisme* (1955), p. 176.

the bare fact or in the significance inferred from it. The first of these two contrasts has occupied our attention elsewhere. What we want to do now is to gain more insight into the second. If Christian allegory differs from pagan allegory with respect to its basis, it differs no less from it with respect to its *term*. By the latter no less than by the former, it stabilizes history, rather than refining it or seeing it as no more than a mere "support." If it is in the final analysis a plunge into "mystery," it by no means follows that it is a "flight from history," as some have accused it of being.[16]

Let us recall the extremely expressive phrase which we read in Sallust the Philosopher: "It is not that these things ever happened!" When he set down the stories of which he made himself the exegete, Sallust "did not let himself be taken in by unbelievable fables or by absurd miracles"; he saw in them nothing but "poetic fictions," as his friend and panegyrist Julian tells us.[17] But on the other hand—and this is the aspect which interests us here—what Sallust found to be signified in these fables were also, as he said himself, "things which had occurred at no moment in time, and yet last forever." [18] In other words, they were abstract truths, outside of time; they were ideas about the world, about the soul, about divinity; they were speculations of the moral or metaphysical order. And thus Julian himself recognized in the manly attributes of Mercurius Quadratus the fullness and the fecundity of reason, or in the episodes of the myth of Attis the vicissitudes of the soul in search of the divine. Others saw in the labors of Hercules a symbol of the struggle against good and evil, and so on.[19] For a long time, it seems as if no one looked farther than vegetal or agrarian symbolism to find an interpretation for myths such as that of Adonis.[20] It was thus, Origen remarked, that the subtler minds of paganism tried to spiritualize their fables; it was thus that they dealt with their

16. See Daniel Lys, "A la recherche d'une méthode pour l'exégèse de l' Ancien Testament," *Etudes théologiques et religieuses,* 1955, pp. 28, 36.
17. Julian, *Disc.* 8, 251–252.
18. Sallustius, *Concerning the Gods and the Universe,* c. 4.
19. Examples given by Marcel Simon, *op. cit.,* pp. 33, 77.
20. Origen, *Selecta in Ez.,* c. 8 (*PG,* 13, 800A).

"mythical theology." [21] Whether it was elementary naturism or transcendent spirituality, nothing more than theories was ever involved, in any event. An eighteenth-century scholar excellently defined the essence and spirit of this pagan allegory, and possibly the conscious intention of the authors of the myths themselves, when he said about those who devoted themselves to this game: "They wrapped up in fictions almost all the secrets of theology, morality, and physical science." [22]

Now he thereby expressed the exact antithesis of Christian allegory. Here again, verbal analogy is misleading; no more can be based on it than on others, the analogy of the word *"sacramentum,"* for example,[23] or the analogy of the word *"mysticum."* [24] In Christian exegesis there is neither myth, on the one hand, nor naturalistic thought or philosophical abstraction, on the other. What is proposed here is to "introduce through figures" —the events and the laws of the Old Covenant—"to the view of Truth," which is nothing other than "the fullness of Christ." [25] In this way we really are going, at least taking a first step, from history to history—although certainly not to history alone, or at least not to the mere exterior of history.[26] We are led through a series of individual facts up to another individual Fact; a series of divine interventions, whose very reality is pregnant with mean-

21. *Ibid.* Augustine, as we know, actually reproached Varro for calling theology something which in reality was only physiology or cosmology. But his fundamental criticism, like Origen's, went much further, as we shall see. See Macrobius, *Saturn.,* l. 1, cc. 18–24: Prétextat reduces all the gods to the *Natura solis* (Eyssenhardt, 104–128).

22. Massion, *Ac. des Inscript.,* 1706 (quoted by Lombard, *L'abbé du Bos,* p. 185). He says of the ancient poets what might better be said of their interpreters.

23. Tertullian, *Adv. Marc.,* l. 1, c. 13: the lions of Mithra are the *sacramenta* of dry and burning nature (307).

24. See Augustine, *Civ Dei,* l. 10, c. 21: *"hoc mysticum significante fabula"* (PL, 41, 299).

25. See Origen, *In Jo.,* l. 6, c. 3, nn. 14–15 (109).

26. So it is not sufficient to define the contrast between Christianity and paganism at the time of Diocletian, or in any other era, by saying with F. C. Burkitt that it is "the contrast between an historical account and a philosophical account, or rather . . . between an annalistic and a systematic account" (*Church and Gnosis,* 1932, p. 127; see pp. 138, 139, 145).

ing, leads up to another kind of divine intervention, no less real, but more profound and more decisive. Everything culminates in a Great Fact, which in its unique individuality has multiple repercussions; which dominates history and is the bearer of all light as of all spiritual fecundity: *the Fact of Christ*. Just as Cassiodorus says, a little clumsily perhaps but still forcefully, this is not some theory or other, some invention of philosophy, *"quae in cordibus nostris phantastica imaginatione formatur"*; it is not simply an idea, however just, however happy and fertile: it is a reality *"quae personam habet existentem,"* a reality inserted in our history at a given moment, a reality which expands within the Church, *"Collectio fidelium sanctorum omnium, anima et cor unum, sponsa Christi, Jerusalem futuri saeculi."* [27] If then we wish, with Cicero, to call philosophy "all knowledge of those things which are best and all exercise related thereto," we can surely say that the fruit of Christian allegory is "philosophy," but on the condition that we add that it is, very precisely, "Christian philosophy," the "heavenly" or "divine" [28] philosophy, that "philosophy of Christ" which is contrasted by exegetes to pagan or secular philosophy as the principle of the only knowledge and the only exercise of "those things which are best," namely, the mystery hidden in Scripture, from which flow knowledge of Christ and life in Christ. It is "the true philosophy," the life of charity in the Trinitarian life and in the image of the Trinitarian life; [29] it is the wisdom which the "true Plato" teaches from the top of the Cross. In a more radical phrase, which is fully worthy of Origen, it is the Philosophy which Christ is himself, just as he himself is the Kingdom: *Ipsa Philosophia Christus.*[30]

[27.] *In Ps. 4* (*PL*, 70, 47C).
[28.] Adam of Perseigne, *In l. s. Bened.* (*Collectanea OCR*, 4, 1937). Adam of Bremen, *Gesta Pont. Hammab. Eccl.* (*PL*, 146, 459A). Bernard, *De consideratione*, l. 3, c. 4, n. 15 (*PL*, 182, 767A); *In Ps. qui hab.* (*PL*, 183, 206D); *Vita Bernardi*, 1. 7, c. 13, n. 19 (*PL*, 185, 423D). Peter Cantor, (*PL*, 205, 29C). Aldhelm (*PL*, 89, 133C).
[29.] William of St. Thierry, *De contemplando Deo*, c. 25 (M. M. Davy, 60).
[30.] H. Rochais, "Ipsa philosophia Christus," in *Mediaeval Studies*, 1951, pp. 244–247.

"The Old Testament is one vast prophecy whose governing principles are not at first apparent; a land of mystery in which we have to learn to discern the royal roads that lead to Christ." [31]

And yet the early apologists of the Church, especially Origen, St. Augustine, St. Gregory of Nazianzus, have frequently been reproached for inconsistency and polemic partiality and for falling into the "error of the mote and the beam" when they criticized the philosophers of paganism for an attitude which they had adopted themselves. Surprise has been expressed that so "paradoxical" a situation existed—in both instances, after all, the allegorical exegesis was the same, both as to its goal and as to its point of departure, and the Christian, basically, could only reproach the pagan—and the pagan the Christian—"for the choice of objects to be submitted to this exegesis." But in reality Christian exegesis and pagan exegesis are based on two very different distinctions which cannot overlap each other. When St. Paul, and all Christians after him, distinguish letter from spirit, or biblical history and the mystery borne by it, or figure and fulfillment, or shadow and truth, they do not in the least draw their inspiration, even indirectly, from the Platonic distinction between opinion and true knowledge, so as to contrast, as Antisthenes or Zeno had done, an exegesis κατὰ ἀληθείαν and an exegesis κατὰ δόξαν. The latter distinction, between a banal meaning, purely a matter of appearances or in no wise transcending the truth of appearances, and a profound meaning, which was alone truly real, was a familiar distinction for the Greeks, and there can be no doubt that it was responsible for an exegetical tendency among commentators on Homer. But it does not provide us with a general definition of allegory which is valid for all cases and all circumstances. It would not be found in St. Paul, either in the Letter to the Romans or in Second Corinthians, nor would it be found even in the author of the Letter to the Hebrews,[32] despite the amount of "Platonism" which can be discerned in him, nor in the cloud of witnesses who comment on

31. A. Gelin, *The Key Concepts of the Old Testament*, p. 9.
32. Rom. 5, 14; 2 Cor. 3, 13–17; Heb. 9, 6–10.

165

them or are inspired by them. It is not enough to speak here, in a vague way, about the parables and about the tendency of the Fathers of the Church "always to look, in the stories contained in the Holy Books, for a deeper meaning hidden under the literal meaning."[33] Two meanings which are added together,[34] or two meanings, the first of which, real enough in itself even though extrinsic, must make way for the other or be transformed into the other after the occurrence of a creative or transfiguring event, are not the same sort of thing as two meanings which are mutually exclusive, as are appearance and reality, or "fallacy" and truth. The appearance or "fallacy" of which the Greek mythologist speaks does not correspond to the "letter" or the "history" of the Christian exegete. And neither does the "truth" of the former correspond, even from a completely formal point of view, to the truth of the latter—to the *"ventura Veritas,"* the *"futura Veritas"* who is Jesus Christ, as prefigured in Scripture, the Word of God made man for the salvation of men. Jesus is "truth," he is "full of truth," because he has done away with "all shadow and all cloud": we have here one reality which follows upon another, replaces it and assumes it, which justifies it and makes it understood while at the same time surpassing it and superseding it.[35] Clearly then, the Christian pairings which we have been studying do not in any sense constitute the analogue, even approximate, of the Greek pairings to which we might be tempted to liken them. They are, rather, their antithesis. Their two terms are united in distinction, as are the two "Testaments" and the two "Economies": this union in distinction introduces us into a world of thought which was never suspected by the philosophers who spent their time reasoning over and polishing their myths. To sum it all up in one word, this union is one of the forms in which the *Christian Newness* appears.

In various ways, then, the very structure of the symbolism is different. Needless to say, the contrast is not brought out in all

33. Jean Seznec, *La survivance des dieux antiques* . . ., 1941, p. 79.
34. κατὰ διπλῆν ἐκδοχήν is what Chrysostom says (*PG,* 55, 209), expressing a thought which was common at the time.
35. See Origen, *In Jo.,* l. 13, c. 26 (251); *In Jo.,* fr. 9 (481); *In 1 Cor.,* fr. 17 (*JTS,* 9, 353).

its force on every page. Above and beyond a portion of the vocabulary, above and beyond grammatical usage and terminology, Christian writers, let us repeat, have more than one method in common with pagan writers. In their works of controversy, the writers of the Patristic Age, if not those of the Middle Ages, sometimes liked to bring out certain analogies which could easily mislead the hurried reader—although even then they were likely to discuss them sufficiently to make the divergences apparent.[36] Whether their purpose is to justify the Christian position as against those who attack it, or to try to win over to Christ a still-unbelieving soul, such a tactic is common to apologists of all periods.[37] The apologists of the early centuries frequently suggested relationships between the pagan myths and the basic principle of their faith. Clement of Alexandria, for example, noted that the enigmas of the Egyptians resembled those of the Hebrews in their obscurity, and that the Greeks themselves had a taste for this kind of veiled language.[38] More boldly still, he made use of the "poetic psychology" of fable to introduce his readers "into the divine dance," that is to say, to bring them to the Mystery of Christ by explaining it to them "in images familiar to them." [39] But for Clement, just as for all who believe they discern "diabolical antics" in myths, the

[36.] In "Saint Augustin et la fonction protreptique de l' allégorie," *Recherches augustiniennes,* I (1958), J. Pépin rightly points out, in relation to the *Contra Celsum,* l. 4, c. 50 (324), that Origen "is careful to distinguish radically Christian allegory from pagan allegory; the Bible includes an authentic signification which is prior to any interpretation, and this insures for it a large audience, whereas the substance of mythology is without any real existence in the literal sense"; and "this is how Augustine will evaluate the risk of the esoteric which is connected to the optional function of allegory, and how he will reconcile the privilege of subtle exegesis with universalism." In the same author's *Mythe et allégorie,* Paris, 1958, p. 460, it is brought out how Origen noted, as against Celsus, "that the author of the biblical stories was always preoccupied with the intention of giving his work a genuine literal value."

[37.] Origen, *Contra Celsum,* l. 4, c. 38 (309–310). See *Histoire et Esprit,* pp. 30–34: "Origène contre Origène."

[38.] *Protrept.,* c. 12, 119 (Mondésert, *SC,* 2, 188–189).

[39.] *Stromata,* l. 5, c. 4, nn. 19, 24 (Stählin, I, 338–341). On the Christian allegorism of Clement see, in addition to the work of Claude Mondésert, J. Moingt, *RSR,* 37 (1950), pp. 534–545.

basic Christian principle, whether taken in its prophetic foretelling or in its realization "in the fullness of time," is always
the norm; their explanations themselves negate the analogy or
the parallelism too often attributed to them.

It is quite clear that anyone who failed to recognize for himself *the Fact of Christ,* in all its individuality, would encounter
a bit of difficulty in fully understanding the impact of that great
Fact on the consciousness of those who first perceived it and
interpreted the Bible consistently with it. Even so, every historian can perceive at least something of the extraordinary surge
which it produced; and every historian can also discern, in the
biblical allegorism of the early Christian centuries, the vital role
which was played by the major datum called the "New Testament." He then can ask himself this simple question: Where can
one find, in the facts of history, or simply in the thought or
imagination of the Greek allegorists, the incursion of any "new
testament" analogous to the New Testament of the Christians,
an incursion which would in one day have startled the ancient
exegesis of the Homeric poems by startling the very being of
their exegete? Where can one find, among men like Cornutus
and others, anything which even remotely resembles the contrast
between the *decrepitude* of the letter and the *newness* of the
spirit? "Christ was struck, was put on the Cross, and in this way
he caused the springs of the New Testament to gush forth. . . .
If he had not been struck, if blood and water had not flowed
from his side, we would all be suffering still from thirst for the
Word of God," for we would still be chained to the letter of the
Old Testament. "The Sun of Justice, our Lord and Saviour,
rose up, a man appeared of whom it was written: behold him,
his name is the Daystar; and then the light of the knowledge of
God spread forth over the entire world," for the lamp of the
Law was transformed into a brilliant star.[40]

Whether their names be Irenaeus, Clement, or Origen, the
great Christian writers of these early centuries left us, in the very
exegesis which they practised, innumerable proofs of the intense
feeling of newness which stirred in Christ's faithful and made the

---

[40.] Origen, *In Ex.,* h. 4, n. 2 (253); *In Lev.,* h. 13, n. 1 (468–471).

springs of an inexhaustible gladness well up in them. Let us consider, for example, Origen. It was when he was setting forth his principles of spiritual interpretation, in the *Peri Archon* which is the most "Greek" and the most debatable of all his works, that Origen proudly proclaimed: "This wisdom of ours has nothing in common with the wisdom of this world." [41] He often vigorously denounced "the dogmas of the philosophers, erroneous and shameful dogmas," which he symbolizes by the waters of Egypt.[42] He exhorts his listeners not to desire "the deceitful nutriments of philosophy, which turn one away from the Truth." [43] He celebrates him who, in his coming and in the revelation of himself, made the walls of Jericho fall crashing down,[44] that is to say, who "destroyed the philosophical dogmas right down to their foundations." [45] Although it sometimes happened that Origen, who like all men was fallible, distorted a scriptural text to support one of his own ideas, he did not consider allegory to be a method for "transforming everything into idea." [46] Allegory was not the "intellectual alchemy" by which he sought, as certain historians have claimed, to change the vile matter of the letter of the Bible into the pure gold of science through rediscovering in the sacred writers the doctrines which the Greek philosophers were thought to have taken from them in the past.[47] His exegesis was not looking for "metaphysical truths" [48] but for traces of the living Word, personal, incarnate, life-giving. If we were not already convinced of this, surely the

41. *De princ.*, l. 4, c. 2, n. 1 (305).

42. *In Ex.*, h. 4, n. 6 (178).

43. *In Lev.*, h. 10, n. 2 (444). *In Gen.*, h. 10, n. 2: *"elatam Graecae facundiae arrogantiam"* (96).

44. *Selecta in Jer.*, 51, 3 (*PG*, 13, 599C). *In Jos.*, h. 7, n. 7 (334–335). Richard, *L. except.*, p. 2, l. 4, c. 2 (J. Châtillon, 279).

45. *In Jos.*, h. 7, n. 1 (328). *In Gen.*, h. 11, n. 2 (103; *SC*, 7, 231). *In Num.*, h. 13, n. 2 (109). See Henri Crouzel, *Origène et la philosophie*, Paris, 1953.

46. A. Vaccari, *Scritti di erudizione e di filologia*, II (1958), p. 352: Origen's allegorizing *"trasforma tutto in idee."* This can be accepted, of Origen as of all Christian spiritual exegesis, provided agreement exists on the word "idea."

47. *Ibid.*, I (1952), pp. 90–91.

48. Etienne Vacherot, *Histoire critique de l'Ecole d'Alexandrie*, I (1846), pp. 282–283.

passages which have just been quoted would suffice to assure us that this allegorist, as his long posterity has understood perfectly, had no intention of contrasting philosophy with philosophy, system with system. Against doctrines which were a-temporal and impersonal in character, employing a method which was fully appropriate to them, against human and abstract teachings, he did not set up another doctrine or another teaching whose character was the same though its content was different. He resisted the very enterprise of "philosophy" and the form of exegesis it entailed as something which was idolatrous and fallacious. What he set up against the "philosophers," just as St. Paul and all faithful followers of Christ had done, was "the Foolishness of God" which confounds their wisdom.[49] Once again, it was a Fact: *the Fact of Christ*. He showed this unique Fact, this wondrous reality, for which no analogue exists, with all that it presupposed and all that it entailed: and he everywhere discerned their foretelling in the Scriptures and their flowering in the Church. The Summit of history, the Fact of Christ presupposed history, and its radiance transfigured history. In this sense, which is critical and too often overlooked, there is no more "historical" thought than Origen's.[50] As such, it was merely expressive of the Christian reality itself, as lived by the Christian community as a whole, but reflected with particular power by this great mind (though expressed too with his particular failings, as is true of every human work). Thus it is not surprising that we find it everywhere reproduced, adapted, and expanded upon in the commentators of the great patristic era,

[49.] Origen, *In Rom.*, l. 2, c. 14 (*PG*, 14, 919–920); *In Jer.*, h. 16, n. 9 (140); h. 8, n. 7 (61–62). For C. Hanson, *Allegory and Event* (1959), there can be no doubt "that Origen, though a believing, devout and orthodox Christian, was at the same time a prince of rationalists" (224). What a strange notion! It would appear that, for this author, any Christian who makes use of philosophical reason, or does not sacrifice human freedom to predestination, or does not confound the miracles of Jesus with the prodigies of Apollonius of Tyana, must be a rationalist; in that event, there is not a Catholic theologian who is not a rationalist.

[50.] See, for example, the beautiful sixth chapter of the second book of the *Peri Archon*.

170

then in those of the Middle Ages, particularly in the West.[51] This immense diffusion cannot be explained solely by the influence, direct or indirect, of a thinker of genius. It presupposes the ever-living activity of the same reality with which each Christian generation continued to saturate its faith.

The early Christian exegetes practised "allegory," then—if we really want to get to the bottom of things—in a very different fashion than the ancient philosophers did. It is certain that they saw in it, whether rightly or wrongly, one of the requirements of their faith in Christ, as they do not cease to assure us. Thus the early Christian exegetes who criticized pagan allegorism were guilty of no "imprudence" and fell into no "contradiction." They might often practise the most immoderate imaginative interpretation of the Bible; they might boast of the benefits of allegory in terms strikingly similar to those which had been used by pagan authors, and even in thought which was not very far from the thought of pagan authors—and yet, in essence, they were not talking about the same allegory. We can see this clearly when Origen, for example, contrasts the story of Jesus with the fables of Dionysus.[52] Therefore, we should not conclude that, during those centuries, "pagans and Christians were in agreement in acknowledging the benefits procured for religious philosophy by myth"; or even that "by the admission of Christian as well as of classical antiquity," merely because of the mutual recognition of certain characteristics in common, "mythical or allegorical expression was found to be naturally adapted to the object of religious philosophy"; or, again, that pagans and Christians professed the same doctrine on "the prophetic value of myth and allegory." It is not possible to treat pagan exegesis and Christian exegesis, pagan thought and Christian thought in this way, without innumerable distinctions or limitations; nor is it possible to put them both over a common denominator which would assert the philosophical unity of mythology. It is more sound to maintain

---

[51.] Thus Rhabanus Maurus, *In Ex.,* l. 1, c. 13, following Isidore, who mirrored the thought of Origen, *In Ex.,* h. 4, n. 6 (177); see cc. 15, 21 (*PL,* 108, 35A, 37C, 45A).

[52.] *Contra Celsum,* 3, 23.

"the incontestable originality of Christian allegory" and "the novelty of Pauline allegorism," [53] whose basic principles have never been absent from the Christian consciousness. When they looked everywhere in Scripture—whatever the illusions or inadequacies of the quest—for prefigurations of everything which goes to make up Christianity, the Christian exegetes were not attempting to harmonize, as has rightly been said of many "allegorical" interpretations of Homer, "myth" with "reason," that is to say, with the knowledge, the feelings and the ideas which were current in a later period.[54] They did not wish to extract from the ancient sacred books, considered independently, an abstract science or wisdom—whether "physical," "moral," "metaphysical," or "theological." Their purpose was not to construct a "religious philosophy," in the manner of the "philosophers," with the aid of a certain kind of interpretation of biblical "myth." [55] What they wanted to construct was something else again. It was, to use a formula which first gained currency at the time of St. Gregory the Great, "the edifice of faith." Because they had a particularly keen sense of this, indissolubly linked to their faith, they wanted to show in a detailed way, with the instruments at their disposal, how all of biblical history bears witness to Christ. They also wanted to show how this history, contemplated now in the light of Christ, thanks to the *sensus Christi* of which St. Paul spoke,[56] to "the sense of Christ which no one who has not reclined on the breast of Jesus can obtain," [57] wholly takes on a Christian meaning.

[53.] J. Pépin, *Mythe et Allégorie,* Paris, 1958, pp. 478–483; but see 261. See Augustine, *Contra Faustum,* l. 12, cc. 39–41 (*PL,* 42, 275).

[54.] See Milburn, *Early Christian Interpretations of History* (1954), p. 43, on Theagenes of Rhegion and others: "their attempt to harmonize mythology with reason and to maintain old and honoured truth side by side with the ideas of a newer age." This was certainly not true of Origen. See P. Hartmann, "Origène et la théologie du martyre," *ETL,* 34, p. 824.

[55.] See Augustine, *Contra Faustum,* l. 12, c. 40 (*PL,* 42, 275–276).

[56.] Origen, *De prin.,* l. 4, c. 2, n. 3 (310–311); *Contra Celsum,* l. 5, c. 1 (2, 2). 1 Cor. 2, 16.

[57.] Origen, *In Jo.,* l. 1, c. 4 (8).

172

## 2. The Christian Dialectic

Christian thought, entirely directed as it is to showing the Fact of Christ in all its dimensions and under all its aspects, is essentially dialectical on the subject of mutual relationships of the two Testaments. It contrasts these relationships, to the point of making them contradictory, and it also unites them, to the point of blending them into one. It passes unceasingly from one point of view to another, making analogies follow upon contrasts, and is itself constituted by these processes of passage and alternation. It thus becomes important to make a closer study of the nature of this alternating movement, which can quite properly be called the Christian dialectic.

There are any number of texts in the exegesis of the ancients which set forth, sum up, or presuppose this dialectic. If we fail to perceive the orientation of these texts, we might very well view them as grossly exaggerated, or as oftentimes mutually contradictory, —exactly like the texts of St. Paul,[1] and the words of Jesus himself. Is it not true that in the Gospel "two apparently contradictory features become immediately apparent: Jesus' immense respect for the Temple; his very lively criticism of abuses and of formalism, yet above and beyond this, his constantly repeated assertion that the Temple is to be transcended, that it has had its day, that it is doomed to disappear"?[2] And we might very well accuse our exegetes of ignoring historical realities. We are inclined to be startled that St. Augustine, for example, who shows an informed sense of history in other works and refuses to judge the behavior of the Patriarchs by our standards, should, in the *Contra Faustum,* "totally lack historical perspective" and "ignore the progress of revelation."

1. "There is no point whatever in saying that Paul was not always coherent," according to a recent historian. Sedulius Scotus was more accurate, *In Rom.,* c. 3: *"Non est praetereundum quod contraria sibi scribere videtur Apostolus, . . ."* (*PL,* 103, 46A-C).

2. Congar, *The Mystery of the Temple,* p. 112.

The fact is that judgments about "Old Testament" matters differ utterly, according to the time and the situation involved. Our early authors would fully approve of Karl Barth's remark that "the Old Testament . . . as such, and in and for itself, the Old Testament of which this must be said is not a reality at all, but a Jewish abstraction." [3] In its Law, in its prophecy, in the unfolding of its facts, in the growth of its light, it constituted an "introduction" to Christianity.[4] It was Christianity's "preparation" [5] and, in some sense, "protracted childbirth." [6] When considered before the coming of Christ, it is, therefore, rich and fertile, full of development and promise, living. After the coming of Christ, *"post Evangelii veritatem,"* [7] it becomes wretched and sterile if one insists on recognizing it alone, if one persists in saying, with the Synagogue: "Just as God is one, his Testament, exactly as he gave it to Moses, is also one, and nothing in it can be changed from now until the end of the world"; [8] the living spirit of prophecy is no longer within it; it is a body to which one remains attached even after the soul has been taken from it; [9] it is dead.[10] As we look upon this cadaver, we can only say: *"Quantum distat inter nigredinem corvorum nitoremque columbarum lactearum, imo et amplius, distat inter occidentem litteram et vivificantem spiritum"* (The distance between the letter which kills and the spirit which gives life is as great as, and even greater than the distance between the blackness of ravens and the whiteness of milky doves).[11]

Thus there is a real *destitutio* about this Testament, all of

3. *Church Dogmatics*, I, II, p. 89.
4. Origen, *Contra Celsum*, l. 2, c. 4 (I, 130).
5. Primasius, *Super Ap.*, 1.2 (*PL*, 68, 835A).
6. Bede, *In Sam.*, l. 3, c. 4 (*PL*, 91, 632A).
7. Jerome, *In Is.* (*PL*, 24, 624A). There are many texts which insist on this point, thus, Rhabanus (*PL*, 108, 160B, 899B).
8. Martin of León, *Sermo 4*, c. 20 (*PL*, 208, 284D); *Sermo 2 de Nativ.* (548A).
9. Augustine, *Sermo 10*, (*PL*, 38, 94).
10. See Jerome, *In Gal.*, l. 2, c. 4 (*PL*, 26, 376C). Gilbert Foliot, *In Cant.*, c. 4: *"vetus interiit . . ."* (*PL*, 202, 1258D).
11. Rupert of Deutz, *In Cant.*, 1. 5 (*PL*, 168, 923B).

whose figurative aspects shall henceforth be merely *"vetusta via."* [12] It is now nothing but *"umbra depulsa"* [13] and its literal meaning is nothing but a "dead meaning." [14] This is one of the connotations of the epithet "old" which is applied to it; it is not only "aged," but "abrogated." *"Veniente Domino, cessavit."* [15] But for the Christian, who sees how it has been fulfilled, the Old Testament, in another sense, is preserved intact. Because the Christian is its *"intellector,"* he can go on being its *"venerator."* He understands that Jesus is its *"finis perficiens, non interficiens"* (perfecting end, rather than extirpating end).[16] This Old Testament does not remain exactly as it was, however: *"non sine immutatione,"* as St. Gregory [17] says; but, as St. Leo said, *"dum mutatur, impletur."* [18] Its glory fades away before the glory of the Gospel, or rather *in* the glory of the Gospel, just as childhood disappears to give way to maturity,[19] or as the seed gives way to the fruit in which the seed again appears. In short, the Old Testament lives on, transfigured, in the New.[20] It is now one with it, both signifying the same thing.[21] It could even be

[12.] Peter of Celle, *Sermo 36* (*PL,* 202, 742C); *Sermo 20* (699B). It was at the Last Supper that the *destitutio* was accomplished. See Heb. 8, 13.

[13.] Rupert of Deutz, *In Cant.,* 1. 1 (*PL,* 168, 851C).

[14.] Gilbert of Holland, *In Cant.,* sermo 16, n. 7 (*PL,* 184, 85D).

[15.] Alcuin, *Disp. puer.,* c. 7 (*PL,* 101, 1120D). See Heb. 7, 18.

[16.] Augustine, *Contra Adimantum,* c. 15, n. 1 (*PL,* 42, 152). *In Jo.,* tr. 55, n. 2 (*CCL,* 36, 464). See C. H. Dodd, *New Testament Studies,* Manchester, 1953, p. 129: the term "fulfilment includes denial upon one level and total reaffirmation upon a new level."

[17.] *In Ez.,* 1. 1, h. 6, n. 17 (*PL,* 76, 836D). Peter the Venerable, *Tr. c. Jud.,* c. 4 (*PL,* 171, 19, 575D).

[18.] Leo, *Sermo 58,* c. 1 (*PL,* 64, 333A). See Odo of Cluny, *Occupatio,* 1. 6, v. 7 (A. Swoboda, 119). Samuel Marochiani, *L. de Messiae adventu praeterito,* c. 19 (*PL,* 149, 357D).

[19.] Sedulius Scotus, *In II Cor.,* c. 3 (*PL,* 103, 166B).

[20.] Origen, *In Rom.,* III, II: Christ destroys the Law just as perfect glory destroys partial glory (*PG,* 14, 957B). —as he absorbs in his own glory that of Moses and Elijah. See William of St. Thierry, *Speculum fidei,* c. 1: *"Nec tamen fides et spes peribunt, sed in res suas transibunt"* (Déchanet, 50).

[21.] Bruno of Segni, *In Ap.,* 1. 2, c. 4 (*PL,* 165, 628C).

175

said that, in a certain way, the New was already in the Old—
and the more one looks at it from God's point of view, the more
true this is.

Barth also says that the Old Testament did not know the real
face of its Lord; it did not appreciate the full extent of its ignorance of it. St. Augustine said: *"Illa prophetia, quando in illa
Christus non intelligebatur, aqua erat";* and yet this was not just
any water: *"in aqua enim vinum quodammodo latet."* And the
Spaniard, Beatus: *"In lege ignis Spiritus sancti latet."* [22] As soon
as the ignorance was dispelled, as soon as the miracle of transformation was accomplished in Christ, the pretense of preserving
the prior state of reality by preserving the prior reading of the
Book becomes a doomed undertaking; in point of fact, it can be
nothing but a regression, if not a corruption. In spite of appearances, the water with which one still longs to slake his thirst is
no longer the water it once was. There is no hidden wine in it
any more. It is a water without power.[23] But it is not even pure
water any more: it is contaminated by parasitical germs. In days
gone by, it had been drinkable in its historical meaning, but now
it communicates the evils of heresy.[24] To the extent that it has
been emptied of the Spirit, the letter is defiled by idolatrous
blemishes and various superstitions.[25] If the water refuses to be
changed into wine, see how it becomes blood, exactly as occurred in the first of Egypt's plagues.[26] The Lord's vineyard
grows parched, the rod of Aaron withers, the one-time paradise
is transformed into a desert, the springtime of the Law gives
way to a winter without hope. It is a real suicide.[27] *Judaica
siccitas!* The fatal dryness of the north wind, dispelling the life-
bringing rain clouds, that is, all spiritual understanding of the

22. *In Jo.,* tr. 9, n.3 *(CCL,* 36, 91–92). Beatus, *In Ap.* (194).

23. Jerome, *In Is.,* l. 2, c. 3, n. 1 *(PL,* 24, 58A-B).

24. Bruno of Segni, *In Ap.,* 15, c. 16 *(PL,* 165, 692C-D).

25. John Scotus, *In Jo.,* fr. 1 *(PL,* 122, 304B).

26. Etherius and Beatus, *Ad Elip.,* l. 1, c. 51 *(PL,* 96, 924C).

27. Hildegarde, *L. div. operum simplicis hominis,* p. 3, vis. 10, c. 18
*(PL,* 197, 1021B-C). Gerhoh, *De invest. Antich,* c. 35 *(L. de lite,* 3,
344). See Jerome, *In Is.,* l. 1, c. 2 *(PL,* 24, 42A).

Law and the Prophets! [28] Even without any change on the outside, and under the deceitful appearance of continuity, the
*"veteranus usus"* has thus become the *"nova superstitio."* [29] Long
ago, in the middle of the desert, the Cloud had been obscure to
the Egyptians but obvious to the Hebrews; and now the Hebrews
have taken the place of the Egyptians.[30] It is, after all, one
thing to be entrusted with the *"mysterium velatum,"* but something else again to be left with nothing but the *"mysterii velamen."* [31] The Immanuel is no longer present under the letter to
which the unbelieving Jew remains attached. Hardened in his
hostile immobility, unjustly withholding the truth whose bearer
he had been, his worship of a dead letter leads him back to the
position of a pagan. *"Populus Judaeorum, amissa fide, in tor-
tuosam silvam gentilitatis est versus"* (The Jewish people, once
they had lost the faith, turned towards the twisting forest of the
gentiles).[32]

In one sense, the dialectic thus described is certainly immanent
in history. As can be seen from the texts we have quoted, a mere
sampling of all that are available, the Middle Ages were perfectly well aware of this fact—even though they explained it in
different words. There was no need for them to borrow the concept or the term "dialectic" from an outside philosophy, for
dialectic was an old Christian idea, derived from the situation
created by the Fact of Christ. It was the idea of St. Paul and the
Fathers. It is more exact to say that it was the positive evidence
in faith of a real dialectic; it was the Christian interpretation of

28. Rupert of Deutz, *In Is.,* l. 2, c. 19 (*PL,* 167, 1336D); see *In Jer.,*
c. 9 (1374A). Berengarius, *In Ap.,* vis. 3: *"siccatus est torrens"* (*PL,*
17, 835B). Absalon, *Sermo 36* (*PL,* 210, 209D).
29. See Rhabanus, *In I Mach.,* l. 1 (*PL,* 109, 1165D). Agobard, *De
jud. sup.* (*PL,* 104, 87B). Joachim of Flora, *Sup. 4 ev.,* 105: *"Noluerunt
ipsi Judaei mutari cum tempore"*; thus the spirit of truth withdrew from
them.
30. *Glossa in Ex.,* XIV, 20 (*PL,* 113, 226B). Gilbert of Holland, *In
Cant.,* sermo 5, n. 2 (*PL,* 184, 32D).
31. Bernard, *In Cantica,* sermo 73, n. 2 (*PL,* 183, 1134D).
32. Gregory, *Moralia,* l. 27, c. 28, n. 52 (*PL,* 76, 430–431). Hervé,
*In Is.,* 1.4 (*PL,* 81, 279D). See Gaston Fessard, S.J., *Libre méditation
sur un message de Pie XII* (1957), pp. 71–73.

salvation-history. Furthermore, tradition never repudiated such a dialectic, —even though we in modern times might very well have failed to appreciate its fecundity, once it was pirated by an unconnected philosophy. Again we see that Christian truth, as the Ancients said, must be taken back, after it has been purified, from its "unjust possessors." [33]

This whole line of argument was based, it is obvious, on the consideration of *Time* and *Act* as sketched out in the second chapter of this work. *Domini resurrectio tempora permutavit* (The Lord's resurrection has altered time profoundly).[34] The Christian understanding of the Scriptures does not merely take account of an historical evolution, nor does it stem simply from a changed intellectual perspective. It assumes the occurrence of a spiritual revolution and it results from a dialectical movement in which symbols are reversed. Hence the perpetual transition from continuity or succession to antithesis, and from antithesis to harmony, *"ut omnis contentio pacifica quiete finiatur"* (so that all contention might end at last in peace and quiet).[35] And hence the change of one inclusion into another: at first mysteriously contained in the Old Testament, the New in turn contains the Old, but in another way. The Old Testament is not merely annulled by the proclamation of the New, as Faustus fancied in his controversy with St. Augustine: [36] the New does not come along simply to be added on to the Old, which would have made it acceptable to certain Jews [37] and which some Jewish historians today are tempted to see as Jesus' purpose.[38] To "fulfill" the Law is not a matter of "completing" it by "adding on" to it a

33. See de Lubac, *Sur les chemins de Dieu;* ET *The Discovery of God,* New York, 1960, p. 173.

34. Hugh of Rouen, *Tr. in Hexaem.,* 1. 1 (Fr. Lecomte, *AHDLMA,* 25, 19). Paschasius Radbertus, *In Matt.,* 1. 12, c. 27 (*PL,* 120, 964B).

35. Augustine, *In Ps. 17,* n. 17 (*CCL,* 39, 880–881). Origen, *In Matt.,* t. 2 (Robinson, *The Philocalia of Origen,* c. 6).

36. In the *Contra Faustum,* 1. 15, c. 1 (*PL,* 42, 301; Monceaux, c. 21, 1).

37. See Gilbert Crispin, *Disputatio Christiani cum gentili;* Judaeus (Blumenkranz, 18; see 32–33). He relied on 1 Tim. 1, 8, *"Bona est lex."*

38. S. W. Baron, *A Social and Religious History of the Jews,* II, New York, 1952, p. 67: "The probable Aramaic original, preserved in the Talmud, 'I am come not to detract from the Law of Moses, but to add to it,' has an even more authentic ring."

certain number of new precepts or new teachings, which is the
way it has been viewed even within Christianity by theoreticians
who had lost their awareness of one of the essential notes of early
Christian thought.[39] Each of these viewpoints undoubtedly has
some truth of its own, but only superficially. In the eyes of the
Christian, the two Testaments sometimes seem to be opposed to
one another in absolutely categorical contrast, but sometimes
they seem to be identified with one another. It sometimes seems
that Moses, the "Moses of the Ancients," is, for the Christian,
nothing but an antithesis and that the Law of Moses is but a
foil; [40] and yet, through this very Law of Moses, he sometimes
hears God speaking to him *"os ad os."* [41] These two assertions
are unquestionably real; there is a central point of vision which
brings them together, but each, if viewed in isolation from the
other, becomes deceptive.

Indeed, more than one historian has been deceived. They
sometimes thought they detected a stale smell of Manicheism in
the first assertion, and in the second an uncalled-for exaggeration of the role of the Old Testament through a neglect of the
differences in favor of the resemblances; and in both a tendency
to "suppress history." When both were discovered in a single
author, they were tempted to conclude either that the author was
contradicting himself or that he had been led to make "concessions" to the thesis which he had combatted, and they then were
surprised to find him so close to modern historical viewpoints
after having at first seen him so very far removed from them.[42]

[39.] One example might be Abelard, who was in favor of another
logic, *Problemata Heloissae,* p. 15, sol.:*"Ad moralia itaque tantum
legis praecepta referendum est quod Dominus ait . . ."* (*PL,* 178, 703AC);
the passage is characteristic of a change in ways of thinking. See also the
Abelardian commentary *In Hebr.;* "[Lex] *ut Apostolus dicit nihil ad
perfectum perduxit; cui quod deerat doctrina Christi perfecta et
praedicatio superaddidit"* (Landgraf, 661). Also, *Dial. inter Philosophum,
Judaeum et Christianum* (*PL,* 205, 241C).
[40.] St. Avitus, *Sermo 20: "Quid mihi laudet antiquus Moysen suum,
. . ."* (*MGH, A. Ant.,* 6, 134).
[41.] Origen, *In Num.,* h. 7, n. 2: *"Nunc enim os ad os loquitur per
legem Deus"* (39).
[42.] Thus, C. Hanson, *Allegory and Event* (1959), with respect to
Origen: "the reader is constantly tempted to conclude that for him
there is no fundamental distinction between the revelation given in the

The reason for this is that they did not take account of the dialectical movement which, starting with history, gives rise to both assertions and alone makes it possible to understand their relationship. Again we must make it clear that this movement took place within the fabric of historical reality before it was recorded in the mind of the believer. We should note, in the language of traditional exegesis, the perpetual recurrence of such frequently underestimated words as *prius, antea, tunc, olim,* on the one hand, and, on the other, *postea, modo, nunc, jam nunc,* as well as of the conjunctions which indicate distance or explain the transition from the first to the second, such as *quamdiu, donec.* Under divine action, Time first did its work. But, on the critical Day, the seed did not get removed from its wrapping all by itself; the pure essence of the victim was not released without the iron of the Sacrificer. And neither did the believer become unbelieving nor the religious man superstitious by the sole action of time or reflection. Everything was altered, and everything renewed, *quia ille Homo novus venit.*[43] In a single καίρος, the Act of Christ effected the transition. He traced out the line which separated time. He separated and he united. The Cross of Christ, with its double beam, changed all the symbols. We might call it the pivot of the Christian dialectic.

No matter how fair, how positive, no matter how eminently real the principle was, we should admit that the Christian dialectic, as commonly expressed, was very much tainted by the polemic spirit. This had been true since the days of St. Paul. We should also admit that it ran the risk, if not of losing sight of the permanent, although still incomplete, values of the Old Testament, then at least of occasioning the neglect of them. More-

---

Old Testament and that given in the New" (202); "On several occasions Origen makes a distinction between the gospel and the law" (210–211); "The consequence of these concessions is that Origen very occasionally speaks of the Bible in terms not very different from those which a modern exegete, . . ." (212–213). And with regard to Augustine, Paul Cantaloup, *L'harmonie des deux Testaments dans le Contra Faustum* (1955): "The idea of Revelation is divided in two, the Old Testament and the New Testament" (pp. 125–126); "As he sees it, the message of the Old Testament already contained the further perfections introduced by Christ" (p. 177).

over, it became ever more subtly, sometimes too subtly, refined but at the same time rigidified as it became necessary to reply, by turning it back on them, to the dual reproach of "eccentric" and "pagan" made by the Jews to those who were faithful to Christ. Even after ten or twelve centuries, the Christian dialectic remained contentious. The reason for this was that it did not proceed solely from a calm and vaguely retrospective reflection on the crisis in which it had originated. The problem which had to be resolved by it was somehow a permanent one, and was rediscovered by every generation; the accident of a new controversy or of a disciplinary problem could always bring it completely out in the open again.[44] This was not only a problem *for* the Church, but also a problem *in* the Church. Christianity had always had to define itself in relation to the faith of Israel, and it was constantly surrounded by and confronted with the witnesses to that faith. The Jewish objection found some favor with the common man, and the Jewish mentality found no less favor, perhaps, with theologians and churchmen whenever allegory lost for them some of its quality of spiritual understanding and became narrowed down, externalized, and hardened into pure typology. Then the dominant concern for harmonizing the two Covenants reduced sensitivity "to the unconditional newness of what had occurred," perception of the great metamorphosis became blurred in the erection of a parallelism, and "shadow" received a protracted firmness which no longer yielded completely to "truth." [45] The books of Joshua and Judges could very easily become manuals for the holy war; the kings had to be, literally, new Davids or new Josiahs; even the priesthood had to take up the sword, etc. The spirit of the Old Testament was being reborn. This was a permanent temptation, yet it must not be thought that there was any lack of minds who were on guard against it.[46]

---

[43.] Augustine, *In Jo.*, tr. 30, n. 7 (*CCL*, 36, 293). Origen, *In Lev.*, h. 10, n. 2; h. 16, n. 7 (445, 506).

[44.] Gregory, *Ep.*, 1. 13, 1 (*PL*, 77, 1253–1254). See H. Lietzmann, *Geschichte der alten Kirche*, I, 219.

[45.] Chenu, *La Théologie au douzième siècle*, 219, 213.

[46.] Thus Gerhoh, *De invest. Antichristi*, c. 39: "*Quod pro illius temporis ratione in sacerdotibus Domini non solum inculpabile, sed et laudabile fuit, vid. in gladio percutere, in Christianismi sacerdotio culpa*

It is a temptation which, in various guises, is ever present; we can see its effects a good deal closer to our own times in a number of pages from the *Politique tirée de l'Ecriture sainte,* and perhaps, even closer to us, in several experts of the recent "biblical movement." [47] It means that men have forgotten the cardinal truth that the reason why Christianity is a "Judaism fulfilled" is that Christianity is, at the same time, a "Judaism transfigured." [48]

## 3. *"The Abridged* Word"

Jesus Christ, the end of the Old Law, bestowed unity upon that Law in advance. Age after age, everything in the Law was converging upon him. It was he who long since had constituted, from the material multiplicity of "the whole body of Scripture," "the single Word of God." Rupert of Deutz suggests that Moses and the Prophets wove the tapestry of Holy Scripture solely through conceiving Christ in their hearts by the action of the prophetic spirit and then bringing him forth from their mouths.[1] The *Word* made flesh, he is the new Ezra who, once for all, preserves the Holy Books from loss during the Babylonian diaspora and makes them new again by gathering them together.[2] In him, the *"verba multa"* of the biblical writers be-

---

*etiam sacerdotii peremptoria carere non arbitror"* (*L. de lite,* 3, 347). See Bonizo of Sutri, *Ad amicum,* 1. 9: *"Si licet Christiano armis pro veritate certare"* (Jaffe, 2, 686), and the declaration of Anselm of Liege (*ob.* after 1056). *Gesta episc. leod.,* 1. 2, cc. 7, 64 (*MGH, Scr.,* 7, 194, 228).

[47]. For the ninth century, see E. Delaruelle, "Charlemagne et l'Eglise," *RHEF,* 39 (1953), pp. 165–199, which seems, though, to force things a bit; for the eleventh and twelfth centuries, G. Funkestein, *Das Alte Testament im Kampf von regnum und sacerdotium* (1928; see *BTAM,* 4, 728).

[48]. See Stanislas Fumet, *Devant la question juive. Le retour d'Israel,* May 15, 1928, pp. 10–11. Newman, *A Grammar of Assent* (Harrold ed.), New York, 1947, pp. 332–333.

[1]. Rupert of Deutz, *De S. Spiritu,* 1. 1, c. 6 (*PL,* 167, 1575–1576). *In Reg.,* 1. 3, c. 14 (1157C).

[2]. Rupert, *De vict. Verbi,* 1. 7, c. 32 (*PL,* 169, 1380A).

came the *"Verbum unum"*[3] forever. But, without him, the bond becomes undone—once again, the Word of God is fragmented into "human words"; multiple words, not in number only, but also in essence, and lacking all possible unity. Just as Hugh of St. Victor asserts, *"multi sunt sermones hominis, quia cor hominis unum non est"* (the words of man are many, because there is no unity in man's heart).[4] The unbelieving Jew, whose *perfidia* is a faith without consistency, a faith turned around, is therefore left with nothing but a Law which is going to pieces, a dusty collection of memories and "superstitious" rites. The Christian, in contrast, possesses unity in its very principle. For him, the *Word* made flesh is the *Verbum abbreviatum.* He understands the wonder of which the Prophet sang: *"Verbum abbreviatum fecit Deus super terram."*

In the Bible, under the figures and enigmas which foretold him, this *Word,* who in himself is one, who is the very Son of God, still revealed himself only as "many and various." On the lips of countless "holy men," he was still "dilated" and, as it were, stretched out.[5] The *"verbum sacrae paginae"* could still be nothing more than an earnest pledge of God's mildness towards men,[6] for it still rang out in a hundred different ways, all of them incomplete, through the hearts and mouths of many holy men. It was indeed *"aut declamatorie praedicatum, aut figuraliter significatum, aut imaginarie somniatum";* sometimes spoken, sometimes effected, its appearance was always transitory and parcelled out.[7] *"Plane multa sunt, verba digesta calamo prophetarum"* (The words set down by the Prophets' pens are extremely numerous).[8] When we think back on this ancient era,

[3.] Rupert, *In Jo.,* 1. 7 (*PL,* 169, 494D). Jerome, *In Eccl.,* XII, 16–17 (*PL,* 23, 1113–1115). See Augustine, *In Jo.,* tr. 28, n. 9 (*CCL,* 36, 282–283).

[4.] *In Eccl.,* h. 13 (*PL,* 175, 204D); h. 17 (237D).

[5.] Origen, *In Gen.,* h. 14, n. 1 (121). Augustine, *In Ps. 103,* sermo 4, n. 1 (*CCL,* 40, 1521).

[6.] Peter Cantor, *Verb. abbr.,* c. 1; and School of Peter Cantor (Landgraf, *Gregorianum,* 1940, pp. 50–51).

[7.] Bernard, *Super missus est,* h. 4, n. 11 (*PL,* 183, 86B-C). Augustine (n. 57).

[8.] Rupert, *De S. Spiritu,* l. 1, c. 6 (*PL,* 167, 1575D).

we can only say: *"Semel locutus est Deus, et plura audita sunt"* (God spoke but one word, yet many were heard).[9] This was the era of the Old Testament. But the new age has come: *"Judaeo ista dicta sunt, et Christianus audivit"* (These things were said to the Jew, and it is the Christian who heard them).[10] The words of revelation discover their unity when they receive their definitive meaning in the Spirit. Just as the Word eternally pronounced is in reality one, so too now is its hearing by men, for time and eternity have been brought together in the *Word* made flesh.

Here then is the one *Word.* Here he is among us, "coming forth from Zion," [11] after having taken flesh in the Virgin's womb: *"Omnem Scripturae universitatem, omne verbum suum Deus in utero Virginis coadunavit"* (The whole universe of Scripture, the whole of his word, have been brought together by God in the womb of the Virgin).[12] "Behold the *Word* opened before us. Behold the *Word* unfolded before us and we can read in him as in an open book." [13] Everything contained in the Law and in the Prophets is summed up substantially in him, and in him for the first time takes on all its meaning. For it really is this same *Word,* today brought forth by the Virgin, who had been brought forth by the Prophets long ago. It was under another form then, but under the action of the very same Spirit.[14] The Word of God was really sent forth to Mary, and it was always the very Word of whom the apostle John says in the prologue to his gospel: *"In principio erat Verbum."* For God has only one *Word,*[15] his only Son: *"Eloquium Dei, Verbum Dei; Verbum Dei, Filius*

9. Ambrose, *In Ps. 61,* nn. 33–34 (*PL,* 14, 1180B-C).

10. Ambrose, *In Ps. 118,* sermo 13, n. 6 (*PL,* 15, 1382).

11. Oration for Advent, *Or. vis.,* 21: *"Lex tua verbumque, Deus Pater, de Sion prodiens, . . . ."*

12. Sacramentary of Lyons, eleventh-century, Feast of the Annunciation: *"Deus qui hodierna die Verbum tuum beatae Mariae virginis alvo coadunare voluisti."* Rupert, *In Is.,* l. 2, c. 31 (*PL,* 167, 1362B-D).

13. Paul Claudel, *Un poète regarde la croix;* ET *A Poet Before the Cross,* Chicago, 1958, p. 54.

14. Rupert, *De S. Spiritu,* l. 1, c. 8 (*PL,* 167, 1577C-D). Arno of Reichersberg, *Apol.* (Weichert, 90). See Bernard, *De circumcisione,* sermo 1, n. 3 (*PL,* 183, 133D).

15. Origen, *In Jo.* (52); *In Jo.,* fr. 20 (486); *In Jer.,* h. 9, n. 1 (64). Haimo of Auxerre, *In Os.* (*PL,* 117, 11A).

*Dei."* [16] In each instance, this is so completely the same Word that the play between them is known, in the language of theology, as "communication of idioms." [17] Under each form, there is in reality the very same mysterious being, the very same divine nourishment, which deserves the name of "manna"; "questioning, or rather wondering, name," a name which thereby denotes its singular effectiveness as well as its unprecedented novelty.[18] Behold it now, total, unique, in its visible unity. Abridged *Word*, "concentrated" *Word*, not only in the primary sense that he who in himself is immense and incomprehensible, he who within the Father is infinite, is enclosed in the Virgin's womb or is reduced to the proportions of a little baby in the stable at Bethlehem, as St. Bernard [19] and his disciples loved to repeat,[20] as M. Olier repeated in a hymn for the Office of the Interior Life of Mary,[21] and as Père Teilhard de Chardin [22] repeated only yesterday; but also, and simultaneously, in the sense that the wealth of material

[16.] Adam of Perseigne, *Fragmenta mariana* (*PL*, 211, 750D).

[17.] Helinandus, *Sermo 4* (*PL*, 212, 513A). See Rhabanus Maurus (*PL*, 108, 248).

[18.] Helinandus, *Sermo 3* (*PL.,* 212, 502B-C).

[19.] Bernard, *In vig. nat.*, sermo 1, n. 1 (*PL*, 183, 87B). *In nat. Dom.*, sermo 1, n. 1 (115B). *In circumcisione*, sermo 1, n. 1 (131D). *In annuniatione*, sermo 3, n. 8: *"excelsus, humiliatus; immensus, abbreviatus"* (396D). V. Lossky, "Etudes sur la terminologie de Saint Bernard," in *Bulletin du Cange*, 17 (1934), pp. 87–90, does a good job of setting forth this meaning of *"abbreviare, abbreviatus"* in Bernard; contrary to his opinion, though, this is not "a new meaning."

[20.] Guerric of Igny, *De nativitate*, sermo 5, n. 1 (*PL*, 185, 43B-D). Earlier, Etherius and Beatus, *Ad Elip.*, l. 1, c. 37: *"Judaei et haeretici, qui Verbum abbreviatum id est hominem factum non credunt esse Filium Dei"* (*PL*, 96, 914D). Absalon, *Sermo 15* (*PL*, 211, 94B).

[21.] *"Christi Mater, Patris Verbum—Verbo carnem efficit—Fitque Verbum breviatum—Et si sensus deficit,—Ad Filium sic formandum—Matris fides sufficit," Vie intérieure* . . . , Rome, 1866, 2, p. 430.

[22.] *The Divine Milieu*, New York, 1960: "When the time had come when God resolved to realise His Incarnation before our eyes. He had first of all to raise up in the world a virtue capable of drawing Him as far as ourselves. He needed a mother who would engender Him in the human sphere. What did he do? He created the Virgin Mary, that is to say He called forth on earth a purity so great that, within this transparency, He would concentrate Himself to the point of appearing as a child" (p. 114).

in Scriptures spread out through centuries of Awaiting is all gathered together *to be accomplished,* that is to say, to be unified, completed, illuminated, and transcended in him. *Semel locutus est Deus:* God utters only one word, not only in himself, in his changeless eternity, in the immobile act in which he begets his *Word,* as St. Augustine pointed out, but also, as St. Ambrose had already taught, in time, and among men, in the act in which he sends his *Word* to dwell on our earth. *"Semel locutus est Deus, quando locutus in Filio est"* (God uttered only one word, when he spoke in his Son): for it is he who bestows meaning on all the words which foretold him, and everything is heard in him and in him alone: *"et audita sunt etiam illa quae ante audita non erant ab iis quibus locutus fuerat per Prophetas"* (And then were heard even words which had not been heard before by those to whom he had spoken through the Prophets).[23]

*Word,* then, doubly abridged, since at the moment of his incarnation, "he recapitulated in himself the long unfolding of human history, and offered us salvation, condensed in himself." [24] Double abbreviation, of a *Word* who is neither mutilated nor diminished thereby. Double abbreviation, that of time and that of eternity, which come together so as to make only one, just as time and eternity come indissolubly together in this abridged *Word.* Double recapitulation, that of the Word eternally uttered within the Father and that of the Word addressed to men down the course of centuries, the first to allow the second, and the second no less to reveal the first, so that we can and must say, in two interconnected senses: *"Verbum abbreviatum de Verbo abbreviato audivimus"* (We have heard an abridged word coming forth from the abridged *Word*).[25] Double abbreviation, double recapitulation, but always of a unique *Word,* since God has but one *Word* within himself and holds out but one Word,

---

[23.] Augustine, *In Ps. 61,* n. 18 (*CCL,* 39, 786). Ambrose, *In Ps.* 61, n. 33 (*PL,* 14, 1180C). Rupert (n. 84). For the contrast with an apparently parallel theme in Buddhism, see *Aspects of Buddhism,* pp. 121–123, 178–179.

[24.] Irenaeus, *Adv. Haer.,* l. 3, c. 18, n. 1 (*PG,* 7, 832B).

[25.] Garnier of Rochefort, *de nat. Dom.,* sermo 5 (*PL,* 205, 599C).

—which is never any word other than this *Word,* this same in-carnate *Word;* this is so true that we can and must say, in two interrelated senses: *Semel locutus est Deus, quia unum genuit Verbum* (God spoke only once, because he begot only one *Word*).[26] This is a double marvel, which nonetheless is single for us forever, since made manifest in a single moment in the mystery of Christmas:

O brethren, if we gaze piously and diligently on this *Word* which the Lord has made today and has shown forth unto us, what great things might we learn of him, and with what ease! For it is an abridged Word, but in such wise that there is found consummated in it every word of salvation, because he is himself the *Word* who consummates and abridges in justice (Is. 10, 23). . . . But how can we be surprised that the *Word* of God should have abridged for us all his words, when we see that he willed to abridge and in some sense to diminish himself, to the extent that, beginning from his incomprehensible immensity, he somehow shut himself up in the narrow confines of a womb, and, though he contains the world, let himself be contained in a manger? [27]

Yes, this is an abridged *Word,* "greatly abridged"—*"brevissi-mum"* [28]—but substantial, par excellence. An abridged *Word,* but greater than what it abridges. Unity of fullness. Concentration of light. The incarnation of the *Word* is the opening of the Book, whose extrinsic multiplicity will facilitate the perception of the unique "marrow," the marrow on which the faithful will be nourished.[29] See how, by Mary's *Fiat* in response to the angel's announcement, the Word, which until then had merely been "audible to the ears," became "capable of being seen by the eyes, touched by the hands, carried on one's shoulders." [30]

26. Bernard, *De diversis,* sermo 73 (*PL,* 183, 695B). See *In Cantica,* sermo 5, n. 1 (554B-C). Bede, *In Cantica* (*PL,* 91, 1119C).
27. Guerric of Igny, *In nat. Dom.,* sermo 3, n. 3 (*PL,* 185, 44C-D). See *In Purificatione,* sermo 2, n. 5 (70D).
28. Absalon, *Sermo 22* (*PL,* 211, 130C). Here, as in the works of Etherius and Bernard, Jesus is the abridged *Word* as related no longer to Scripture but to his status as eternal *Word.*
29. Rupert, *In Jo.,* 1. 6 (*PL,* 169, 441D; see 444C-D).
30. Bernard, *Super Missus est,* h. 4, n. 11 (*PL,* 183, 86B).

And even more, capable of "being eaten."[31] None of the ancient truths has perished, nor any of the ancient precepts, but all have passed over to a superior state.[32] All the Scriptures are gathered together, in the hands of Jesus, like the eucharistic bread,[33] and when he carries them it is he himself whom he bears in his hands: "the whole of the Bible in substance, so that we could have it all in a single mouthful. . . ."[34] "In many and various ways," God had distributed to men, page by page, a written book which, under many words, concealed a single Word: today he opens this book for them, in order to show them all these words united in the unique Word. *Filius incarnatus, Verbum incarnatum, Liber maximus:* the parchment of the Book now becomes his flesh; what is written thereon is his divinity.[35] Thus the New Testament follows upon the Old, the Old is found once again in the New, and both together make only one; and, just as in God unity expands into Trinity, and Trinity then communes with itself in unity, the New Testament is expanded into the Old and the Old is condensed in the New: *"Atque ita fiet ut et Vetus Testamentum constringatur in Novo, et Novum in Vetere dilatetur."* [36]

Here then we see the final realization of the supreme wish. Here, in all its richness, we finally encounter unity. Here we have the one Sacrifice and the one Priest, and the one Victim. The

31. Helinandus, *Sermo 3* (*PL*, 212, 503B).

32. Hildegarde, *Scivias*, 1. 1, vis. 5 (*PL*, 197, 435D).

33. Rupert, *In Jo.* (*PL*, 169, 443C-D).

34. Paul Claudel, *Apocalypse,* has in his own way brought this traditional theme back to light: "Behold this *Word,* expanded by the measure of the Infinite, here restricted, in contact with itself, in the hand of the Angel, down to the dimensions of a small book, βιβλαρίδιον, no longer the imposing Scroll of a moment ago, but a slender sheaf of pages and verses, the substance of the whole Bible now reduced to a small morsel. . . . Of this abridgement, let us say that it consists in the single word which the same St. John gives us in his Letter: God is Love. And you too will love" (p. 50). See Rev. 10, 9-10). This is the interpretation of Jerome and of Sedulius Scotus (pp. 193-194).

35. Garnier of Rochefort, *De nat. Dom.*, sermo 6 (*PL*, 205, 609D; 610A, C). Absalon, *Sermo 25* (*PL*, 211, 148D). Gerhoh, *In Ps. 21* (*PL*, 193, 1015-1016). See Heb. 1, 1.

36. Jerome, *In Ez.*, 1. 14, c. 48 (*PL*, 25, 482C). Rhabanus Maurus, *In Ez.*, 1. 20 (*PL*, 110, 1072D).

great passage is accomplished, *"a multis sacrificiis ad unam hostiam translatio"* (the passage from many sacrifices to the single offering): [37]

> *Ordine multiplici signatus Patribus olim*
> *Mactatur legi, vatibus et canitur.*[38]

Here then is the perfect holocaust. Here is the holocaust which God will never disdain, the holocaust who dwells always before his Face. It is he whom we hold, entirely, in the eucharistic mystery. Odo of Cluny explains it thus in his *Occupatio,* a great but flawed poem, which we quote solely for its teaching:

> *Porro facit Verbum, promisit ut, abbreviatum;*
> *Muneribus variis et pluribus inde rejectis,*
> *Frumentum et vinum, cunctis hoc praetulit unum.*
> *Hoc sacrat, hoc nimirum quod fit breve, quod nimis altum.*
> *Tam modicum sumptu, tam perfacile atque paratu,*
> *Tam sublime tamen, quo totam habeat deitatem.*[39]

In this abridged *Word,* who covers the whole earth, we have the remedy for all our sores,[40] the perfect cure: *Sufficit hoc solum mundi purgare piaclum.*[41]

Here is the purity of the Gospel.[42] *"Abbreviatus atque perfectus sermo Evangelicus est"* (The Word of the Gospel is an abridged and perfect word).[43] Moses had said a great many

---

[37.] Leo, *Sermo 68,* c. 3 (*PL,* 54, 374D). See *Sermo 50,* c. 7 (341C). Origen, *In Lev.,* h. 4, n. 8; h. 5, n. 3 (327, 338). See G. Salet, S.J., "La Croix du Christ, unité du monde," in *Le Christ notre vie* (3d ed., 1958), pp. 47–100.

[38.] John Scotus, *De Christi resurrectione,* vv. 23–24 (*PL,* 122, 1228C).

[39.] L. 6, cc. 27–32 (Swoboda, 120). The "pathetic style" of this poem is still not without its particular beauty, in the opinion of Zumthor, p. 73. See Augustine, *In Ps. 49,* n. 15 (*CCL,* 38, 588). Helinandus, *Sermo 3* (*PL,* 212, 498D).

[40.] Evagrius, *Alterc. Sim. et Theoph.: "Verbum breviatum faciet Deus in omni terra. Hoc est Verbum, quod verbera nostra sanavit"* (Bratke,10). Bodo of Prüfning, *De st. domus Dei,* 1. 2 (494A).

[41.] Odo, *Occupatio,* v. 33.

[42.] Jerome, *In Is.,* l. 1, c. 1, v. 11 (*PL,* 24, 33–34).

[43.] Jerome, *In Is.,* l. 4, c. 10 (*PL,* 24, 140A). J. Béleth, *Rationale,* c. 40 (*PL,* 202, 49D). Peter Comestor puts it in the opposite way, *In f. Trin.* (*PL,* 171, 595D).

things, and yet his Law had led nothing to perfection. By a single word from Jesus, the definitive perfection is taught.[44] *"Verbum abbreviatum et abbrevians, salubre compendium"* (Abridged and abridging *Word*, health-giving summary).[45] The whole essence of revelation is contained in the precept of love; in this one short word, we have "the whole Law and the Prophets." [46] But if this Gospel announced by Jesus, this word uttered by him, contains all things, the reason is that it is nothing other than Jesus himself. His work, his doctrine, his revelation, his word is he! The perfection which he teaches is the perfection which he brings. *Christus, plenitudo legis.*[47] It is impossible to separate his message from his person, and anyone who tried to make such a separation would soon be led to betray the message itself: in the final analysis, person and message are one. *Verbum abbreviatum, Verbum coadunatum: Word* condensed, unified, perfect! Living and life-giving *Word.*[48] Contrary to the laws of human language, which becomes clearer when it is explained, it is when the *Word* appears in abridged form that what had been obscure becomes manifest: *Word* first uttered *"in abscondito"* now *"manifestum in carne."* [49] Abridged *Word, Word* always ineffable in himself, and yet explaining all things. A Garnier of Rochefort needed only two long sermons in which to celebrate this ineffable *Word* and this abridged *Word,* and to develop the interrelated themes suggested thereby to the reflection of the Christian.[50] *Word* fulfilled, summing up all things, fulfilling all

[44.] Abelard, *Ep. 8* (*PL,* 178, 294B-C). See Rupert, *In Ap.,* l. 1, c. 1 (*PL,* 169, 858A-B).

[45.] Bernard, *De diligendo Deo,* c. 7, n. 21 (*PL,* 182, 986–987). *Glossa in Rom.,* IX, 28–29 (*PL,* 114, 502D).

[46.] Sedulius Scotus, *In Rom.* (*PL,* 103, 93C-D). Gilbert Crispin, *Disputatio* (Blumenkranz, 39).

[47.] *L. moz. sacram.* (517, 622).

[48.] Bernard, *In Cantica,* sermo 59, n. 9 (*PL,* 183, 1065D).

[49.] *Or. vis.,* oration for Advent (32).

[50.] Garnier of Rochefort, *De nat. Dom.,* sermo 5: *"Verbum caro factum est. Verbum abbreviatum de Verbo abbreviato audivimus. Sed,*
   *Dum brevis esse laboro*
   *obscurus fio* (Horace, *Ars Poetica,* 26–26), *quippe quia per verbum abbreviatum et obscurum de verbo abbreviato et obscuro loquimur. Sed verbum meum, quia abbreviatum, obscurum. Verbum vero illud, quia obscurum, abbreviatum. Obscurum enim erat,*

things, concluding all things, making all things sublime, making all things united:

Jesus, abridged and yet consummating Word, bringing perfection to earth, and the Law and the Prophets to their end in the double precept of charity. . . . O Word consummating and abridging all in justice! Word of charity, Word of all perfection.[51]

All Christians are in accord on this extremely simple truth, in which all Christian faith is actually summed up and consummated. Jerome, echoing Origen, agrees with Augustine; Peter Abelard is reconciled with St. Bernard; the Benedictine Rupert of Deutz and the Cistercian Garnier of Rochefort vie with one another in lyrical subtlety in extolling it.

This is not, as might be thought and as has been said of St. Bernard in particular, a "disparagement of the divine Word to the advantage of the divine *Word*," a disparagement which, by good fortune, remained "completely speculative and, we might even say, oratorical." [52] This is profound doctrine, contained radically in the prologue of St. John,[53] and borne out by a long series of witnesses and by the liturgy itself. By making us see in the ancient Scripture the mode in which "the divine Word, sole-begotten Son of God, has stooped down to our level," [54] by affirming, through expressions whose power is perhaps para-

---

*antequam esset abbreviatum, et abbreviatum est ut esset manifestum. Antequam esset abbreviatum, videri non poterat oculis mentis; abbreviatum vero, videri potuit oculis carnis. Verbum erat non breviatum, nec dici poterat; verbum abbreviatum fuit, et dici potuit. Dici forte potuit, non quid erat, sed quod erat; sed dici non potuit quid erat, sed quid non erat. . . . O Verbum ineffabile, et infans fabilis! O Verbum ineffabile apud Patrem, et infans fabilis apud matrem!"* (PL, 205, 599C-D). *"Ex multis igitur verbis, quorum scientia prolixa et incomprehensibilis erat, excepit Sapientia Patris Verbum abbreviatum, cujus doctrina salubris est et compendiosa"* (605D).

51. Aelred of Rievaulx, *De Jesu duod.*, n. 13 (*SC*, 60, 76); *Speculum caritatis*, l. 1, c. 16 (*PL*, 195, 520A). For the meaning of St. Paul and of Is. 10, 22–23, quoted by Paul, see Huby-Lyonnet, *Epître aux Romains* (1957), pp. 354–355.

52. A. Humbert, *Les origines de la théologie moderne*, I (1911), 52.

53. See C. H. Dodd, *New Testament Studies*, Manchester, 1953, pp. 141–142.

54. Louis Bouyer, *Le sens de la vie monastique*; ET *The Meaning of the Monastic Life*, London, 1955, p. 170.

doxical, the ontological bond between it and the Word in which God is revealed, this doctrine enhanced rather than disparaged the divine Word, and expanded its actuality through the entire duration of Christian time,[55] —while steadfastly refusing to canonize in it the *littera sola.* Luther had understood this well, when, during the wiser period of his biblical reflection, in his first commentary on the Psalms,[56] and then in the commentary on the Letter to the Romans,[57] he again took up the old theme of *"Verbum consummans et abbrevians."* [58] St. Augustine had expressed it well in his reply to Faustus, and all who say it with him are right: the Christian neither adds to nor subtracts from Scripture. He extracts from it its substance. He abridges it, condenses it, unifies it, without losing anything from it, he holds it all intact in Jesus Christ: *liber quippe sufficiens omnibus* (a book which is sufficient for all).[59] He receives from the chosen people all the books of the former Testament; he venerates them; he never ceases to explore them, to meditate on them, to admire in them the ways of God, —but always as leading to Christ. Everything which he discovers in them—and there is no end to his discoveries—he sees ultimately transfigured in Christ. Always, somehow, whatever be the learning at his command, whatever be the methods of the exegesis of his time, and perhaps after many a detour, he once again finds Christ in them. There comes to him a ray of the inner light which filled the soul of Jesus when, in the days of his life on earth, he took the Bible in hand:

Jesus discovers himself, recognizes himself when he reads the Old Testament. He sees himself as the term of all the History "prophesied until now in the Law and the Prophets." He sees in it the expectation of his coming. From all the scattered features of

[55.] Hans Urs von Balthasar, *A Theology of History,* New York, 1963, pp. 79–81.

[56.] *In Ps.* (W. A., 3, 262).

[57.] *In Rom.,* XI, 28 (Ficker, 232).

[58.] The origin of this theme is to be found in Origen: *In Rom.,* 1. 7, c. 19 (*PG,* 14, 1153–1154); see *In Luc.,* h. 34 (199–200). See J. H. Crehan, S.J., *JTS,* 6 (1955), pp. 87–90.

[59.] Absalon, *Sermo 25* (*PL,* 211, 149A).

the prophecies: the Messiah, King of peace, the Immanuel in
Isaiah, the Son of Man in Daniel, the Judge, the Shepherd, he does
not infer what he must be through some inductive process; in them,
he quite simply recognizes himself. . . . He lets the wrapping fall
again into the shadows. . . . In divine fashion, he synthesizes all
these features, not from without, but from within. He casts his
own interior light on the prophecies, and then they come together,
lose the marks of the circumstances in which they were first proclaimed, are harmonized and fulfilled. . . . When he discoverd
the Bible, Jesus saw the reflection of the Light shining within him,
and heard a feeble echo of the Word which resounded in his human
consciousness.[60]

Some recent exegetes, in agreement with the theologians, and
with them in agreement with the ancient tradition, view the matter thus: in everything reported to us by the apostles and the
evangelists about Jesus, we find again, melted down and purified,
the ore of the Old Testament, and this entirely Christological
orientation is not imposed, somehow or other, on this Old Testament, but is intrinsic to it and penetrates it in all its parts.[61] The
two forms of the *Word,* abridged and expanded, are inseparable.
Thus, the Book remains, while at the same time it passes over in
its entirety into Jesus,[62] and meditation on it by the Christian
means the contemplation of this passage. Mani and Mohammed
wrote books, but Jesus wrote nothing. Moses and the other
Prophets "wrote of him." The relationship of the Book to his
Person is, therefore, the reverse of the relationship which we
observe elsewhere. Thus, the law of the Gospels is in no way a
*lex scripta.* Properly speaking, Christianity is not "a religion of
the Book,"[63] but the religion of the World—but neither solely

[60.] Louis Richard, PSS. See Karl Rahner, S.J., *Réflexions théologiques
sur l'Incarnation* (tr. G. Daoust, *Sciences ecclésiastiques,* 12, 1960, 19):
in the *Word* made flesh, "the Word of God expressing itself and the
hearing of it make but one."

[61.] See Hoskyns in *Mysterium Christi,* quoted by Hebert, *The Authority of the Old Testament,* p. 118.

[62.] Absalon, *Sermo 25* (*PL,* 211, 148D).

[63.] E. R. Curtius, *European Literature and the Latin Middle Ages,*
New York, 1963, ch. 16. "Christianity, religion of the sacred Book,"
says Curtius, even though he devotes but a few pages to the Bible.

nor principally of the Word in its written form. It is the religion of the *Word*—"not a written and speechless *Word,* but one which is incarnate and living." [64] The Word of God is now here, among us, so that we have looked upon it and touched it with our hands: [65] a "living and effective" [66] Word, unique and personal, making one and sublime all the words which give witness to it.[67] Christianity is not "the biblical religion": it is the religion of Jesus Christ.[68]


## 4. The New Testament

In the doctrine of spiritual understanding of Scripture, just as in the Pauline formulas which are at the base of it, the Old Testament is always thought of in its relationship to the New. One can and should, though, also ask the question: how about the New Testament itself?

Modern treatises on hermeneutics ordinarily put the question in the following way: are there "prophetic types," "spiritual meanings," "allegories" in the New Testament writings as well? There are some who deny it; the nineteenth-century Patrizi,[1] for example, denied it emphatically. Others, who answer the ques-

[64]. Bernard, *Super Missus est,* h. 4, n. 11, where Mary is made to say: *"nec fiat mihi verbum scriptum et mutum, sed incarnatum et vivum"* (*PL,* 183, 86B).

[65]. Jn. 1; 1 Jn. 1, 1–3. Georges Auzou, *La Parole de Dieu,* (2d ed.), Paris, 1960, p. 426.

[66]. Martin of León, *s. de J. Bapt.* (*PL,* 209, 18B).

[67]. See Gerhoh, *In Ps. 19* (*PL,* 193, 961D), taking up yet once more the Origenian symbol of the transfiguration.

[68]. We speak freely today of biblical religion, biblical thought, biblical metaphysics; but no matter how legitimate the use of such expressions might be, we should never forget that they do not suffice to define the Christian faith. *"Verbum abbreviatum"* sometimes simply has the meaning of Creed; Origen, *In Rom.,* 1. 7, c. 19, on Rom. 9, 27–33 (*PG,* 14, 1154A—a gloss by Rufinus?—see Rufinus, *Exp. in symb.,* I, *PL,* 21, 336B). Bernard, *In Cantica,* sermo 79, n. 2 (*PL,* 183, 1163C).

[1]. *Institutio de interpretatione Bibliorum,* iterum edita (1876), pp. 200–201, 222–225.

tion in the affirmative, limit the affirmation by various reservations and evasions. No one will be surprised by these wavering opinions, if he bears in mind that the basic constitution of spiritual understanding was a "function" of the Jewish Scriptures. How could it possibly have been otherwise for St. Paul, who was obviously unacquainted with any others? We know that, up until the year 150 or so, "when a Christian speaks of Γραφή, he understands by that the Γραφή of the Jews, which until that time had been the Γραφή of the Christians, or the books of our Old Testament." [2] A little later on, this is still the habitual usage of a St. Irenaeus.[3] This situation will for a long time remain more or less constant, and the spiritual meaning which must transform "Jewish letters" into Christian letters [4] will continue to be sought in the former. When St. Eucherius writes: *"Universam porro Scripturam tam Veteris instrumenti quam Novi ad intellectum allegoricum esse sumendam,"* the exception is only apparent, for the quoted passage only alludes, as far as the New Testament is concerned, to the interpretation of the parables.[5] Even in the twelfth century, Adam Scotus will write, when referring to the time of the Mosaic Law: *"tempus Scripturae."* [6] Still more strik-

2. G. Jouassard, "Aperçu sur l'importance de l'A.T. dans la vie liturgique des pemiers siecles chrétiens," in *Mélanges Salaville* (1958), p. 105.

3. Thus *Adversus Haereses,* l. 2, c. 35, n. 4; l. 3, c. 21, n. 5; l. 4, c. 10, n. 1; c. 24, n. 2; c. 26, n. 1; l. 5, c. 17, n. 1; c. 34, n. 3. See H. D. Simonin, in *Angelicum,* 1934, 15. H. Holstein, in *RSR,* 36 (1949), pp. 259, 269–270; *La Tradition dans l'Église* (1960), p. 70–76.

4. Thus Isaac of Stella (*PL,* 194, 1725D).

5. *Intelligentiae spiritualis formulae,* praef. (C. Wotke ed., 3). See R. P. C. Hanson, *Allegory and Event,* London, 1959, pp. 112–113: ". . . Irenaeus is the first writer to allegorize the New Testament; we have already glanced at his elaborate exposition of the parable of the Good Samaritan. . . . Irenaeus . . . will . . . apply allegory to the text of the New Testament without restraint. In spite of the efforts of some modern French scholars to defend this practice, one cannot but feel that Irenaeus is thereby placing his readers one stage further away from the real meaning of the New Testament." This is nothing but confusion.

6. *Sermo 6,* c. 14 (*PL,* 198, 133B).

ingly, *Scripturae sanctae* will be understood by the Fathers of the Council of Trent to designate primarily the ancient Scriptures, or Prophecy.[7] If we readily admit that the works of the two Testaments comprise a single *corpus,* a single Book, the reason is that these works are interrelated in such wise that the early grouping makes up the history, or letter, while the later grouping is the allegory, or spirit, of the former. Through Jesus Christ, mankind did indeed enter upon the age of the Spirit.[8] Is not "sacred history" the term which we traditionally use, even today, for the history of the former people of God? Sacred history in its entirety was prophetic because in its entirety it foretold Christ. He himself is prophecy or figure no longer, but Presence and Truth:

When the emperor comes, his images are taken away. We look upon the image when the emperor is absent. But once he whose features are reproduced by the image is present, the image is put aside. The images were, therefore, set up before the Lord Jesus Christ, our emperor, came. Now, with the images taken away, we see the glory of the emperor's presence.[9]

*"Magna distantia inter litteram et spiritum, inter figuram et veritatem, inter umbram et corpus"* (There is a great distance between letter and spirit, between figure and truth, between shadow and body).[10] Spirit, truth, "body" or solid and definitive reality: these are what are shown by the gospel accounts when they proclaim that Jesus is the Messiah. By that very fact, *"revelant arcana secretorum, et quae Prophetae operuerant, ipsi aperiunt."* [11] This is what the authors of Acts and of the Letters do when they explain Christ. They are exegetes; their writings

[7.] Decree *De Can. Scripturis* (Denzinger-Rahner, 1953, 783).

[8.] Alcuin, *In Ap.* (*PL,* 100, 1120A). Bruno of Segni (*PL,* 164, 584B).

[9.] Augustine, *Sermo 74,* n. 5 (*PL,* 38, 474). See *De div.,* q. 83, q. 58, n. 2 (*PL,* 90, 42). Atto of Vercelli, *In Col.,* c. 2 (*PL,* 134, 627A-B). See Bede, *In Lucam,* X, 23 (*PL,* 92, 467C). Chromatius of Aquileia, *Hom.* 19 (*RB,* 73, 201; J. Lemarié).

[10.] John Scotus, *In ev. Jo.,* fr. 2 ( *PL,* 122, 320B). Atto of Vercelli, *In Col.* (*PL,* 134, 623A-B).

[11.] John of Ford, unpublished sermon, *In Ramis palm.* (Talbot, *Collectanea O.C.R.,* 7, 1940, 37).

were called "the apostolic exegeses." [12] They comment "allegorically" on the Scriptures, which is to say that they disclose their ultimate significance. For the matters of which they treat really are the ultimate things, towards which were directed all the shadows and figures, by which these shadows and figures were to be illumined, in which they are now realized at last.[13] This is what St. Paul, in writing to the Galatians, was intent upon demonstrating to them; *"omnia illa quae in typis et imaginibus praecesserunt . . ., gratia Evangelii subrepente cessasse"* (all the things which had preceded by way of types and images disappeared, once the grace of the Gospel arrived).[14] Thus we had on the one hand the Prophets, and on the other the apostles; that is to say, on the one hand Scripture, and on the other the Christian preaching or the explanation of that Scripture by the Fact of Christ. To the fullest possible extent in earthly conditions, the grace of the New Testament, casting a retrospective light [15] on prophecy, brings out the mystery which had lain hidden, sealed, impossible to understand until then under the letter. Henceforward, all the modes of understanding of which the letter is susceptible—would they were seven in number!—are theoretically elucidated.[16] During the generations which would follow that of the apostles, this work of elucidation was to be carried on by Fathers and Doctors. It is beyond doubt that they would no longer enjoy the same charism of inspiration as the apostolic authors had enjoyed, and this makes a radical

12. *Homélies sur la Pâque*, 1, n. 5 (Nautin ed., *SC*, 36, 56). See above, I, ch. X, 5 (vol. II, p. 668–681). See Dom Hilaire Duesberg, "Vulgaris Liberalitas," in *Parole de Dieu et Sacerdoce* (1962), p. 174: ". . . Gospels like Letters, Apocalypse like Acts of the Apostles, are nothing other than an exegesis, enthusiastic, universal, guiding souls towards Jesus through the Old Testament, . . ."
13. John Keble, "On the Mysticism Attributed to the Early Fathers of the Church," no. 89 of *Tracts for the Times*, London, 1868, c. 5, n. 22, p. 136. See Bruno of Segni (*PL*, 164, 846A-B).
14. Jerome, *In Gal.*, prol. (*PL*, 26, 309–310). See Rom. 7, 6; 2 Cor. 3, 6.
15. Ambrose Autpert, *In transfiguratione Domini*, n. 18 (*PL*, 89, 1317D).
16. Haimo of Auxerre, *In Ap.*, 1. 2 (*PL*, 117, 1014B, 1016D).

difference as far as insight and authority are concerned; but, even so, the analogous quality of their work, which in both instances is an exegesis, is not effaced. The exegesis of all Christian generations will have as its primary task the preservation of the exegesis of the first generation as an absolute norm. When we ask whether the New Testament has, like the Old, an allegorical meaning, this seems to come down to asking if the exegesis of the Book has the same qualities as the Book itself, or in other words if an allegorical commentary must be made on an allegorical commentary. But how could such a question be answered except in the negative?

We must make a few preliminary distinctions, however. We begin by recalling the fact that the expression "New Testament" is today an ambiguous one. The ancients very clearly distinguished, as we have seen, between the Testament itself, or the Covenant, and the writings which were, so to speak, its charter; or, to use the terminology which was retained by some, between *testamentum* and *instrumentum*.[17] Before they stopped to consider the text in one or another of its parts, their doctrine on understanding of Scripture viewed the *instrumentum* in its essential relationship to the *testamentum*. Now, a basic piece of evidence becomes more apparent in this overall perspective. If the Old Testament and the New are, as Isaac of Stella said, two worlds, the world of history and the world of allegory,[18] and if the New Testament is precisely defined as the allegory of the Old, it becomes clear that it could not in its turn be allegorized. If the New Testament is the spirit of the Old Testament, which is the letter of the New, it is clear that it cannot be treated anew like a letter from which the spirit was still to be extracted. This would be to embark on a *processus in indefinitum,* the fruit of an extravagant imagination, and something destructive of Christian reality. If we were to admit an explanation of the New

---

[17.] Thus Sedulius Scotus (*PL,* 103, 338A-B). See Augustine, *Contra duas epistolas Pelagianorum,* l. 3, c. 4, n. 12 (*PL,* 44, 595). The usage came from Tertullian.

[18.] *In nativitate Beatae Mariae,* sermo 54 (*PL,* 194, 1874B-C). Isaac posits yet a third world, the world of anagoge.

Testament analogous to the explanation of the Old which the New in fact is, we would be stripping the word "spirit" of all specific content; we would be admitting that the New Testament is, as the Old had been, susceptible of a later transformation or surpassing; that it is in its very substance a call to something other than itself. This would make of faith in Christ a relative and transitory faith, and would be to view in Christ and his Gospel the figures of another Saviour to come, a Saviour who would in turn have the power to transform and to surpass these figures *"in spiritualem intellectum"* [19]—while, undoubtedly, waiting for a third Saviour, who would not be the supreme and real Saviour either, to come along and displace him by allegorizing him. . . . We must, therefore, say, borrowing the language of the two Spaniards, Etherius and Beatus, that the New Testament *"pro se stat sicut auditur; non est allegoria; non significat alterum Christum, sicut Patriarchae et Prophetae hunc significaverunt et praedicaverunt esse venturum"* (it is just as we hear it; it is not an allegory; it does not signify another Christ, such as him whose coming was signified and foretold by Patriarchs and Prophets).[20] When we believe that the New Testament, taken in its full and universal acceptation, no longer entails any allegorical or spiritual meaning, we are, then, simply believing in Jesus Christ, whose testament is *"novissimum,"* that is to say, last, definitive, eternal; new, in the absolute sense.[21] We are believing that, "with Jesus, eschatology has entered into history."[22] After Jesus Christ, we have nothing more to learn, nothing more to receive. Outside of Jesus Christ, we have nothing more to hope for.

And yet, always in this primary acceptation, the New Testament remains a complex whole. Even if it does not entail any

---

[19.] Anselm of Laon, *In Matthaeum* (*PL*, 162, 1318C).

[20.] *Ad. Elip.,* l. 1, c. 105 ( *PL*, 96, 958D).

[21.] On the many senses of *"novus"* in Scripture, see Innocent III, *Sermo 2 de Sanctis, in Nat. Dom.* (*PL*, 217, 455–456). See Walter Daniel, *Centum Sententiae,* 30: *"Superveniente novo, facta sunt omnia nova: nova vid. lex, nova plebs, novus rex, novus pontifex, novum sacrificium, novum sabbatum, novum pascha, et novum alleluia"* (C. H. Talbot, *S. Er.,* XI, 1960, p. 287).

[22.] *R.bibl.,* 49 (1940), 284 (reviewing H. D. Wendland).

meaning other than *of itself,* even if it does not make the least allusion to some reality or other above and beyond it, whose figure and foretelling it would be and to which it would one day have to yield, we are nonetheless obliged to recognize, *at the very heart of the New Testament,* a series of diverse relationships, which oblige anyone who wants to see it in its entirety to adopt successively diverse points of view. In other words, it is spiritual understanding, but this spiritual understanding takes on its fullness only through the totality of the diverse meanings into which it is subdivided. Open the *Fons Philosophiae* of Godfrey of St. Victor, which contains a statement of the quadruple meaning, and read strophe 136, which follows that statement:

> *Qui cum, sicut diximus, sit quadripartitus,*
> *Veteris historia plus infirmat ritus*
> *Et ob hoc ad alterum magis vergit litus*
> *Nobis est vicinior modus tripartitus.*

Lest there be any hesitation about this reading, the verses are preceded by a title in prose: *"Nota historiam ad vetus et reliquos tres modos ad novum magis pertinere sacramentum"* (Note that history concerns rather the old "sacrament," and the other three modes rather the new).[23]

The substance of the New Testament is the Mystery of Christ. Now this Mystery is pre-eminently a great Fact: it is what can be called, to be brief about it, the redemptive Fact or the Fact of Christ. It is the Fact of his incarnation, his earthly life, his death, his resurrection, and his ascension. It is also the Fact of the Church, which, as his Spouse and his "Body," cannot be separated from him. It is the mysterious Fact, or the effective Mystery, of the nuptials of the *Word* with mankind. This is the nature of the decisive Act, the unique Fact—not only with the uniqueness proper to any fact, but with a uniqueness vis-à-vis every other fact—whose foretelling the Christian reads in the ancient Scripture. *"Patres Veteris Testamenti figuris et aenigmatibus designabant universa quae verus Pacificus in Ecclesia fac-*

---

23. Vv. 451–455 (P. Michaud-Quantin, 54). See Delhaye, *Le Microcosmus* (1951), p. 278.

*turus erat"* (The Fathers of the Old Testament designated in figures and in enigmas everything which the true Solomon was to accomplish in the Church).[24] At the same time that it is the allegory of the Old Testament, its "Truth," and its "Mystery," this great Fact is, at least up to a point, the equivalent of what *historia* was in the Old Testament. For it is a real fact indeed, which occurred in a definite place, at a definite time; consequently, it has an entire extrinsic aspect and, like *historia,* it is really the basis of everything which must still be taken account of within the New Testament, which is to say within itself, by means of *tropologia* and *anagogè.* It really is the sign, or the figure, of everything which the latter two meanings must set forth. And yet, what an abyss lies beneath this analogy! This Fact is not a simple history any more than it is the simple letter of a text. It is sign indeed, but efficacious sign. Neither is it mystery alone: it is in its basic principle *the entire mystery.* Tropology will do no more than describe its fruit, and anagoge will only suggest its consummation. It would not be grasped in all its depth, but would actually be mutilated, unless it were contemplated in this dual extension. Yet the very word "extension" is inadequate, for the investigation of these two latter meanings really adds nothing at all to the Mystery of Christ; it brings us neither outside nor beyond that Mystery, but simply makes its fruitfulness apparent. Everything which remains hidden within the New Testament is still part of the New Testament. While the *historia* which made up the ancient Scripture guided the reader to an *allegoria* by prefiguring a reality which was *other,* ulterior and superior, namely the very Mystery of Christ which is the New Testament, the Mystery of Christ does nothing else but spread forth its own intrinsic dimensions before the eyes of the believer who studies it. Whereas the three meanings mentioned after the original *historia* led us from the Old Testament to the New, the two meanings which are still mentioned after the new *historia* which has now become *allegoria* remain dependent upon it and cause us to explore it in depth. Thus it can be called, as

---

24. *Glossa, In I Paral.,* XXVIII, II (*PL,* 113, 663C).

was the earlier one, their foundation, but in a much more basic and much nobler sense.

Thus, however paradoxical it might seem, it will be asserted: *"In Domino totius Ecclesia figura versatur"* (The figure of the entire Church is contained in the Lord); *"Christus Ecclesiam suam praefigurare dignatus est"* (Christ has deigned to prefigure his Church); *"Suae sanctae Ecclesiae signum nobis Christus occurrit"* (Christ becomes for us the sign of his holy Church).[25] The redemptive facts are "sacraments," that is to say, they are before anything else figures, signs: *"Passio Christi salutis nostrae continet sacramentum"* (The passion of Christ contains the mystery of our salvation);[26] *"Satis elucet mysterio Dominicae mortis et resurrectionis figuratum vitae nostrae veteris occasum et exortum novae"* (In the mystery of the death and resurrection of the Lord, we find quite clearly prefigured the death of our old life and the arising of the new); today the Church is still waiting for the realization of what was in the past foretold in Christ: "The universal Church, in the pilgrimage of this mortal life, awaits at the end of the age the very thing which was shown in advance in the body of our Lord Jesus Christ."[27] Bossuet, faithful to the tradition of the Fathers, will express this magnificently:

It must be acknowledged that everything which is, so to speak, the most utterly true in the Christian religion is both mystery and sacred sign. The incarnation of Jesus Christ is for us a figure of the perfect union which we must have with the divinity in grace and in glory. His birth and his death are figures of our birth and of our spiritual death. If, in the mystery of the Eucharist, he deigns to come near to our bodies in his own flesh and blood, he thereby invites us to

[25.] Optatus, *Sermo in nat. Innoc.,* n. 7 (Hauwart ed., I, 291). Etherius and Beatus, *Ad Elip.,* l. 1, c. 12 (*PL,* 96, 901A); see *L. moz. sacr.* (283); Guitmond of Aversa, *De corp. et sang. Dom. veritate in euch.,* 1. 2 (*PL,* 149, 1459A-B).

[26.] Leo, *Sermo 55,* c. 1 (*PL,* 54, 323B). Ambrose, *Explanatio symboli,* n. 6: *"Totum hoc* [from the incarnation to the resurrection] *sacramentum tuae est resurrectionis"* (O. Faller ed., 7, 91).

[27.] Augustine, *De spir. et litt.,* c. 6, n. 10 (*PL,* 44, 206); *Ep. 55,* c. 2, n. 3 (33,206); *Enchiridion,* c. 14, n. 53 (198).

the union of spirits, and he is the figure of it; ultimately, until we have come to the full and manifest truth which will make us eternally happy, every truth will be for us the figure of a truth still more intimate: we shall only enjoy Jesus Christ in his own form, pure and unalloyed by any figure, when we shall see him in the fullness of his glory at the right hand of his Father.[28]

Thus we see again that the New Testament itself is in a certain way comparable to the Old. "As the actions of the Word in the New Testament appear to be prefigured by the actions performed by that same Word in the Old Testament, they now appear to us as types of the actions which that same Word will perform in the Church and in the kingdom." [29] It should be noted, however, that the new figurative relationship, as thus perceived, simultaneously appears as the opposite of the Old, so that one might even speak, as Bossuet did, of "ambiguity"—so delicate a task it is to handle such words as figure, sacrament, and mystery. Here, it is figure which is the dominant reality, a reality not only active and efficacious, but also assimilating. The life of the Church, the life of the Christian soul, the life of the eschatological kingdom are not only signified, nor only caused inasmuch as they are signified by the efficacious sign which the Mystery of Christ is, but they are wholly constituted by man's assumption into the heart of the Mystery of Christ. It was not very long ago that the figure was destined to be accomplished in the superior and substantially other reality which it had the mission of prefiguring, but now we must say of the redemptive facts, on the contrary, that "they were mystically accomplished and are called sacraments in Scripture, so that the Christian life might be configured to them." [30] It was not long ago that the figure yielded to the reality or passed over into it, that the figure somehow subsisted only by being transformed into the reality, but now this other figure says to each of those which it signifies: "You shall not change me into yourself, but you shall be changed

[28.] *Histoire des Variations,* l. 4, n. 12 (Lachat, 14, 1863, pp. 150–151). See Rupert of Deutz, *Ep. ad Cunonem (PL,* 167, 194–195).
[29.] Jean Daniélou, *Approches du Christ;* ET *Christ and Us,* New York, 1961, p. 138.
[30.] Fragment from the School of Laon (Lottin, *RTAM,* 1946, p. 246).

into me." [31] We see, then, that this figure neither yields before another nor is it transformed into another: "The mystery of the incarnation, foreseen and predestined before all ages, remains unto ages of ages." The *novitas* of the incarnation of the *Word* suffers no surpassing and no repetition of any kind.[32] The Mystery of Christ, in the saving Act which is its constitutive principle, remains ever-present, always perfectly including everything of which it is the source: *"Jesus Christus heri, hodie, ipse et in saecula."*

Here we have the solution of a scholastic problem which, since the Middle Ages, has frequently divided theologians or has found them indecisive. Which is uppermost, the literal meaning of the Bible or its spiritual meaning? Which is the more "worthy"? The answer will vary, depending on whether one considers the Old Testament or the New. It cannot be doubted that in the Old Testament the spiritual meaning has greater dignity than the literal, which is to the Old Testament what the Old Testament is to the New; the Mystery of Christ is superior to all the prefigurations of it. Just as the fruit outshines the leaves, so does allegory outshine any history.[33] If we look at the New Testament, the answer is going to appear less simple. Here the literal meaning is itself spiritual, since the Mystery of Christ, even in its primary aspect as an historical fact, is the "truth," that is to say, "the spirit" of the Old Testament. Moreover, since this Mystery also contains in itself, in the way which we have just described, the latter two meanings which flow from its "letter," this letter itself will have to be called the more worthy.[34] The assimilating figure will obviously outshine the assimilated reality. The personal Act of Christ towers over the constitution

31. Augustine, *Confessions,* l. 7, c. 10, n. 16. See our *Corpus Mysticum,* p. 200.

32. *Glossa in Eccli.,* XXIV, 14 (*PL,* 113, 1208D). Augustine, *De civ. Dei,* l. 12, cc. 19–20 (*PL,* 41, 368–372).

33. *Alleg. in V. T.,* l. 9, c. 2 (*PL,* 175, 737D). In other words, *"Vetus Testamentum est minus quam novum,"* Thomas, *In II Cor.,* III (Vivès ed., 21, 78).

34. Thus Tolet, *In Primam,* q. 1, a. 10: *"Nam semper spiritualis sensus potior est. Nam in Veteri Testamento quod figura erat, saepe ita fit, at in Novo, quae ad litteram de Christo sunt, praecipuum habent litteralem*

of his "mystical body," the Head is superior to the members. However, the constitution of this "body" is not the purpose of this Act; the Head wills the members, the *Word* of God became incarnate only *propter nos et propter nostram salutem,* and the Church is the "pleroma" or the fullness of Christ. The intention of the Spirit is that one stop no more at the letter of the New Testament than at the letter of the Old, and since the spirit of the letter of the New, that is to say the tropology and the anagoge whose sign and foundation it is, does not really surpass the letter but finds all its substance in the letter, it is perfectly proper to say that this Mystery taken in its totality, the ultimate reality willed by God, constitutes the meaning which, if not the most "worthy," is at least the most complete and in the final analysis the most important.

If, from the New Testament considered in its essence, we now go back to the slender collection of writings which comprise the *Novum Instrumentum* and more particularly to the four gospels, and consider them simply in faith as a series of inspired accounts, as texts of *historia,* we shall see that the question of understanding them is now posed in different conditions. A moment ago, the New Testament was the spirit of the letter which was the Old Testament. This spirit was not made up of the externals of the Gospel accounts, of the *historia* alone, but of the entire *mysterium,* that is to say, of everything which Christ was to accomplish beginning with the incarnation, right down to his Church, his sacraments, the souls faithful to him, and ultimately the heavenly Jerusalem. The two *instrumenta* now comprise one letter in the same meaning of the word, and under that letter the spirit can be concealed:

*"Duas manu tenens spicas" (Is., 9). Duae spicae, duo sunt Testamenta, quia sicut in spica vel in arista granum est cum palea, ita sunt sacramenta latentia sub littera.*[35]

---

*sensum, quam cum moraliter de nobis intelliguntur"* (56). The problem is analogous to that of knowing *"an corpus Christi verum sit melius corpore Christo mystico, an e converso,"* (Turrecremata, O.P., *Summa de Ecclesia,* 1. 1, c. 62; 1. 2, 83 [Venice ed., 1561], fol. 74 and 215–216),

[35.] Garnier of Rochefort, *Sermo 32 (PL,* 205, 778B).

Thus nothing prohibits us from seeing in the gospels or in the Acts of the Apostles, just as in the stories contained in the books of the Old Testament, the various traditional meanings with their traditional applications and in their traditional senses. *"Novi vel Veteris Testamenti intelligentia duplex, historialis scilicet et spiritualis"* [36]; or, *"(Invenimus) historiam, allegoriam, tropologiam et anagogen in duobus Testamentis."* [37] This is why we find collections of *Allegoriae in Novum Testamentum* which are strikingly similar in appearance to the collections of *Allegoriae in Vetus Testamentum,* and every bit as well supplied. And although Etherius and Beatus warned us just a moment ago that the New Testament contains no allegorical meaning whatever, the same authors can now unhesitatingly tell us: "All of Scripture, the Old Testament as well as the New, must be taken in an allegorical meaning." [38] The reason is that, a moment ago, they were talking about the "New Testament" itself, the New Economy in Christ, while now they are talking about the "writings in the New Testament" and about the external facts related therein. As long as we pay attention to the difference in viewpoints, there is no contradiction whatever, not even in the words.

In our four gospels, it turns out, just as in the old historical books, there is a *"facies lectionis,"* [39] and there is a *"superficies verborum,"* a *"superficies historici sensus,"* [40] which must not be confused with what is elsewhere called the *"plenitudo Evan-*

---

[36]. Richard of St. Victor, *In Ap.,* l. 2, c. 6 (*PL,* 196, 766A). Othloh, *Dial. de trib. q.,* c. 15 (*PL,* 146, 79D). On this subject, Origen used the same turns of phrase for both Testaments; thus *In Cant.,* h. 1, n. 4 (*SC,* 37, 68). Godfrey of Admont, *H. dom.,* 32 (*PL,* 174, 218D). See Volcuin of Sittichenbach, Hom. (Leclercq, *Studi Med.,* Spoleto, 1962, p. 339).

[37]. Martin of León, *In dedic,* sermo 2 (*PL,* 209, 91A). In his *Enarrationes in ev. Mat.,* Anselm of Laon carefully distinguishes *historia, moralitas, allegoria* (*PL,* 162, 1229–1263); it seems nevertheless that *"allegoria"* denotes rather a relationship of the Old Testament to the New, or else an allegory in the common meaning; for the spiritual understanding of a gospel fact, Anselm uses the term *"mystice."*

[38]. *Ad. Elip.,* l. 1, c. 98 (*PL,* 96, 955C).

[39]. Peter Chrysologus, *Sermo 95,* (*PL,* 52, 467A).

[40]. Othloh, *Lib. de curs. spir.,* c. 3 (*PL,* 146, 146D); *Vita S. Wolfg.* (*PL,* 146, 397A).

*gelii* " [41] or, more simply, as by the Council of Trent again, the
*"Evangelium."* All the facts and doings of the Saviour himself, at
least as to the external details which we are told about them—
*corporaliter gesta*—do not fully participate in the redeeming Act.
At all events, we can begin by viewing them in themselves, independently of their relationship to that Act. This is only the
more true of any number of other notes pertaining to other
persons, of any number of other points of every conceivable
nature—places, circumstances, names, numbers, etc.[42] These
have to do with a letter under which, as under every letter in
Scripture, *"latet mysterium."* [43] We are invited to seek therein,
in the same way and with the same discretion, *"sublimiora
secreta."* [44] After having explained it as history, we must still
explain it *"juxta mysticum sensum,"* [45] extract from it the *"sensus
allegoricus"* [46]; it will be rare indeed if we find we are unable
to discover in it *"aliquid mysticae significationis."* [47] *"Nota haec
est evangelicae lectionis historia: quaeramus mysteria."* [48] For
example, St. Augustine, with regard to these extremely simple
words, *"Accessit ad eum centurio,"* remarks: "The profundity
of the mystical language of the holy evangelist must not be lightly
considered." [49] In short, then, the letter of the gospels, or even
of the Acts, conceals, in the proper sense of the word, an alle-

[41.] Gregory of Elvira, tr. 2 (20). Claudius of Turin. *In Reg.,* 1. 4 (*PL,*
104, 779B).
[42.] Peter Chrysologus, *Sermo 146* (*PL,* 52, 592C). Bernard, *In dom.
Palm.,* sermo 3, n. 1 (*PL,* 183, 259D).
[43.] Nicholas of Clairvaux, *In Act.,* VI, 8 (*PL,* 184, 846D). Origen,
*In Matt. ser.,* 32 (57); *In Matt. X,* 1 (2); *In Luc.,* h. 38, n. 1 (*SC,* 87,
442); *In Jo.,* 1. 20, c. 36 (375); *In Cant.,* h. 1, n. 4 (*SC,* 37, 68). See
*Histoire et Esprit,* pp. 195–197.
[44.] Aelred of Rievaulx, *De Jesu duod.,* c. 1, n. 7 (A. Hoste ed., *SC,*
60, 60).
[45.] Ambrose Autpert, *S. de lect. evang.,* n. 4 (*PL,* 89, 1295A). Arnobius the Younger, *In Matt. XIII: "Facta sunt ista omnia, sed habent
spiritualem intellectum"* (Morin, *Anal. Mareds.,* 3, p. 3, 139; see
133, 140, 150).
[46.] Gregory, *In Ev.,* 1. 2, h. 40, nn. 1–2 (*PL,* 76, 1312).
[47.] Augustine, *De cons. ev.,* 1. 2, c. 30, n. 75 (*PL,* 34, 1114); c. 47,
n. 99, on the calming of the tempest (1127).
[48.] Gerhoh, *De quarta vig. noctis,* c. 11 (*L. de lite,* 3, 508).
[49.] Augustine, *De cons. ev.,* 1. 2, c. 20, n. 49 (*PL,* 34, 1101); n. 50.

gory (*allegoria facti*), and this allegory, just like the allegory hidden under the letter of the Old Testament, enjoys some relationship to one of the aspects of the Mystery of Christ. Consider, for example, the approach of Jesus to the gates of the city of Nain: "Allegorically, this means that the Word made flesh introduces the gentiles into the heavenly Jerusalem through the gates of faith." [50] The healing of the paralytic at the pool of Bethesda can be considered as an allegory of baptism, exactly like the ancient episode of the rock at Horeb:

This pool was in every particular the image of future baptism. But, there is no less distance between the image and the truth than there is between the grace obtained in this pool and the grace of saving baptism.

Similarly, we can say of Mary, the sister of Martha and Lazarus, who poured perfume over the feet of Jesus: *"Secundum allegoriam vel mysticam rationem, figuram Ecclesiae praeferebat"* (According to allegory, that is, the mystical reason, she prefigured the Church). Of the man lame from birth whom Peter and John cured at the gate of the Temple which was called Beautiful, St. Chromatius of Aquileia declares: *"In claudo, si consideremus, etiam mystica sacramenta cognoscimus praeostensa"* (In the lame man, we find, if we look carefully, mysteries shown beforehand).[51] When speaking of the miraculous escape of St. Peter from prison, Lothar of Segni says: "Since we clearly see the historical meaning, let us explore deeply into the allegory: let us look for the spirit underneath the letter, like the kernel underneath the husk." [52] The forty days which the Saviour spent in the desert cannot be considered as lacking in mystery, any more than were the forty days of Moses or Elijah or the forty years of wandering by the Fathers after their departure from Egypt: Isaac of Stella [53] brings this out, and it had been a commonplace for centuries prior to him. The allegorical explana-

---

[50.] Werner, *Deflorationes SS. Patrum*, 1. 2 (*PL*, 157, 1154A). Bede, *Sup. Act.* (*PL*, 92, 961D).

[51.] Unpublished homilies of St. Chromatius of Aquileia, 14, 1; 11, 3; I (J. Lemarié, *RB*, 72, 1962, pp. 267–268, 260, 232).

[52.] *Sermo 4 de sanctis* (*PL*, 217, 561D).

[53.] *Sermo 31,* init. (*PL*, 196, 1790C).

tion of a scene is sometimes, just as it was for certain passages in the ancient Scriptures, reflexive in one way or another: it justifies itself in its principle, by providing the symbols for its own development. We see an example of this in a homily of Paul the Deacon. St. Luke tells us that one day some men, in order to bring a paralytic to Jesus, made an opening in the roof of the house where Jesus was staying:

We must climb onto the roof of the house in which Jesus is teaching; that is to say, we must want to know the sublime meaning of Scripture. . . . Once the roof was broken through, the sick man went down to Jesus, because, by opening the mysteries of the Scriptures, we arrive at the knowledge of Christ; that is to say, we descend through piety to the humility of faith. And the house of Jesus is indeed described as covered with tiles, because, under the crude veil of the letter, if someone is there to open it, we find the divine virtue of spiritual grace. . . . Indeed, to take away the tiles which cover the dwelling of Jesus is to open a passage, through the letter's crudeness, to the spiritual meaning and to the heavenly secrets.[54]

Thus everything which was said of the letter of Scripture in general we can repeat, in the same terms, of the letter of the gospels. Its allegorical exegesis is based on the same principles. This exegesis is practised with the same abundance, the same scrupulousness, the same pedagogical methods, and often, we must admit, the same eccentricity.[55] *"Omnia plena sunt sacramentis, et non dico una hora, sed dies vix sufficiet ad interpretationem"* (Everything therein is filled with mysteries, and I do not say an hour but a day would be barely adequate for explain-

---

[54.] Paul the Deacon, *H. 154 de temp. (PL, 95, 1350–1351).* Werner, *Deflorationes SS. Patrum,* 1. 2 *(PL, 157, 1179C-D).*

[55.] This is not the doing of the Latins alone. The homilies of John Chrysostom on St. Matthew "attribute a prophetic significance to the least detail reported in the text. . . . This is largely the result of subjective interpretation as to the determination of the prefigurations, not merely in the Old Testament but also and especially in the New, where, of necessity, recourse to any scriptural argument must be renounced. He recognized, besides, the purely hypothetical character of some of his explanations." René Leconte, *Saint Jean Chrysostome, exégète syrien* (mimeographed thesis, Institut Catholique de Paris, pp. 246–247).

ing it), is what St. Jerome said about a page from St. Luke; and it was about St. Mark's gospel that he wrote thus, in completely Origen-like terms:

There are those who love the history who keep to the Judaic meaning, who follow the letter which kills rather than the spirit which gives life. . . . As for us, we do not deny the history, but we prefer the spiritual understanding. For such is the meaning which we make our own: we follow the meaning of the apostles, and principally that of the "vessel of election" who did not deny the history, but who discovered its mysteries; and who did not say: "We understand that these are the two Testaments" but: "These are the two Testaments . . ."[56]

Along with Paschasius Radbertus in his commentary on St. Matthew, there is a multiplication of formulas such as *"mystice factum," "mystice promulgatum," "mystice scriptum," "mystice prolatum."*[57] The four standard meanings are spelled out in the gospel episodes every bit as much as elsewhere; thus Gerhoh of Reichersberg comments on the wedding feast at Cana:

In this single page of the gospel, we can see the four different kinds of wedding banquet: the historical, the moral, the allegorical, the anagogical. The historical banquet is the one of which we read, according to the letter, that it took place at Cana in Galilee. The allegorical is the one which takes place in a universal way between Christ and the Church, with their nuptial union celebrated at Cana in Galilee, that is to say, in the zeal of the transmigration, with Jesus passing over from the Jews to the Gentiles. The moral banquet is the one which takes place every day, when the believing soul is united to the Word of God and takes his meal with him, in his eagerness to pass over from earthly things to heavenly ones. The anagogical banquet is that in heaven, when, after the foolish virgins have been excluded, the wise virgins pass from this world to the nuptial bed where, in the fire of a fervent charity, they will eternally love their spouse and be loved eternally by him.[58]

[56.] *Hom. In Luc.* (Morin, *An. Mareds,* 3, p. 2, 383). *In Marc.* (348).
[57.] *In Matt., passim (PL,* 120, 39B, 53A, 355B, 709C, 858C).
[58.] *In Ps. 36* (Van den Eynde ed., 2, 574–575). Speaking analogously, we can also distinguish within the Church her profound life, which is not other than the Mystery of Christ, and the external detail of her rites, which is also capable of being allegorized (something which occasioned the same kind of abuses).

We should also note that if the Mystery of Christ, in its primary and determinative reality, begins at the time of the "first coming," that is to say, at the time of the incarnation of the Word, it must, so as to be complete in itself and to be revealed externally even before it finds fulfillment in the Church, none-theless pass through the stages of death, resurrection, and ascension. The events related by the evangelists over and above the great saving facts are, then, not merely *exterior* to the Mystery, but are also *anterior* to it. Consequently, it would not be too much of a paradox to hold that they still belong, to a certain extent, to the era of signs and figures, which is to say to the era of the Old Testament. For if the New Testament can be dated from the moment of the incarnation, this is only inasmuch as that moment is seen as preparing for the redemptive Act be-cause of which the incarnation itself took place. In other words, inasmuch as the entire "unfolding of this incarnation" is kept in mind.[59] This is, though, an anticipatory view, and if it can be said that "God appeared in the flesh, revealing the mysteries of the Scriptures," it is said by way of summary and involves a consideration of the entire work of the incarnate Word, rather than the precise moment which inaugurated it. Jesus was "born under the Law," and lived under the Law.[60] The new Covenant was established by him at the Last Supper; the veil which still concealed its true nature was not completely removed until his death, followed by his resurrection and ascension; until then, his disciples and he himself observed the Jewish Law according to

[59.] Leo, *Sermo 48*, c. 1:*"Nec alia fuit Dei Filio causa nascendi, quam ut Cruci possit affigi"* (*PL*, 54, 298A); *Ep. 16*, c. 2 (697–698). See Dom Olivier Rousseau, in *La Maison-Dieu*, 65 (1961), p. 91: Augustine dates the *Adventus Domini* either from his birth, or from his first preaching, or from the preaching of John the Baptist; for him, the sixth age, that of the New Testament, only really begins with the birth of the new man, *"qui jam spiritualiter vivit,"* *Gen. c. Manich.*, l. 1, c. 23, n. 40 (*PL*, 34, 192). J. Guillet, *Jésus-Christ hier et aujourd' hui* (1963), p. 9.

[60.] Thomas of Perseigne, *In Cantica*, 1. 7 (*PL*, 206, 529A-B). It is in this extremely simple sense that we can allow the observation of Rudolf Bultmann that Jesus was not a Christian but a Jew. We might recall that it was only in the sixth century that the chronological system which counted years *"ab incarnatione Domini"* was adopted (Dionysius Exiguus, *ob.* 544).

the letter. As long as the course of the Saviour's *corporea ac dispensatoria minoratio* was incomplete, as long as the condition of *"mortalitas"* and *"temporalitas"* [61] which he assumed was not yet abolished—and as long as the apostles whom Jesus had chosen, "still coarse and not yet enlightened by the Holy Spirit, believed in a Jewish sense"—the new Covenant was still not definitively established.[62]

This way of conceiving the chief line of demarcation between the two Covenants is in conformity with the views of the first generations of Christians. The nucleus of the most ancient confessions of faith actually consists in the reference to the exaltation of Jesus and to the title of Lord which is then definitively conferred upon him.[63] Even in the theology of St. John, notwithstanding the initial proclamation of the *Verbum caro factum,* it is the end of the earthly life of Jesus which constitutes "the decisive event"; it is what St. John calls his glorification.[64] Our exegetes continue to feel as their earliest ancestors did, and this is a second reason for them to acknowledge the presence of a properly "allegorical" meaning under the letter of the gospels, in just the same way as under the letter of the prior stories. Gerhoh of Reichersberg explains the phenomenon very neatly:

We say that an allegorical meaning is involved when, reading what happened before the coming of Christ or during his earthly life

[61.] See Arno of Reich., *Apol.* (Weichert ed., 230, 196).

[62.] Pseudo-Gregory (*PL,* 79, 664C). This is why Patrizi correctly specifies that if there are "types" in the gospels, we should say *"nullos tamen post Christi mortem, id est post sublatum Vetus Testamentum, vel certe post adventum Spiritus Sancti, id est post Novum Testamentum promulgatum"* (*op. cit.,* p. 200); *"saltem post adventum Spiritus Sancti"* (222; see 225). Erasmus will write, *De magnitudine misericordiarum Domini* (1524): *"In confinio Veteris ac Novi Testamenti factus homo"* (Leyden, vol. 5, col. 560).

[63.] Oscar Cullmann, *The Earliest Christian Confessions,* London, 1949; J. B. Montini, *Pastoral Letter* (1949): the Incarnation "prepares for the Pasch and finds in it its own term."

[64.] H. Van den Bussche, "Structure de Jean, I-XII," in *L'Evangile de Jean, études et problèmes* (1958), p. 65; Van den Bussche, "L'attente de la grande révélation dans le quatrième évangile," *NRT,* 85 (1953), pp. 1009–1019. Similarly, in 1 Cor. 15, 47, St. Paul is less concerned with the incarnation than with the resurrection. Joseph Huby, *Saint Paul, Epîtres aux Corinthiens,* p. 392.

before the historical revelation of grace, we understand that this was accomplished anew in the universal contemplation of Christ and the entire Church.[65]

*Neque enim Evangelium ante Crucem Christi est.*[66] As long as the great "passage"[67] has not been crossed, history and allegory cannot, therefore, be absorbed into one another. They are not yet fully united in the "Mystery".[68]

In quest of the spirit under the least significant letter of the gospels, a zeal which is frequently even redoubled is brought to bear, stemming from the natural conviction that nothing can possibly be as "filled with mysteries" as the words and actions of the Saviour: "Each of the words of the most gentle Saviour is heavy with mysteries, and filled with sacred doctrines."[69] The believer must, therefore, redouble his attention as he reads, for "the things which he did, and not only the things which he said, were parables, that is, signs of hidden realities."[70] "Everything which he said, everything which he did, everything which he suffered: let no one doubt that all was filled with mysteries."[71]

[65.] *In Ps. 36* (573–574).
[66.] Jerome, *Adversus Jovinianum*, 1, 26 (*PL*, 23, 245A).
[67.] Bernard, *In die Paschae sermo*, n. 14 (*PL*, 183, 281B-C).
[68.] The same duality of aspects, or the same ambiguity in evangelical times or in the mystery of salvation viewed "at the level where it was lived by Christ the Leader on the stage of our historical experience," have recently been analyzed by Père Grelot, "Les figures bibliques," *NRT*, 84 (1962): "There is a fragment of human time which is rather difficult to define precisely: does it belong to the time of preparation or to the 'last time'? On the one hand, it is prior to the 'consummation of time' which is constituted by the Cross-Resurrection event (Heb. 9, 11–12). But on the other hand, heaven and eternity are, in the incarnate Word, already made present on earth and in time; the Kingdom is inaugurated in the person of Jesus (*autobasileia,* following the formula of Origen . . .)" (p. 687).
[69.] Paschasius Radbertus, *In Matt.*, 1. 6 (*PL*, 120, 440D); 1.12 (958B). Gregory the Great, *In ev.*, h. 29, n. 1 (*PL*, 76, 1213D); h. 22, n. 2 (1175A).
[70.] Bede, *In Marc.* (*PL*, 92, 168D). Robert of Melun, *Sent.*, l. 1, p. 1, c. 6 (Martin ed., 178). Walafrid Strabo, *De subversione Jerusalem*, on the vendors cast out of the temple: *"Quod tunc Dominus per semetipsum egit corporaliter, quotidie agit in Ecclesia spiritualiter"* (*PL*, 114, 973D).
[71.] Bernard, *In ascensione Domini*, sermo 4, n. 2 (*PL*, 183, 310A). Leo, *Ep. 16*, c. 2 (*PL*, 54, 697–698).

Special attention is paid to his miracles, whose character as sign stands out more brilliantly. And it is thus that the "corporal" or "sensitive Gospel" is transformed unceasingly, through an unceasing meditation, which continues throughout the centuries, into "the spiritual Gospel."

Yet here we are, brought back almost despite ourselves to the substance of the Gospel after having wandered away from it. For when we are talking about the person of the Saviour, even what seems at first glance to be only the "sensitive" or "corporal" Gospel touches upon the substance; correlatively, the substance itself is not without a "sensitive" and "corporal" aspect. Inside and outside are not cut off from one another. Each individual fact pertaining to Christ in his earthly existence participates in the great Fact of Christ in its permanent singularity. Each of them manifests to us a "parcel" of it, to use an expression of Dom Odo Casel's.[72] Or, to employ the language of St. Leo the Great, all the mysteries of the life of Christ are joined together in the unity of his person.[73] In each of these facts, the connection between *historia* and *allegoria* thus tends to become interiorized. Some facts touch still more closely upon the single Mystery, to such an extent that the "allegorical" commentary on them tends, as we have seen above, to become nothing other than a tropological and anagogical application. This is the case for the scenes of the Nativity,[74] or the Epiphany.[75] When speaking of the adoration of the kings, the scene of the baptism of John and of the miracle at Cana, it will be said: "The mysteries and the joys of our salvation are contained in each of these

---

[72.] *Le mystère du culte dans le christianisme* (Hild trans.), p. 136: "*The mystery* thus reveals to us all the meaning of the historical acts and deeds of the Saviour. It takes nothing away from the concrete reality of these actions, but it does directly relate them to the divine order, and shows us in them parcels of the great plan of redemption."

[73.] *Ep. 16*, c. 3 (*PL*, 54, 698–700).

[74.] Berengarius, *In Ap.*, vis. 3 (*PL*, 17, 848A). Maximus of Turin, h. 11, *De nat. Dom.*, 6 (*PL*, 57, 246A). See the beautiful text, Bernardine in inspiration, published by H. M. Rochais in *Studia anselmiana*, 50, 1962, pp. 116–117: "*Quid significent ea quae Christus gessit corporaliter.*"

[75.] Leo, *Sermo 35*, c. 1 (*PL*, 54, 250A).

scenes." [76] And it will be said, first and foremost, of the events which mark the three sacred days of the Lord's passion, burial, and resurrection; "the entire triduum is quite clearly unfolded as a sacrament of man's salvation." [77] There are the immediate externals of the saving facts, there are the saving facts themselves, and there are the "mysteries" in which the Mystery is, in the eyes of faith, realized and expressed more particularly and which consequently find a privileged place in the liturgy. This external aspect of the Mystery is past, as is true of everything which pertains to time—Christ, having now entered into his glory, suffers and dies no more—but its internal aspect remains, so that, as St. Leo says, "the Lord's pasch is less to be celebrated in the memory as a past fact than honored as a present reality." [78] This brings us to the very heart of Pauline morality.[79]

Nevertheless, even though the divergence between evangelical *historia* on the one hand, and *allegoria* and *tropologia* on the other is thus suppressed, there may yet remain a final divergence within the New Testament, and at its very heart. To put it another way, the New Testament, even in the present fullness of

[76.] Maximus of Turin, *hom.* 22 (*PL*, 57, 270C). See Aelred of Rievaulx on the progress of the child Jesus, *De Jesu duod.*, c. 2, n. 11: *"Ita ejus profectus corporalis, noster est profectus spiritualis, et ea quae ab eo in cunctis aetatibus acta describuntur, in nobis per singulos profectuum gradus spiritualiter agi a bene proficientibus sentiuntur"* (*SC*, 60, 70–72). J. Guillet, *Jésus-Christ . . .:* "Everything which Jesus said or did belongs not to the past but to the present" (p. 221).
[77.] Peter Damian, *Sermo 48·* (*PL*, 144, 774A-B). Augustine, *Ep. 55,* c. 14, n. 24 (*PL*, 33, 215). Origen, *In Rom.*, V, 10 (*PG*, 14, 1048–1049). Bernard, *In dom. palm.*, sermo 3, n. 1 (*PL*, 183, 259–260). Hugh, *Did.*, l. 7, c. 27 (*PL*, 176, 838B).
[78.] *Ep. 16*, c. 3 (*PL*, 54, 699A). *Sermo 64*, c. 1 (358A). See *Sermo 63,* c. 6 (356B). *Sermo 22*, c. 1 (193B). See Origen, *In Luc.*, h. 7, n. 7: "When we gather together everything which is reported about Jesus, we shall see that everything which was written about him is considered to be divine and worthy of wonder: his birth, his education, his power, his resurrection, all these took place not merely at the time indicated but are still working on us today" (*SC*, 87, 161).
[79.] See Erasmus, *Ecclesiastes*, 1. 1 (*Opera*, 1703, vol. V, col. 830): *"Paulus vero vitam omnem Christi commonstrat mysticis typis esse refertam, exponens quid sit illi commori, quid cum illo sepeliri, quid resurgere, quid in caelum adscendere."*

its Mystery, is still susceptible of a further explanation: the anagogical one. We said above that, with Jesus, eschatology entered into history; but, in very precise terms, the history which continues to unfold still retains the full manifestation thereof—we are still under the dominion of the "luminous cloud," which heralds broad day. In this way, we rediscover the triple schema of salvation history, whose eternal fulfillment is prepared, as it is prefigured, by the two stages of that history which are committed to the two successive Testaments:

God made earthly man in an earthly universe; he made the second man spiritual in a spiritual universe; he will make the third man heavenly in a heavenly universe. The first universe is historical, and its creation and governance are recounted in the Old Testament. The second universe is moral and allegorical, and its creation and governance are recounted in the Gospel. The third universe is anagogical; its estate is known only by him to whom it has been given. What the Old Testatment does is to recount the creation of the first universe and announce the work of the second; the New Testament proclaims the reconciliation of the first universe, which is the creation of the second, and it promises, while prefiguring it, the estate of the third.[80]

But this triple schema relates only to knowledge.[81] The Mystery of Christ, once bestowed, is bestowed in its entirety. The anagogical meaning can only be glimpsed, but the underlying reality is already there. Let us acknowledge the full force of the unique Fact by which the new Covenant was inaugurated: the redemptive incarnation of the Word of God. This must be repeated, because it is the basis of all ancient exegesis just as it will always remain, no matter what the ever-changing variety of our disciplines, the basis of our faith, and also because the

[80.] Isaac of Stella, *Sermo 54·* (*PL,* 194, 1874B-C). See Ambrose Autpert, *S. in Transfig.,* nn. 6–7 (*PL,* 89, 1309). Edmond Ortigues, *Le discours et le symbole* (1962), p. 57: "Letter, allegory, anagoge, that is to say the past of history, the present of faith, and the future of eschatology."

[81.] Bernard, *De diversis,* sermo 37, n. 6 (*PL,* 183, 642A-B); *In Cantica,* sermo 48, n. 7 (1016A). See Henri Crouzel, "Origène et la 'connaissance mystique.' " *Studia Patristica,* 5 (Paris, 1962), pp. 272–273.

ancient texts which express or assume this truth are the object of a stubborn misconception on the part of many historians. This incarnation is a unique fact, not simply in the obvious sense, common to every fact, to every event, that it happens only once in time; it is also unique in the totally unique, totally singular sense that this Fact, alone among all facts, was prefigured by the long series of facts in the old Covenant—which, in its fundamental reality, does not lend itself to allegorization either, and finally, never ceases, from the very first instant, to bear fruit within itself for centuries to come and for eternity.

## 5. The Unity of the Quadruple Meaning

The doctrine of the four meanings of Scripture (history, allegory, tropology, anagoge) is fulfilled and finds its unity in traditional eschatology. For Christianity is a fulfillment, yet it is, in this very fulfillment, also an expectation. Whether mystical or doctrinal, whether taught or lived, real anagoge is, therefore, always eschatological. It stirs up in us the desire for eternity. And this is another reason why this fourth meaning is necessarily the last one. It can no more be followed by a fifth than it can do without the other three. The expectation is never absent, nor, in our earthly condition, is it ever surpassed, even though it might even now encroach upon the term.

There are many texts which express this expectation, and in various ways. All are summed up, we might say, in the famous hymn: *"Coelestis urbs, Jerusalem, beata pacis visio."* But what the majority of the texts do not show in explicit fashion, and, ordinarily, still less adequately the more complete and the more didactic they are in setting forth the four meanings, is the theory's secret soul. This is the dynamic unity, the reciprocal interiority of the four meanings. We speak, as we must, of various meanings; we explain this meaning, that meaning, yet another meaning, so as to distinguish them one from another; we superpose them, or juxtapose them, or we oppose them to one another; we count them out and put them in sequence just as if they were so many separate entities. This is language's inevitable parade, but it did not deceive the ancients—any more than a good Thomist would take the elements of being, whose real distinction he affirms, for so many "things." We should say of these four meanings what an early author said of the four degrees of contemplation: they are connected like the links of a single chain, *concatenati sunt ad invicem.*[1] Let us call again to mind Ezekiel's "wheel within a wheel," on which St. Gregory commented with such extraordinary ingenuity and whose full significance will soon become apparent. Each of the wheels possesses a propulsive force, so that one drives the other *"per incrementa intelligentiae, quasi quibusdam passibus mentis."* "The word of history" is fulfilled by "the meanings of allegory," and "the meanings of allegory" in turn naturally incline "to the practice of morality."[2] There is a passage, by a natural and necessary motion, *"de historia ad allegoriam, et de allegoria ad moralitatem."*[3] Allegory is truly *the truth* of history; the latter, by itself, would be incapable of an intelligible self-fulfillment; allegory brings this about in history by bestowing upon it all its meaning.[4] The mystery which allegory thereby uncovers merely initiates yet another cycle; in its first phase, it is simply an *"exordium";*[5] in order to be fully itself, it must find a double fulfillment. To begin with, it moves inward upon itself and produces its fruit in the spiritual life, which is treated in tropology: this spiritual life must then open out into the sun of the kingdom, at the end of time, which is the object of anagoge—for what we now realize in Christ through deliberate acts of will is exactly what will one day, after it has been freed of all obstacles and all obscurity, be the essence of eternal life.[6]

[1] Guigo the Carthusian, *Scala claustralis,* c. 12, n. 13 (*PL,* 184, 482C).

[2] Gregory, *In Ez.,* l. 1, h. 10, n. 1 (*PL,* 76, 886C). *Mor., ep. miss.,* c. 1 (*PL,* 75, 512A).

[3] Luke of M. Corn., *Mor in Cant.* (*PL,* 203, 550D).

[4] Gaudentius, *Tr.* 10 (100). Rhabanus Maurus, *In Ex.,* l. 1, c. 8 (*PL,* 108, 27A).

[5] Alcuin, *Div. off.,* c. 26 (*PL,* 101, 1226D).

[6] See Basil, *Treatise on the Holy Spirit,* c. 15: "The Lord, in preparing us for the life that follows on the resurrection, lays down for us the evangelical manner of life by proposing that we be gentle, resigned,

This process of development is temporal first of all. In time, history comes before mystery; figure comes before truth; history is "prefiguration": "Do not the acts which must be accomplished spiritually follow upon those which have been bodily accomplished?" [7] For us, eternal life is future life, and the spiritual world is the world to come.[8] But succession in time is not the whole of it. There is a development, from one meaning to the other, which can be called logical. The object of the second meaning constitutes, vis-à-vis the object of the first, a reprise, an internal progression, a much more wonderful "recapitulation." With reference to the nativity of the Virgin, Isaac of Stella made note of this fact in dramatic terms, and in a broadened perspective:

Everywhere that which is wonderfully said or done is still more wonderfully resaid or redone in mystery. "Beginning with the head, then, everything comes back together again." For all things which come initially are figures of what will come later, and the latter, which now begin to be revealed in their proper time, are themselves what might be called envelopes or exemplars of those which will come in the future. And just as the latter are more true and more evident than the first-mentioned, so the things which are to come are still more true, so that there is a constant passage experienced by every nativity, every living man, from image, in a sort of vanity, until he arrives at the naked, obvious, and stable face of truth.[9]

The term *"involucrum"* accurately indicates the relationship of the historical meaning, as historical, to allegory. It is the latter which really gives us Christ, who is the *"adeps frumenti,"* the *"granum tritici."* Now *"nullum granum potest ad maturitatem*

---

that we guard ourselves intact from the love of pleasure, that we live a life detached from wealth, so that even now we might, by deliberate willing, achieve what the life to come will possess, as of its inherent nature" (*SC,* 17, 171).

7. Hilary, *Tr. myst.,* 1. 1, c. 22 (*SC,* 19, 112).

8. See E. Molland, *The Conception of the Gospel in the Alexandrian Theology,* Oslo, 1938, p. 152: "[Origen's] spiritual world is the world on high but it is also the world to come."

9. *Sermo 54* (*PL,* 194, 1873A). Bede, *In Sam.,* 1. 2, c. 9 (*PL,* 91, 592A).

*venire, nisi intra paleam latitaverit"* (no seed can come to maturity unless it has first been hidden in straw).[10] "In order to arrive at the future, one must first pass through the present." The most "allegorically-minded" of our ancient authors are not the ones who insist the least on the need for temporal maturation. But the bond among these three latter meanings is even more interior. The New Testament is homogeneous, and this is the reason why these new relationships could no longer be very satisfactorily expressed by the term "allegory," even though a mystical or spiritual meaning is still involved. The history of Abraham, the history of David were "allegorical," but the history of Jesus is not.[11] *Non significat alterum Christum.* Henceforward, everything is produced, prolonged, and locked within an identical mystery: *Christus substantialiter semper idem; Christus seipsum significat* (Christ is, substantially, ever the same; Christ signifies himself).[12] The passage from one meaning to the other is, more precisely, the passage of the one meaning into the other, the becoming of the one by the other. "The works of Christ which were accomplished in time become, within the heart of the believer, wondrous sacraments of eternity."[13] *Translatus est Christus ad Ecclesiam.*[14] The Church will be the fullness of Christ—let us repeat the extremely beautiful phrase of St. Ambrose—"it is in souls that the Church is beautiful."

In addition to being a temporal succession and a logical development it is also a living evolution. The quadruple meaning puts forth an organism. "From the root of history, allegory produces spiritual fruit," which is gathered up and stored for eternity.[15] Thus "there is an entire chain of correlations which links

10. Etherius and Beatus, *Ad Elip.,* l. 1, c. 98 (*PL,* 96, 955B).

11. *Ibid.,* l. 1, c. 105 (*PL,* 96, 958D).

12. See Guitmond of Aversa, *De corp. et sang. Dom. ver. in euch.,* 1. 2 (*PL,* 149, 1459A, 1461C).

13. William of St. Thierry, *Speculum fidei* (*PL,* 180, 387D). Langton, *In Gen.,* III, 19: *"Verbum Dei debet converti in opus"* (Smalley, *The Study of the Bible in the Middle Ages,* 249, n. 1). See Cerfaux, *Christ in the Theology of Saint Paul:* "The risen Christ is seen as 'the Son of God displaying his spiritual might'" (p. 275).

14. Paschasius Radbertus, *In Lam.,* 1. 2 (*PL,* 120, 119A).

15. Gregory, *Moralia,* l. 6, c. 1, n. 2 (*PL,* 75, 730C).

together the aspects and stages of the Design of Salvation which unfolds here below for an ultimate consummation which is beyond history." [16] Each meaning tends towards the other as towards its end.[17] Thus although they are several, they together make but one. There is unity as to source and unity as to convergence; by means of them, Richard of St. Victor says in an extract which is difficult to translate: *Scriptura multa nobis in unum loquitur.*[18] There is mystical identity. And the same is true of anagoge and tropology: the soul, says St. Bonaventure, *"intrando in seipsam, intrat in supernam Jerusalem"* (entering within itself, enters into the heavenly Jerusalem); [19] and Raoul of St. Germer said much the same thing: *"Jerusalem vero, id est visio pacis, debet esse anima nostra, civitas utique quam Deus inhabitare dignetur"* (Our soul must be Jerusalem, that is, the vision of peace, the city in which God deigns to dwell).[20] And again of allegory and anagoge: the Church in time, as we have seen, is not another Church than that of eternity,[21] although it does remain in another condition: *"nondum re, tamen spe . . ."* (not yet in reality, yet already in expectancy).[22] *"Caelum est sancta Ecclesia."* [23] History itself, even in its relative exteriority, participates in this mystical identity, for, as Rupert of Deutz also explains, the saving facts, even those which are as yet saving only from afar and by way of preparation, are no more without

[16.] P. Grelot, in *Introduction à la Bible,* I (A. Robert and A. Feuillet eds.), p. 208.

[17.] Gregory, *In Ez.,* l. 2, h. 3, n. 18 (*PL*, 76, 968A).

[18.] *Benjamin major.,* l. 4, c. 14 (*PL*, 196, 151C).

[19.] *Itinerarium,* c. 4, n. 4 (Quaracchi, V, 306).

[20.] *In Lev.,* l. 16, c. 1 (198H). See Origen, *In Num.,* h. 26, n. 7 (254–255).

[21.] Dom Olivier Rousseau, "La Jérusalem céleste," in *La Vie spirituelle,* 86 (1951), p. 380: "We believe that Origen has been wrongly criticized for having sometimes applied the notion of maternity to the heavenly Jerusalem and sometimes to the Church on earth, as if this involved an inconsistency attributable to an imperfect ecclesiology (Plumpe)." See Origen, *In Jer.,* h. 6 (Jerome trans.), (*PL*, 25, 634A); *In Jos.,* h. 21, n. 2 (431–432).

[22.] Rupert, *In Zach.* (*PL*, 168, 791D); following Augustine. see above, I, p. 627 (*Exégèse médiévale*, Paris, 1959).

[23.] Richard, *In Ap.,* l. 2, c. 1 (*PL*, 168, 744A-B).

"reason" than the Father is without the *Word,* and "just as the eternal Father does nothing without the coeternal Son, so none of the acts which, for man's salvation, were bodily posited either in the Law or in the Gospel suffers from any lack of spiritual signification." [24] Thereafter, the identity is still more clearly asserted: it is the "mystery" which is "example," [25] and this, the substance of it, is "the very thing which must be carried within one's heart." [26] In mystery, nothing will suffer separation. The coming of Christ, through each of its phases, "is something indivisible." [27] If the traditional understanding of Scripture perfectly assures in the history of our salvation that "meeting of event and meaning" [28] which is one of the major preoccupations of every cultivated mind, it is in Christ and through Christ that it is assured, at every stage along the way. It always shows forth the Mystery of Christ, indivisible. The same unique mystery is also the mystery of ourselves and our eternity. Each phrase of Scripture has many meanings; but, in a still more real fashion, all of Scripture's phrases have but a single meaning.[29] All of Scripture's "letter" contains a single treasure, "our treasure." [30] In each instance, the *visio imaginis* is different, but the *intentio mentis* is always the same.[31] Each phrase, in what it is aiming at, comes together with all the others; they all converge on the single Focus in which they, secretly, originated.

*Mysterium Christi:* this mystery has infinite depths—and the mind of each believer has varied capacities with which to under-

[24.] *In Jo.,* 1. 2 (*PL,* 169, 284–285).

[25.] Guerric of Igny, *De annutiatione,* sermo 2, n. 4 (*PL,* 185, 122D).

[26.] Augustine, *Contra Adimantum,* c. 16, n. 2 (*PL,* 43, 156).

[27.] F. Nogues, *Revue des questions liturgiques et paroissiales,* 1937, p. 240.

[28.] M. Merleau-Ponty, *Eloge de la philosophie* (1953), 17; ET *In Praise of Philosophy,* Evanston, 1963.

[29.] See Albert the Great, *In I Sent.,* d. 1, a. 5. Bouyer, *The Meaning of the Monastic Life,* p. 181.

[30.] Rupert, *In Ez.,* 1. 2, c. 17 (*PL,* 167, 1479A).

[31.] *Moralia,* 1. 29, c. 31, n. 69: all the pages of the Bible *"unum praedicant"; "divisi quidem fuerunt tempore, sed non praedicatione"* (*PL,* 76, 515C-D).

stand it. As a result of this, there is an incurable character of non-fulfillment which marks all spiritual understanding, just as we saw to be especially true of anagoge. But as St. Gregory's word *volatus* suggested in reference to anagoge, this fatal non-fulfillment should be considered primarily in its positive and dynamic aspect. The Word of God never stops creating and burrowing within a man who makes use of his capacity to receive it, so that the understanding which also believes can grow indefinitely. An old text can, by means of allegory, always make further aspects of the newness apparent; [32] the new mystery can always be further interiorized and can always introduce eternity still more deeply into the heart. Just as the knowledge of God, as described by a St. Gregory of Nyssa,[33] constantly goes "from beginning to beginning," the same can be said of the understanding of Scripture, *"cum (Deus) maximam nobis sacramentorum abyssum quasi de novo jam incipiat aperire"* (when God begins to open to us, as if for the first time, the immense abyss of the mysteries).[34] Thus we are called to be "changed into his likeness from one degree of glory to another; for this comes from the Lord who is the Spirit." [35] This is what Origen had taught on the subject of the manna. John Cassian, in his conference on *spiritual knowledge,* had repeated it for the West: "In the measure that our mind is renewed by meditation on Scripture, the very face of Scripture begins to be renewed, and the beauty of the holier meaning somehow begins to grow with our own growth." [36] The *Moralia* of St. Gregory had propagated the same doctrine [37] and they themselves had been echoed by the *Sentences* of St. Isidore of Seville: "Sacred Scripture varies with the understanding of each reader, like the manna. . . . And yet, though the Lord's word might be diversified depending on what

32. See Rhabanus Maurus, *In Ruth,* c. 13 (*PL,* 108, 1218D).
33. See *Sur les chemins de Dieu;* ET *The Discovery of God,* New York, 1960, ch. 6.
34. Aelred of Rievaulx, *De oner.,* sermo 12 (*PL,* 195, 405C).
35. 2 Cor. 3, 18.
36. *Coll. 14,* c. 11 (Pichery, *SC,* 54, 197).
37. *Moralia,* l. 6, c. 16, n. 22 ( *PL,* 75, 741B-C).

223

each reader understands of it, the word itself remains one." [38]
A century ago, Mgr. Gerbet expressed the same thought: "The
symbol has a kind of expansive meaning, which stretches with
the reader's understanding." [39] Only yesterday a philosopher
reminded us of it again: "Depending on the level of understanding involved, Scripture differentiates its responses; and the
latter, we suspect, are worth exactly what the quality of interro-
gation is worth." [40] We can well wonder at the perfect correspondence of the preceding remarks with those of St. Gregory or
of Rhabanus Maurus: "To the extent that each man makes
progress towards the heights, the sacred words themselves keep
pace by disclosing still higher things." [41]

No better explanation of the matter has been given than that
of St. Gregory, which is both very poetical and very precise.
Actually, it is to Gregory that Rhabanus Maurus is indebted,
after Isidore, after Smaragdus,[42] and so many others after them.
Scripture, says Gregory, "moves forward with those who read
it." The reason for this is that Scripture, which contains God's
revelation about himself, is, we might say, expandable—or pene-
trable—to an infinite degree. Gregory therefore applies to it a
law of religious knowledge, elsewhere expressed by him in connection with the meeting between the two travellers and the
risen Jesus on the road to Emmaus. One might think, he explains
in the latter passage, that Jesus was at first hiding his real
identity, so as not to be recognized; but this would be a superficial way of interpreting his incognito, and one which was
hardly worthy of him who is Truth: *"Nihil ergo simplex Veritas
per duplicitatem facit, sed talem se eis exhibuit in corpore,*

38. *Sent.,* l. 1, c. 18, n. 5 (*PL,* 83, 576B).
39. *Esquisse de Rome chrétien,* I, 409.
40. Henry Duméry, *Critique et religion* (1957), 247, n. 3. See Gregory,
*Moralia,* l. 23, c. 19, n. 34: "God caused the sacred Books to be written
so as thereby to answer the many and secret questions of every man. . . .
He composed a Scripture by which he satisfies the questionings of all"
(*PL,* 76, 271B).
41. *In Ez.,* l. 2 (*PL,* 110, 534D).
42. *Diad. mon.,* c. 3 (*PL,* 102, 598A-B).

*qualis apud illos erat in mente"* (It is not that he who is Truth itself does anything through duplicity, but he so showed himself in body as they themselves thought him to be in their own minds).[43] The explanation will be preserved in the Middle Ages.[44] It too had been set forth at length by Origen, in connection with the gospel account of the transfiguration.[45] Gregory returns to this law, in the seventh of his homilies on Ezekiel, when commenting on the great inaugural vision of the Prophet. In his eyes, it constitutes one of the bases of Christian exegesis, and it itself is based on the truth that it is the same God who gives us Scripture and makes it understood; what appear to be two successive acts on his part are in reality but one. God, of course, is not subject to the external play of our temporal succession. Consequently, we can expect to find priority or reciprocal causality between the objective meaning and the interpretation of it, whenever the latter comes from the Spirit. This is in no way similar to the notion that there are dogmas which have been held in reserve, since the Spirit was given to the Church, as a kind of revelation to come. The sacred text must not be thought of as a repository for a series of meanings, all of which are already formed and more or less prepared to be discovered. The Spirit communicates to the sacred text a limitless potentiality, which therefore entails degrees of profundity which can go on and on. No more than this world was Scripture, that other world, created once for all: the Spirit "creates" it still, as if every day, to the extent that he "opens" it.[46] Through a wondrous and precise correlationship, he "expands" it to the extent that he ex-

---

43. *In ev.*, 1. 2, h. 23, n. 1 (*PL*, 76, 1182C). On the idea of a "constant progress" in the work of Gregory, see Leclercq, *L'amour des lettres et le désir de Dieu;* ET *The Love of Learning and the Desire for God,* New York, 1961, pp. 39–41.

44. Bede, *In Luc.* (*PL*, 92, 627A). Werner, *Deflorationes SS. Patrum, s. de resurr.* (*PL*, 157, 931C).

45. *In Matt.*, cc. 32, 35 (58, 65). *Contra Celsum*, 1. 6, c. 77 (2, 146–149). *In Luc.*, h. 3 (20–23). See H. de Lubac, *Aspects of Buddhism,* New York, 1954.

46. Compare *In I Reg.*, 1. 3, c. 5, n. 30 (*PL*, 79, 216C).

pands the understanding of him who receives it.[47] For, just as
Origen had already pointed out, *"extenditur anima nostra, quae
prius fuerat contracta, ut possit capax esse sapientiae Dei"* (then
our soul, which was at first contracted, expands, so as to be
capable of receiving the wisdom of God).[48] The *volatus* of the
contemplative soul, no matter how far into the heavens of Scripture it might carry the soul, will never cause it to collide at any
frontier, for both space and flight are provided, proportionately.
This is a bold view indeed, but, properly understood, the boldness is precisely the boldness of faith. It is, however, a view which
is more than capable of inducing vertigo in our possibly too
human "common sense," and of leading astray the positivist
mentalities of our time, in any event.

This is what St. Gregory, following Origen and Cassian, repeats with a new profundity. He sees it all signified in the fact
that the chariot which was contemplated by Ezekiel in his vision
followed the movements of the Spirit of Life which was within its
wheels. His explanation bears out very precisely the parallel
symbol of the double abyss: *abyssus abyssum invocat.* Was Harnack thinking of something similar to this when, true to a cliché
which goes back to Melancthon [49] and is, we are sorry to say,
sometimes picked up by Catholic historians, he suggested that
the great pope had debased the spirituality of the patristic age
to the level of the uneducated? [50] And was it to this that one of
the masters of the *Aufklärung,* J. Brücker, was referring when
he wrote that the entire doctrine and the entire devotion of
"this Doctor with very poor judgment" could be reduced almost
to the "superstitions of an external cult"? [51] Was it because of

---

[47.] Dom Cuthbert Butler, *Western Mysticism,* p. 124, n. 1, has noted
that such formulas as *"animus dilatatus," "mentis laxatur sinus,"
"cum in Dei lumine rapitur (animus) super se, in interioribus ampliatur"*
are frequent in Gregory.

[48.] *In Jer.,* h. 5 (*PL,* 25, 627C).

[49.] *"Gregorius, quem isti Magnum, ego praesultorem* καὶ δαδοῦχον
*theologiae pereuntis voco"* (*Corp. ref.,* II, 16).

[50.] *Dogmengeschichte,* III (4th ed., 1910), pp. 257–269. See R. See-
berg, *Lehrbuch der Dogmengeschichte,* III (4th ed., 1930), pp. 37–46.

[51.] *Historia critica philosophiae,* III (1743), pp. 560–563: *"doctorem
exigui judicii"; "superstitio, judicii paupertas,"* and so forth. The author

similar passages that so many other historians present to us the faith of this man as a faith "deeply rooted in the fear of hell," [52] feeding the somber flames of the Middle Ages? And was it also because of this kind of thing that Ebert himself, in his really solid history of the literature of the Middle Ages, paid no attention to the homilies on Ezekiel, as "lacking any particular interest for us"? [53] We may at last be able to show a bit more fairness. This feeble, sickly pontiff, overburdened with problems of administration and with cares, speaking to the wretched populace of a half-ruined city at whose gates the enemy soon would camp,[54] not only succeeded in making the radiant but still far-off vision of the heavenly Jerusalem shine in the eyes of his listeners; he drew enough energy from his contemplative faith to be able to probe deeply and serenely, with a liberty of spirit which would one day excite the admiration of St. Bernard,[55] into the most sublime and most mysterious of subjects: the living contact of our understanding with the truth of the God who is revealed to us. And so persuasive was the word of this good shepherd that, by an extraordinary miracle, his flock never stopped following him, from church to church, and experienced a new birth of hope, like the bones which the Prophet saw returning to life under the breath of the Spirit.[56]

---

subjects the practice of the quadruple meaning to the same adverse criticism. The absence of any profound metaphysical speculation in the works of Gregory makes him deny the "exalted spirituality"; but when this profound speculation is found in the other Fathers, they are immediately accused of having betrayed the simplicity of the Gospel.

52. F. B. Artz, *The Mind of the Middle Ages* (3d ed.), New York, 1958, p. 192.

53. A. Ebert, *Histoire générale de la littérature du moyen âge en Occident*, I, Paris, 1883, p. 590.

54. On the tragic circumstances in which these homilies were delivered, see John the Deacon, 1. 4, cc. 66–67 (*PL*, 75, 215–219).

55. *De consideratione*, 1. 1, c. 9 (*PL*, 182, 739B-C).

56. See Denys de Sainte-Marthe, *Hist. de S. Grégoire le Grand* (1697), p. 230: "This fidelity, whether that of the Shepherd in preaching the word of God, or that of the people who came to hear it in spite of all the worries which contemporary events must have caused them, seems to me as great a miracle as the one which is said to have occurred at the same period" (the miracle of the dove).

"Minds become increasingly broader as they receive within themselves, as through narrow chinks, the light of truth." [57] There can be no doubt that Gregory's initial inspiration for his explanation stems from Origen.[58] The basic lines of the symbol which he develops could already be found in St. Ambrose.[59] But the symbol itself, as understood by him, is certainly Gregory's. In the seventh homily, he expresses it in language of such power and beauty that we should be able to quote at least part of it word for word:

*Quocumque ibat spiritus, illuc eunte spiritu, et rotae pariter leva-bantur, sequentes eum. Spiritus enim vitae erat in rotis.*

Wherever the spirit would go, they went, and the wheels rose along with them; for the spirit of the living creatures (life) was in the wheels.

Where the mind of the reader inclines, there too the divine oracles are lifted up: if you seek something exalted in them, these sacred oracles will grow with you, they will ascend the summits with you. For, in the same sentence from Scripture, one reader draws his nourishment from the history alone, while another seeks a typical sense, and yet another, by means of the latter, inclines towards contemplative understanding. Most often of all, what happens is that the three things can simultaneously be found in one and the same sentence.[60]

Thus what is said in the Holy Book grows with the mind of those who read it.

Let us see how the wheels follow the spirit which Scripture calls the spirit of life and says is within the wheels.

In the measure that each reader moves onward towards the heights, the sacred oracles speak to him of higher things. . . . The wheels

57. *In Ez.,* l. 2, h. 5, n. 17 (*PL,* 76, 995B).
58. But, *In Ez.,* h. 1, n. 16. Origen explained the vision of the prophet differently (*PG,* 13, 681C). See Jerome, *Ep. 64,* c. 18 (3, 134).
59. *In Ps. 118,* sermo 4, n. 28: *"O rationabilium equorum grande certamen! O mirandum mysterium! Rota intra rotam currebat, et non impediebatur; Novum Testamentum in Veteri Testamento erat, intra illud currebat per quod annuntiabatur"* (*PL,* 15, 1250A-B). See above, chs. V, IV (*Exégèse médiévale*).
60. There follows the example of the burning bush.

move ahead, stop, rise up, because each reader finds in the Holy Book just what he is looking for. Have you advanced to the active life? It remains steady with you.[61] Have you arrived, by the grace of God, at the contemplative life? It soars above with you.

In the shadows of the present life, this Scripture is our light along the way. . . . Yet we know that even it is obscure to us, unless the Truth throws light on our minds. . . . For created light will not shine for us if it has not been lighted up by uncreated Light. Therefore, because the all-powerful God himself created, for our salvation, everything that is said in the two Testaments, and because he himself has opened up to us their meaning, the spirit of life was in the wheels.[62]

---

61. It will be noted that "*sacra lectio*" in this instance is not reading, but the Book itself. See Cassiodorus, *Inst. div. lectionum* (variant: *litterarum*).

62. *In Ez.*, 1. 1, h. 7 (*PL*, 76, 844–848). Cardinal Humbert will apply the text from Ezekiel not only to the Scriptures, but also to the writings of the Fathers and to Conciliar texts. *Adv. Simoniacos*, 1. 3, c. 28 (*L. de lite*, I, 234). For Maximus the Confessor, *Mystagogia*, the wheel within the wheel meant the two worlds, sensible and intelligible, or reality and the knowledge of it (*PG*, 91, 670).

# APPENDIX

Letters from R. P. Hugues Vincent, O.P. (Jerusalem, Arab Sector).

## 1. To Mgr. Bruno de Solages (April 26, 1950)

. . . By the happiest of coincidences, Père de Vaux, the Director of the School and the Prior of the Monastery, received Père de Lubac's work, *Histoire et Esprit, l'intelligence de l'Ecriture d'après Origène,* in the same post from France. I promptly got hold of the substantial volume, thinking that I would give it a glance before I thanked you for your kind letter. The book was so fascinating that, after devouring the Conclusion in a couple of hours, I read it from cover to cover in two days—even the chapters where his theological mastery completely surpasses my admitted philistinism.

I am really delighted by the position taken by Père de Lubac in the dispute which became so unfortunately complicated in the past by imprudent excesses. I have not the slightest doubt that my beloved and venerated master would have subscribed to it at once. During the years 1891–1900, when Père Lagrange absolutely pulverized my entire attitude towards Holy Scripture, its basic theological notion, its character, and its interpretation, he drilled into me principles which are amazingly identical to those on which the masterly treatment of Père de Lubac rests. As Père Lagrange guided my first steps through the writings of the Fathers, he helpfully sketched out the evolution of the patristic exegesis as adapted to the fluid condition of the Church's own development, in precisely the same style as marks the history which Père de Lubac recounts so brilliantly in his Conclusion. Most of all, he taught me to understand and to love this exegesis, so fruitful for the interior life, and in such perfect alignment with its supernatural character. How many times, in frequent scriptural discussions during our long years of labor together, did I hear him deplore the fact that the harsh demands of the task which was dictated by the needs of the period restricted us to the intricate area of historical exegesis and deprived us of the opportunity of personally enjoying the rich fruits of spiritual exegesis, whose different points of view will never exhaust the treasures of meaning enclosed by God in the Scripture whose Author he is! Père Lagrange never tired of warning his hearers against what he unhesitatingly called "the vain pretensions of historical exegesis." During the last weeks I stayed with him, in October and November of 1937, at St.-Maximin, just after he had become personally acquainted with Paul Claudel—who had little patience with historical method—he told me over and over again how fine, how mutually fruitful it would be for historico-critical exegetes, spiritual-allegorist exegetes (or any other label!) to arrive at a sympathetic understanding of each other, rather than remain compartmentalized and hostile towards one another. He had a presentiment, far better than mine, that present trends and the needs of souls would demand just this collaboration in the interpretation of Scripture.

So I am personally very grateful to Père de Lubac for having discerned so clearly the true nature of the exegesis to which Père Lagrange devoted his life, and for having frequently pointed out his real attitude towards spiritual exegesis. It seems to me that *Histoire et Esprit* is the masterly charter of what the integral exegesis of Holy Scripture must be in the Church today. And because, today no less than yesterday, the labor is immense and calls for varying specializations, I would hope that this book, carefully read and studied, might become the basic norm for spiritual exegesis, in exactly the same way as *La Méthode Historique* endeavored to call forth historico-critical exegetes at a time when they were almost as rare as they were ignored. . . .

## 2. To the Author (June 21, 1950)

... Although the technical field which has taken up the greater part of my life does not qualify me in the least to evaluate the works of theology and religious history in which you excel, everything which has to do with Holy Scripture fascinates me so much that I certainly could not resist pursuing with as much pleasure as profit whatever was accessible to me in your wonderful book. At the very moment that your beautiful book *Histoire et Esprit* arrived at the School, a letter from our mutual friend arrived to tell me that it had just, so very advantageously, been published. I got hold of it with the greatest of eagerness, in that I was at that very moment at work on editing some notes on the exegetical method of my beloved teacher, especially on his innermost attitude towards Scripture. The book fascinated me so completely that, despite my admitted "philistinism," I did not put it down until I had devoured—I would not hesitate to say "savored"—it from first page to last. As soon as I had finished it, I wrote to our mutual friend to tell him of my enthusiastic judgment of it. I cannot be vexed in the least with him for having told you about it. . . . I thought that Père de Vaux himself would review the work in the *Revue biblique* with far greater competence than I could ever have, and I know that he relishes it too. But he wanted me to review it, knowing as he did the joy which reading it had brought me. It goes without saying that readers would have promptly sent me back to my archeological ages if I had presumed to spell out my powerful admiration for your penetrating and profound study of Origen—the man and his work. Thus I discreetly limited myself to a few clinical notes on the structure of the book; but I did try to bring out the benefits of your method.[1] I am very, very grateful to you, dear Reverend

---

[1.] The review referred to by Père Vincent is to be found in *R.bibl.*, vol. 57 (1950), pp. 634–635. There are reviews of *Exégèse Mediévale* in *R.bibl.* by Pierre Grelot: vol. 67 (1960), pp. 261–266; vol. 68 (1961), pp. 423–427; vol. 71 (1964), pp. 413–416.

Father, for having done such perfect justice to the mind of Père Lagrange, by stressing that, even though the needs of the moment required him to devote the major portion of his work to basic literal and historical exegesis, he still considered a spiritual interpretation of the Word of God, based on the powerful and profound spirit of the Fathers of the Church and not satisfied with a mechanical listing of allegories, to be no less indispensable and much more fruitful for the soul. Careful study of the excellent advice you give for revitalizing spiritual exegesis in our own day delights me and brings back to mind the echo of any number of recommendations by my teacher, when he was guiding my first steps through the Bible and was teaching me to enjoy it and to strive to live by it. I ardently hope that *Histoire et Esprit* might become the manual of scriptural hermeneutics both for today's generation and for tomorrow's. Today's generation can fruitfully learn from it that there are much better things to do than waste one's time in swordplay *for* or *against* literalism or spiritual meaning; tomorrow's can derive from it the guiding principles of an integral catholic exegesis, worthy of Holy Scripture and fully capable of answering all the needs of intellect and soul. And, since the labor is infinitely too great for the same men to be able to undertake it with the desired precision, historians will learn that their arduous task simply puts them in the presence or in the possession of honey-in-the-comb, and spiritualists will reckon with the fact that, before one can extract the honey from the wax with any profit for the soul, it is necessary to check on the quality of the comb and see whether it was produced by the divine Bee or by common hornets. And your book will also impress upon each group the essential need, if Scripture is to be understood and interpreted correctly, of *living* one's Christianity with all possible intensity under the living *magisterium* of the Church. I do, then, look upon your book as a great service for our time and I very much want to impress upon you my fervent thanks. . . .[2]

2. It was impossible to suppress from these two letters, without destroying the thought expressed therein, a number of laudatory remarks which are ascribable to the kindness and great courtesy of their author.

# INDEX

Bruno of Segni, 35 n. 18, 86 n. 6, 87 n. 26, 90 n. 51, 103 n. 18, 109 n. 69, 110 n. 86, 112 n. 94, 115 n. 16, 119 n. 45, 122, 131 n. 10, 138 n. 46, 139 nn. 51 and 56, 140 n. 63, 141 n. 70, 143 n. 81, 161 n. 14, 175 n. 21, 176 n. 24, 196 n. 8, 197 n. 13
de Bruyne, E., 127 n. 107
Bultmann, Rudolf, 158 n. 50, 211 n. 60
Burkitt, F. C., 163 n. 24
Butler, Dom Cuthbert, 226 n. 47
Byse, Charles, 70 n. 52

Caesarius of Arles, 20, 28 n. 47, 46 n. 10, 110 n. 77, 140 n. 61, 141 n. 67
Caird, Edwin, 100
Calvin, John, 63 n. 30, 75, 76 and nn. 7, 8, and 10, 77 and n. 12
Cano, Melchior, 57 n. 4, 58 n. 8
Cantaloup, Paul, 180 n. 42
Cantor, Peter, 164 n. 28, 183 n. 6
Capelle, B., 127 n. 108
Casel, Dom Odo, 214
Cassian, John, 49, 56, 68 n. 42, 137 n. 42, 154 n. 30, 223, 226
Cassiodorus, 104 n. 31, 106 n. 47, 108 n. 64, 143, 164, 229 n. 61
Catherine of Siena, 54 n. 39
Cavallera, F., 136 n. 37
Cavallin, Samuel, 128 n. 109
Cellier, Dom, 60 n. 15, 64 n. 30
Celsus, 167 nn. 36 and 37
Cerfaux, Lucien, 36 n. 23, 145 n. 92, 220 n. 13
de Chardin, Pierre Teilhard, 185
Charlemagne, 182 n. 47
Charlier, Dom Célestin, 13 n. 5, 14 n. 10, 15 n. 11, 26 n. 44, 39 n. 31, 40, 60 n. 12, 66 n. 35, 100 n. 3, 154 n. 29
Châtillon, Abbé Jean, 49
Chenu, M. D., 181 n. 45
Chifflot, T. G., 37 nn. 25 and 26, 64 n. 31
Chromatius of Aquileia, 86 n. 3, 109 n. 73, 196 n. 9, 208 and n. 51
Chrysologus, Peter, 130 n. 2, 206 n. 39, 207 n. 42
Chrysostom, John, 14 n. 10, 79 n. 21, 90 n. 49, 119 n. 47, 156 n. 37, 166 n. 34, 209 n. 55
Cicero, 164

Claudel, Paul, 23 n. 38, 34 n. 15, 73 n. 2, 111 n. 89, 184 n. 13, 188 n. 34, 232
Claudius of Turin, 86 n. 17, 87 n. 23, 92 n. 59, 96 n. 73, 91 n. 5, 103 n. 27, 104 n. 31, 109 n. 70, 110 n. 80, 115 n. 23, 118 n. 41, 122, 124 n. 92, 138 n. 44, 142 n. 73
Clement of Alexandria, xii, 22 n. 34, 27 n. 46, 46, 47 n. 12, 167 and n. 39, 168
Cocceius (Koch), 61 n. 20
Combès-Farges, 114 n. 10, 120 n. 59, 146 n. 104, 154 n. 31
Comestor, Peter, 189 n. 40
Comte, Auguste, 70
Congar, Yves, 37 n. 24, 82 n. 31, 102 n. 13, 109 n. 69, 173 n. 2
Coppens, Joseph, 26 n. 43, 32 n. 4, 34 n. 14, 100 n. 1
Cornelius a Lapide, 144 n. 86, 150 n. 9
Cornutus, 168
Crehan, J. H., S.J., 192 n. 58
Crispin, Gilbert, 178 n. 37, 190 n. 46
Crouzel, Henri, 160 n. 11, 169 n. 45, 216 n. 81
Cullmann, Oscar, 13 n. 4, 58 n. 9, 212 n. 63
Cuthbert, 124 n. 89
Curtius, E. R., 193 n. 63
Cyril of Alexandria, 54 n. 41, 60, 106 n. 47

Damian, Peter, 35 n. 19, 51 n. 25, 83 n. 35, 98 n. 81, 99 n. 88, 109 n. 76, 131 n. 10, 215 n. 77
Daniel, 94, 192
Daniel, Walter, 199 n. 21
Daniélou, Jean, S.J., 21 n. 30, 93, 94 n. 66, 136 n. 39, 203 n. 29
Davenson, Henri, 4 n. 3
David, 9, 20 n. 29, 25, 104 n. 36, 140, 181, 220
Delaruelle, E., 182 n. 47
Delhaye, P., 200 n. 23
Denis, J., 45 n. 8
Denys de Sainte-Marthe, 227 n. 56
Desnoyers, L., 33 n. 6
DeZwaan, J., 26 n. 43
Didymus, 19 n. 25, 145 n. 99
de Dietrich, Suzanne, 83 n. 39
Dimier, M. A., 145 n. 91
Diodorus of Tarsus, 48

237